The Rebirth of the Spanish Empire

The death of Carlos II in 1700 and the rise of Felipe V to the Spanish throne sparked a global war – and in New Spain, a cultural and political upheaval. As Bourbon loyalists staged elaborate ceremonies and circulated propaganda to legitimize the new dynasty, priests, artists, and local elites reimagined sacred kingship through vivid metaphors of death, rebirth, and regeneration. Sermons, rituals, devotional images, and unofficial texts anchored the new monarchy in familiar religious frameworks, linking the king's body to Christ's and reinforcing loyalty to both Church and Crown. In this contested public sphere, municipalities, religious orders, and colonial officials vied to display their allegiance and shape a renewed vision of empire. Frances L. Ramos's *The Rebirth of the Spanish Empire* offers a compelling and deeply researched account of how ritual, visual culture, and oratory redefined imperial identity in early eighteenth-century Mexico – illuminating the politics of loyalty and legitimacy during a time of dynastic change.

Frances L. Ramos is Associate Professor of History at the University of South Florida. She is author of the award-winning *Identity, Ritual, and Power in Colonial Puebla*.

"*The Rebirth of the Spanish Empire* should be required reading for any scholar or student interested in understanding how the new Bourbon dynasty managed to impose its authority over the immense Spanish American Empire and secure its survival for more than a hundred years, at a time when it seemed likely that its sovereignty could be easily overturned by its many competitors and enemies."
                                              Alejandro Cañeque, University of Maryland

"This well written and deeply researched study is a timely analysis of the crucial transition between Habsburg and Bourbon rule in the viceroyalty of New Spain. It's a must read for anyone interested in the workings of empire and its permanence and in the consequences of political reinvention in moments of great geopolitical conflict and uncertainty."
                                              Alejandra B. Osorio, Wellesley College

"Frances Ramos has conjured up a profoundly researched and marvelously written cultural history on the soft power of oratory, sermons, and imagery. Clergy, artisans, and pamphleteers sell the Bourbon succession in Mexico. Youthful, vigorous, and fecund Philip V replaces child and hapless Charles II at the helm. A must read for anyone interested in imperial Spanish history."
                              Christoph Rosenmüller, author of *Viceroy Güemes's Mexico: Rituals, Religion, and Revenue*

CAMBRIDGE LATIN AMERICAN STUDIES

General Editors
KRIS LANE, Tulane University
MATTHEW RESTALL, Pennsylvania State University

Editor Emeritus
HERBERT S. KLEIN
Gouverneur Morris Emeritus Professor of History, Columbia University and Hoover Research Fellow, Stanford University

Other Books in the Series

145. *The Rebirth of the Spanish Empire: War and Sacred Kingship in Early Bourbon Mexico*, Frances L. Ramos
144. *An Unholy Pedagogy: Visions of Learning from Mesoamerica, 1300–1650*, Joshua Jacob Fitzgerald
143. *The Making of Brazilian Amazonian Societies: A Study in Ethnographic and Spatial History*, Mark Harris
142. *Armed Citizens and Citizens in Arms: The Military and the Creation of the State of Peru, 1800–1860*, Natalia Sobrevilla Perea
141. *Anchoring an Empire: Gender and Ethnicity in Colonial Panama*, Bethany Aram
140. *Debts Unpaid: Two Centuries of Trouble and Conflict in Mexico's Economy*, Louise E. Walker
139. *Hispanic Technocracy: From Fascism to Catholic Authoritarianism in Spain, Argentina, and Chile, 1945–1991*, Daniel Gunnar Kressel
138. *The Power of Dissent: Urban Political Culture and the Fall of Spanish Rule in Charcas*, Sergio Serulnikov
137. *The Coming of the Kingdom: The Muisca, Catholic Reform, and Spanish Colonialism in the New Kingdom of Granada*, Juan F. Cobo Betancourt
136. *The Shamanism of Eco-Tourism: History and Ontology among the Makushi in Guyana*, James Andrew Whitaker
135. *Fallen from Heaven: The Enduring Tradition of Europeans as Gods in the Americas*, Nicholas Griffiths
134. *Global Servants of the Spanish King: Mobility and Cosmopolitanism in the Early Modern Spanish Empire*, Adolfo Polo y La Borda
133. *Plebeian Consumers: Global Connections, Local Trade, and Foreign Goods in Nineteenth-Century Colombia*, Ana María Otero-Cleves
132. *Peopling for Profit in Imperial Brazil: Directed Migrations and the Business of Nineteenth-Century Colonization*, José Juan Pérez Meléndez
131. *Being the Heart of the World: The Pacific and the Fashioning of the Self in New Spain, 1513–1641*, Nino Vallen
130. *A Tale of Two Granadas: Custom, Community, and Citizenship in the Spanish Empire, 1568–1668*, Max Deardorff

(Continued after the Index)

The Rebirth of the Spanish Empire

War and Sacred Kingship in Early Bourbon Mexico

FRANCES L. RAMOS
University of South Florida

CAMBRIDGE
UNIVERSITY PRESS

CAMBRIDGE
UNIVERSITY PRESS

Shaftesbury Road, Cambridge CB2 8EA, United Kingdom

One Liberty Plaza, 20th Floor, New York, NY 10006, USA

477 Williamstown Road, Port Melbourne, VIC 3207, Australia

314–321, 3rd Floor, Plot 3, Splendor Forum, Jasola District Centre,
New Delhi – 110025, India

Cambridge University Press is part of Cambridge University Press & Assessment,
a department of the University of Cambridge.

We share the University's mission to contribute to society through the pursuit of
education, learning and research at the highest international levels of excellence.

www.cambridge.org
Information on this title: www.cambridge.org/9781009648493
DOI: 10.1017/9781009648462

© Frances L. Ramos 2026

This publication is in copyright. Subject to statutory exception and to the provisions
of relevant collective licensing agreements, no reproduction of any part may take
place without the written permission of Cambridge University Press & Assessment.

When citing this work, please include a reference to the DOI 10.1017/9781009648462

First published 2026

Cover image: Philip V, King of Spain, 1704. Design by Teodoro Ardemans; engraving by
Gérard Edelinck. Chalcographic print in Succession de el rey D. Phelipe V nuestro señor en la
Corona de España by Antonio de Ubilla y Medina. Biblioteca Nacional de España.

A catalogue record for this publication is available from the British Library

*A Cataloging-in-Publication data record for this book is available from the Library
of Congress*

ISBN 978-1-009-64849-3 Hardback
ISBN 978-1-009-64844-8 Paperback

Cambridge University Press & Assessment has no responsibility for the persistence
or accuracy of URLs for external or third-party internet websites referred to in this
publication and does not guarantee that any content on such websites is, or will
remain, accurate or appropriate.

For EU product safety concerns, contact us at Calle de José Abascal,
56, 1°, 28003 Madrid, Spain, or email eugpsr@cambridge.org

For Eric and Ellie

Contents

List of Figures		*page* xi
Preface and Acknowledgments		xiii
	Introduction	1
1	New Spain at War	21
2	An Early Modern Public Sphere	45
3	The Body Politic and Imperial Resurrection	69
4	Prophecy and the Bourbon Succession	92
5	Rebirth	119
	Conclusion	142
Notes		153
Bibliography		187
Index		209

Figures

I.1	Map of New Spain.	*page* 10
3.1	Felipe V, King of Spain. Engraving by Cornelius Vermeulen, 1701.	77
4.1	Felipe V, King of Spain. Engraving by Teodoro Ardemans and Gérard Edelinck, 1704.	106
5.1	The Prince Our Lord Don Luis Fernando, 1710. Oil on canvas by Juan Correa.	138
5.2	Funerary catafalque erected in Mexico City for María Luisa Gabriela de Saboya. Engraving, 1715.	140
C.1	Felipe V, Conqueror of Heresy. Oil on canvas by Felipe de Silva, c. 1712.	146

Preface and Acknowledgments

While flipping through the card catalog at the Biblioteca Nacional de México's Fondo Reservado in 2000, I noticed a marked increase in commemorative sermons printed in New Spain during the first two decades of the eighteenth century – a period that coincided with the War of the Spanish Succession (1702–1714). As a doctoral student in history already deeply engaged with the political culture of the Spanish American viceroyalties, this discovery marked the beginning of a long intellectual journey into the world of early modern kingship and ceremony. That initial encounter with the sources would eventually inform two early publications: an article on the 1701 funerary honors for Carlos II and the oath ceremony for Felipe V in Puebla (2004), and another on the city's 1707 celebrations marking the birth of Luis I (2003).

Although I began seriously contemplating how American subjects understood monarchy and the dynastic transition from Habsburg to Bourbon more than twenty years ago, my interest in sacred kingship, prophecy, and millenarianism – central themes of this book – predates that period of my life. As a high school student, I was introduced to comparative mythology through the teaching of Albert Hernández, who often brought Jungian psychology into our discussions. Only recently have I come to appreciate the lasting impact this early intellectual exposure had on the way I approach and interpret historical sources. While studying at Florida International University, my advisor, the late Noble David Cook, encouraged me to explore the millenarian beliefs of New Spain's early Franciscan missionaries. That formative encouragement would prove invaluable in shaping my historical sensibilities, particularly in reading the many imprints and sermons circulated at the turn of the eighteenth century, as well as the elaborate descriptions of ceremonial life across New Spain's municipalities.

After completing my first book on eighteenth-century Puebla in 2011, I formally embarked on a long-term research project shaped by a central question: how, following nearly two centuries of Habsburg rule, did supporters of Felipe V work to legitimize and promote the Bourbon dynasty in New Spain, the Spanish Empire's arguably most significant viceroyalty? In pursuit of this question, I spent years collecting and analyzing materials from archives and libraries in Mexico, Spain, Chile, and the United States – accumulating many intellectual and personal debts along the way.

My deepest gratitude goes to the institutions that supported the travel, research, and writing that made this book possible. In 2011, I conducted a six-week research trip with a Creative Scholarship Grant from the University of South Florida's Division of Sponsored Research, which allowed me to work in archives and rare book libraries in Mexico City and Puebla. In 2013, I spent nearly six months working with the large collection of Mexican imprints at the John Carter Brown Library with the support of a National Endowment for the Humanities Long-Term Fellowship. In 2016, a USF competitive sabbatical award and a USF College of Arts and Sciences Pilot Study Award enabled me to carry out two months of research in archives in Spain and Mexico. I also spent two additional months working in rare book libraries in Puebla and Mexico City in 2019 with support from a USF Humanities Institute Summer Research Award and a Franklin Grant from the American Philosophical Society. Most recently, in 2021, a highly competitive NEH Fellowship afforded me a full year of writing – time that proved essential to bringing this project to completion. I sincerely hope the NEH continues to support humanities scholarship, free from political interference.

I am also deeply grateful to the many archivists and librarians who assisted me along the way. I am especially thankful to the staff of the John Carter Brown Library for making my time in Providence both productive and inspiring. The exceptional staff at the Biblioteca Palafoxiana and the Biblioteca José María Lafragua made my summer research trips efficient and rewarding. When I could not travel, I was fortunate to count on the generous assistance of colleagues in Mexico, including José Gabino Castillo, Sergio Rosas Salas, and Enrique Cano Galindo. Thank you for answering calls for help with such kindness and collegiality.

I am extremely grateful to the many scholars of seventeenth- and eighteenth-century Spanish America who have offered feedback, encouragement, and camaraderie over the years. Iván Escamilla González and I developed an interest in the discourse surrounding the Bourbon succession around the same time in the early 2000s, though we did not officially meet until 2016. To my good fortune, we ended up collaborating on an article, and he became a dear friend and key interlocutor, even providing feedback on the final manuscript of this book. Aaron Alejandro Olivas and Francisco Eissa-Barroso generously shared sources, and Christoph Rosenmüller has been a steady source of advice and encouragement throughout our long friendship. At a workshop at the Universidad Nacional Autónoma de México, Paula Mues Orts offered incisive commentary on a paper that later evolved into Chapter 5. Longtime friends Patricia Díaz Cayeros and Beatriz Berndt Mariscal opened their homes to me and shared wise counsel and intellectual companionship during many trips to Mexico City.

Over the past decade and a half, personal challenges slowed the progress of this book, but the support, validation, and encouragement of many colleagues helped me to persevere. My late mentor, Sandra Lauderdale Graham, encouraged me throughout my research, and Kris Lane, Charles Walker, and Alejandro Cañeque wrote letters of recommendation. Linda Curcio-Nagy, Sonya Lipsett-Rivera, and Donald Fithian Stevens included me on panels that reminded me why my work matters, and Karen Graubart urged me to apply for funding at a time when I least felt like doing so. Ann Twinam and Jane Mangan read drafts of my fellowship proposal, and Emily Berquist Soule and Christina Bueno provided both constructive feedback and unwavering friendship. Paul Rubinson talked me through numerous frustrations and demonstrated his generosity time and again.

Céline Carayon, Julia Gaffield, Hal Langfur, Guadalupe Pinzón Ríos, Fabrício Prado, Ben Reed, Tamara Walker, and Ken Ward offered intellectual fellowship during my time at the John Carter Brown Library. Rosalva Loreto López, Francisco Javier Fernández Bello, Jonatan Moncayo Ramírez, Lidia E. Gómez García, and Maria Aurelia Hernández Yahuitl brought companionship and welcome distractions during research trips to Puebla. Kenneth Mills prompted my early thinking about the connections between botanical fecundity and human fertility – an idea that recurs throughout this monograph. Francisco Montes González generously shared a copy of his important book on the Dukes of Alburquerque and their patronage of the arts in New Spain.

Silvia Z. Mitchell recommended valuable secondary literature, particularly related to the enigmatic reign of Carlos II (1665–1700), a period shrouded in retrospective distortion. Her insights encouraged me to reconsider his legacy and to reflect on how Bourbon propaganda helped solidify the image of a frail and ineffectual monarch. While this manuscript may not push that argument as far as it might, the historical revision of his reign – and my engagement with it – is far from over. On several occasions, Juan Ponce Vásquez helped clarify questions regarding viceregal administration. I thank everyone mentioned here – as well as Mathew Restall, Kris Lane (again), Cecelia Cancellaro at Cambridge University Press, and my two anonymous reviewers – for their faith in this book.

At the University of South Florida, I have been fortunate to work alongside many accomplished and clear-headed scholars who helped make the process of completing this book more bearable – even during turbulent times. Brian Connolly provided steady leadership throughout his six years as chair of the Department of History, and I am grateful for his early feedback on my proposal. My dear friends David Johnson and Matt King have been constant sources of encouragement, while Davide Tanasi – our department's premier digital humanist and the director of IDEx – graciously assisted with my map. I am also thankful to Tami Davis, Callie Getchell, and Ruth Borrero, whose efforts keep our department and graduate program running smoothly.

I am especially thankful for the family, friends, sitters, and medical professionals who supported me throughout this long process. Jaime Corona Montiel and Martha Juárez Díaz welcomed me to Puebla on multiple occasions; after nearly thirty years of friendship, being with them always felt like coming home. My beautiful mother, Lourdes Garrido, continues to celebrate my accomplishments, and I am lucky to have her in my life – still asking how the book is going. My brother, Paul Ramos, and my mother-in-law, Cindy Amar, have been steady sources of support, as have many of my high school friends, many of whom I reconnected with during the pandemic. Special thanks to Ali Hodin Baier, Debbie Sootin Foley, Michelle Kligman, Ellen Cohen Laddin, Rene Leonard, Melanie Murphy, Ali Nason-Aymerich, and Megan Seigel. I am also grateful to my darling niece, Erin Hidy, who helped care for my daughter, Ellie, while I conducted research in Providence, and to Elissa Salinas, whose support at home made it possible for me to focus during the final stretch of writing.

But there would be no book without the ability to think, write, or function day to day. I thank Dr. Teshamae Monteith and Dr. Marie Labadie-Degennaro for guiding me out of years of chronic migraine, and I extend my gratitude to the scientific community behind CGRP-blockers (calcitonin gene–related peptide inhibitors), which have made daily life manageable again for countless sufferers.

And finally, I am grateful for the loving family I have built with my husband, Eric Amar. I thank our dogs Evie and Coco, and our rabbit Flopsie, for their companionship and emotional support, and I thank Eric for the steadfast love and stability he provides our family. But above all, I thank Ellie. This book, and everything, is for you.

Introduction

The death of Carlos II (1661–1700), the last Habsburg monarch of Spain, triggered a fourteen-year succession crisis that reverberated across the Atlantic Ocean. Upon receiving copies of the monarch's last will and testament, administrators and religious leaders in New Spain choreographed elaborate funerary honors lasting over several days. In Mexico City, two judges on the *audiencia*, or high court, designed the catafalque, the ephemeral funerary structure that held the monarch's symbolic remains, and that served as the centerpiece of the ceremonies in the cathedral. At the top of the pyramidal structure, observers gazed upon four statues representing the four parts of the world, each with its face contorted by grief.[1]

On the walls of the catafalque's foundation, observers could admire a series of nineteen hieroglyphs inspired by the emblem books that shaped festive art in both Europe and America. Along with the popular genre of literature known as "mirrors for princes," these emblem books influenced early modern ceremonial propaganda and helped to create a shared idiom of power that could be deciphered in public rituals across regions. In the late sixteenth and early seventeenth centuries, new heliocentric theories shaped iconographic representations of monarchy, and artists and political theorists developed emblems showcasing kings as the sun at the center of the cosmos, extending protective and nurturing rays throughout their kingdoms. Felipe IV of Spain (1605–1665) represented himself using solar imagery, but with the moniker the Planet King, and his nephew, Louis XIV of France (1638–1715), famously followed suit by fashioning himself the Sun King.[2] Commissioners in charge of Mexico City's catafalque drew on this common association in choosing the theme for the catafalque's design: the eclipse of the sun/Carlos II before he had arrived at his "zenith."[3]

At just four years old, Carlos II became king but with the court under the control of his mother, queen regent Mariana of Austria. During this vulnerable time for Spain, France and the Holy Roman Empire entered into several agreements to dismember the Spanish Empire. Then in 1698, the ailing and seemingly infertile Carlos II named the electoral prince of Bavaria as his sole heir. But as England, the United Provinces, and the Holy Roman Empire all sought to benefit from Spain's succession crisis, the Bavarian prince died, leading most Spanish officials at court to arrive at the same conclusion. To prevent other polities from carving up the empire, it needed to be placed under the care of the strongest military power in Europe. And so, in the month preceding his death, Carlos II made the difficult decision to leave the Crown to Philip of Anjou, the great-grandson of his father, Felipe IV, and the grandson of his half-sister María Teresa and Spain's previous enemy, Louis XIV (1638–1715) of France.[4] Then, on November 1, 1700 – All Saints' Day – the last Habsburg monarch of Spain died shortly before his thirty-ninth birthday.

In choosing to equate Carlos II with the sun, the organizers of Mexico City's funerary honors drew on the potency and multivalency of solar imagery, which, with some thoughtful contextualization, invited associations with those in power; after all, everything revolved around and depended on the sun. By the seventeenth century, the sunburst had become a common design for the monstrance, the vessel that displays the Eucharist. Solar imagery, therefore, invited associations with the divine, associations emphasized repeatedly in both the Old and New Testaments. Furthermore, while many contemporaries likely associated the Eucharist with the sun, they equated the Immaculate Conception with the Woman of the Apocalypse, the travailing woman observed by John in his vision as "clothed with the sun."[5] Both the Eucharist and the Immaculate Conception served as central devotions of Spanish Habsburg piety, and so the sun helped to condense a diversity of meanings.

In representing the death of Carlos II as the eclipse of the sun, the organizers of Mexico City's funerary honors captured the gravity surrounding not only the passing of a king, but the end of an entire ruling dynasty. One somber emblem depicted the cadaver of Carlos II lying on a table, while the sun is visible through the window, completely eclipsed by the moon.[6] However, the sun never darkened for long, and after setting, one expected it to rise again, and so the constancy of the sun reflected the permanency of monarchy. As the imagery on the catafalque made clear, the Spanish monarchy did not die with Carlos II, nor did the last Spanish Habsburg king truly succumb to death. Instead, his individual soul enjoyed an afterlife in Heaven, while the monarchy and his legacy lived on in Felipe V. To help make this point, one emblem depicted a phoenix being consumed by fire only to be reborn.[7] As the two *audiencia* judges explained in the dedication to the printed description of Mexico City's funerary catafalque for Carlos II, Felipe V would rise from his ashes.[8]

The Rebirth of the Spanish Empire focuses on representations of Felipe V and the Bourbon dynasty in early eighteenth-century New Spain, arguably the Spanish Empire's most strategically important viceroyalty. At the most basic level, it illustrates the preoccupation of New Spain's administrators with Spain's succession crisis and the significant ways the war impacted the feelings and circumstances of people from different social groups and municipalities throughout New Spain. During the early eighteenth century, the Spanish Crown's succession crisis dominated public life, and viceregal bureaucrats and prelates who depended on the Crown's stability worked to "sell" the Bourbon dynasty to subjects in New Spain.

By focusing on the symbols, metaphors, and origin myths deployed during this influence campaign, *The Rebirth of the Spanish Empire* recovers how Spanish subjects in New Spain understood kingship and empire at the end of the long seventeenth century (1598–1715), the period preceding accelerated political and economic change under the Bourbon dynasty. For the sake of clarity, I refer to the years of the war as occurring in the "early eighteenth century," but I sometimes use the term "long seventeenth century" to emphasize a point; Bourbon "influencers" or propagandists looked back to justify moving forward. Priests, bureaucrats, artists, and craftsmen created a mélange of propaganda rooted in Judeo-Christian metaphors and symbols related to death and regeneration that undergird medieval and early modern notions of "sacred kingship." As James Frazier argued long ago, the archetype of a "sacred king" can be found across history and cultures and is rooted in dependence on the agricultural cycle; in many examples of sacred kingship, the figure is represented as the sun and, most importantly, is always ready to sacrifice himself for his subjects in order to ensure future fertility and abundance.[9] In the early modern Christian context, a king received his authority directly from God and modeled his rule on other sacred rulers, and scholars have traditionally associated sacred kingship with the late medieval French and English paradigms, in which monarchs literally embodied the divine. Both Queen Anne of England and Scotland (later

Great Britain) (1665–1714) and Louis XIV followed the custom established by their predecessors and performed ceremonies in which they cured scrofula through the royal touch.[10]

Whether monarchs in Castile were perceived as having the divine right to rule has sparked some debate regarding the sacrality of monarchy in the Spanish kingdoms and what exactly it meant to be regarded as a sacred king. While at least one fifteenth-century prince in Aragon claimed thaumaturgic powers, rulers in Castile did not. Although medieval Aragonese monarchs embraced rituals of coronation that underscored the sacrality of their rule, Castilian monarchs did not, as the late medieval Castilian nobility acclaimed their kings.[11] Throughout the early modern period, elites in municipalities throughout the Spanish kingdoms continued to ritualistically "elect" their kings by waving pennants on the day of their *juras*, or oath ceremonies.

Despite the peculiarities of late medieval Castile, both the Spanish Habsburg and Bourbon monarchies emphasized the sacrality of their rule through a variety of symbols and rituals that communicated sacred kingship. Beginning in the fourteenth century, chroniclers claimed that Castilian kings possessed the power to exorcise demons – a belief that distinguished Spanish monarchs as instruments of divine will.[12] Both the Spanish Habsburgs and the French Bourbons also appropriated the cults of sacred monarchs: Saint Fernando III of Castile (1199–1252), canonized in 1671 and venerated as an unofficial patron of the Spanish Crown for his role in the reconquest of Seville and Córdoba, and Saint Louis IX of France (1214–1270), canonized in 1297; leader of the seventh and eighth crusades, he would serve as a model of ideal Christian kingship for the Capetian and Bourbon dynasties. Propagandists for the Habsburgs and Bourbons, moreover, reinforced their rulers' sacred authority by also associating them with biblical figures, especially King Solomon (970–931 BCE), whose reign symbolized the golden age of ancient Israel. In New Spain, artists and intellectuals echoed this association: the second tier of Felipe IV's three-story funerary catafalque in Mexico City (1666), for instance, featured a statue of the king surrounded by four other statues of Solomon.[13]

In the process of championing Spain's Bourbon dynasty, supporters recalled understandings of sacred kingship based in Spain's collective history. This strategy, moreover, made perfect sense; given that monarchical transition often threatened stability, organizers of succession ceremonies typically promised continuity. As art historian Victor Mínguez noted in his foundational study of solar iconography and

Spanish kingship, the funerary honors for Felipe IV in Naples featured the sun setting on one age, and rising on another.[14] However, in 1700, with Spain's subjects facing the prospect of not only a new king but a new ruling dynasty, supporters of Bourbon rule participated in an unprecedented influence campaign that spanned roughly fifteen years. Elaborate ceremonies, ephemeral art pieces, oratory, and printed propaganda all announced a Spanish Renaissance and referenced a variety of symbols and metaphors that had been used to laud the Spanish Habsburg dynasty. Supporters of Felipe V, however, reformulated symbols, metaphors, and myths associated with Spain's Habsburgs to apply them to the Bourbon dynasty. While promising a large degree of cultural continuity, supporters of Felipe V also promised a prosperous future.

From the onset of the conflict, various orators in New Spain argued that the ascension of a new ruling dynasty would "renew" the Spanish Empire, just like the ascension of the sun marks the dawn of a new day. The Franciscan convent of Veracruz's funerary sermon, given on April 23, 1701, relied heavily on solar imagery. The orator Antonio de Posada based it on the premise that life depends on light from the sun and claimed that as Carlos II died, darkness befell the earth. However, he also promised that the ascension of his nephew Felipe V, whose name, according to many, meant "*os lampadis*" or the "mouth of a lamp," would bring forth light and renew life.[15] Preaching Carlos II's funerary sermon in Mexico City's Franciscan convent on May 13, 1701, Blas de Pulgar made clear that the pregnant woman in the Book of Revelation "clothed in the sun" represented the Immaculate Conception. According to the orator, as iconography of the Immaculate Conception depicts her triumphing over sin by standing atop a crescent moon, likewise, Carlos II as the sun triumphed over sin by living a devout life, setting a pious example, and enacting policies to support the Church.[16] Then, in the funerary sermon given in the Franciscan convent of Tlaxcala on August 11, 1701, Maximiliano López de Pro compared both Carlos II and Felipe V to the sun, and Felipe V specifically to a phoenix, emerging from the ashes left by the previous ruling dynasty.[17] The sun, therefore, served as a renewing force and a recognizable symbol of monarchy, deployed by many orators and artisans to mark the transition from Habsburg to Bourbon rule.

While propagandists adopted and adapted long-entrenched symbols of monarchy, contemporary polemics shaped support for Felipe V and how subjects received pro-Bourbon messages. Perceptions of imperial decline, whether accurate or not, could not have but shaped how audiences received and interpreted promises of "renewal." Throughout the seventeenth century, reformist thinkers known as *arbitristas* clamored for economic, political, and religious change and, as Helen Rawlings has observed, *arbitristas* (people who offered *arbitrios* or policy solutions) generally emphasized two primary causes for Spain's progressive weakness: a lack of native industry and a slip in collective virtue, leading to a loss of God's favor.[18] Together, *arbitristas* suggested ways to save the empire, which many imagined as a body politic composed of the king united with his subjects. As early as the 1620s, polemicists declared that the body politic suffered from "disease" and numerous reformers prescribed "remedies."[19] In the 1690s, many surely came to see a weakened Spain mirrored in the king, who had developed a debilitating illness toward the end of his life and around whose health rumors constantly swirled.

This study, however, does not focus on the degree to which the seventeenth-century Spanish Empire experienced decline or the severity of the monarch's health. Rather, it presupposes that claims in both veins have been highly exaggerated. Christopher Storrs has argued that because the Spanish Empire maintained its geographic integrity even without a functioning navy, it needs to be appreciated as evidence of the empire's health, and not its decline.[20] Furthermore, while historians have belabored Spain's supposed decline, the reign of Carlos II saw demographic growth, the inauguration of a variety of cost-saving reforms, and no new taxes for the first time in the history of the empire. While undoubtedly surrounded by a variety of capable figures, the king's supposed incapacity has also been grossly exaggerated, possibly because, as Luis Ribot has suggested, researchers have over-relied on diplomatic correspondence. In the last two decades of Carlos II's life, French ambassadors to Madrid had a vested interest in characterizing both Carlos II and his empire as in need of saving.[21] Diplomats, moreover, periodically alluded to the formidable influence of first Mariana of Austria and then Carlos II's two consorts, Marie-Louise of Orléans (1679–1689) and Maria Anna of Neuburg (1689–1700), on the king. As Silvia Z. Mitchell has speculated, this likely contributed to an image of a feminized monarchy.[22]

Regardless of the incongruence between image and reality, rumors circulated regarding the king's health in the 1680s and 1690s. Between 1679 and 1681, the French ambassador, the Marquis of Villars, depicted Carlos II as stupid, short-sighted, and just barely able to read and write. Furthermore, he described him as physically weak and practically asexual. In the 1680s and 1690s, a series of Venetian ambassadors proved particularly caustic. In 1681, Giovanni Cornaro decried his laziness and described the Spanish king as an "imbecile," and Venice's next ambassador, Sebastiano Foscarini, believed that Carlos II's delicate constitution derived from being a product of an elderly father. Then, in the 1690s, Carlo Ruzzini commented on the king's chronic and debilitating stomach ailments and his general lack of vigor.[23]

News regarding the king's health also circulated inside and outside Madrid. In 1698, amid a physical downturn, Carlos II met with an exorcist from Savoy, even while specific advisors doubted that the king suffered from demonic possession.[24] By the end of the year, the Crown sent a request to Mexico City for prayers and masses for the king's health, leading to rumors circulating throughout the viceregal capital that the king would soon die.[25] Regardless of brief mentions of the king and queen's "perfect" health in the Spanish court's official newspaper, *La Gazeta de Madrid*, rumors about the frailty of the king continued to circulate, and then, in 1699 Madrid erupted in a food riot, leading to the ouster of the king's primary advisor, the Count of Oropesa. In a revealing turn, the crowd only calmed down when Carlos II made himself corporeally visible on the palace balcony.[26] Therefore, while enmeshed in a variety of problematic assumptions, in the final years of the Habsburg era, the image of a weak and infertile monarch loomed large. When the young and healthy Felipe V became monarch of Spain, people surely noted the contrast with Carlos II. To make the transition more poignant and promising, supporters announced that the healthy and fertile Felipe V would revive a moribund Spain.

By the later eighteenth century, Spain's Bourbon monarchy would become synonymous with reform, but supporters of Bourbon rule projected this image early on, casting Felipe V and the Bourbon dynasty as the redeemers of Spain. Given the viceroyalty of New Spain's importance to the Bourbon war effort, the Crown made sure to flood the viceroyalty with material in support of Felipe V, material that promised a revitalization of the imperial body politic. Like the archetypal sacred kings described by Frazier, Felipe V would fertilize the Spanish Monarchy.

But, while promising renewal, pro-Bourbon imprints and oratory harkened back to medieval understandings of messianic kingship, and some orators suggested or outrightly stated that a Bourbon victory would inaugurate a Spanish golden age, ensuring a seamless succession for, perhaps, a thousand years. Orators in New Spain imbued the rhetoric surrounding the Bourbon succession with messianic, and even millenarian, fervor, and thereby sought to invest people spiritually and existentially in the outcome of the war. In this way, Spain's new ruling dynasty transformed into a metaphor for renewal.

Bureaucrats, artists, craftsmen, and priests all amplified this message throughout New Spain, a viceroyalty whose loyalty would prove crucial to the Bourbon cause. After the grandson of Louis XIV became King of Spain, Austria, England, the Netherlands, Savoy, and eventually Portugal banded together to contest the succession and ignited conflict in Italy, the Netherlands, Iberia, North America, the Pacific coast of South America, the Caribbean, and the Philippines, transforming into the first modern war to be conducted on a global scale. At its outbreak, Spain had two primary administrative jurisdictions in the Americas: the viceroyalty of New Spain (established in 1535) and the viceroyalty of Peru (established in 1542), which enjoyed economic primacy throughout most of the sixteenth and seventeenth centuries, thanks to its rich silver mines and especially those located in Potosí in Upper Peru (now Bolivia). But, as the productivity of Potosí's silver mines declined, New Spain, which incorporated all of what is now Mexico, most of Central America, the southwestern United States, Florida, the Caribbean, and the Philippines, ascended in importance. New Spain's viceregal government in Mexico City bore primary responsibility for supplying presidios in the Caribbean and along the coast, areas naturally vulnerable to enemy attack.

Given mainland New Spain's economic and strategic importance, high-level bureaucrats immediately set about tying the region more effectively to Madrid and activated the elite of its "empire of towns," the municipalities scattered throughout the Spanish Empire whose councils, or *cabildos*, ordered town life, administered justice, and reaffirmed ties to the metropole through constant correspondence.[27] Furthermore, municipalities acted as stages for expressing collective loyalty and corporate identity, and in the main plazas and leading parishes of municipalities throughout New Spain, subjects at all levels of society participated in ceremonies in support of the Bourbon dynasty. Felipe V and his advisors worked hard to maintain the loyalty of Spain's oldest American viceroyalty, and the conflict consumed the attention of viceregal administrators and dominated public life, undoubtedly generating intense interest among non-elites. As we will see, it sparked fears of violence and instability in the capital and along the coast, and required the mobilization of large numbers of soldiers and extraordinary resources, placing material pressure on the population.

The war over the Spanish succession also inspired the production and consumption of political pamphlets and the mounting of a series of large-scale commemorations in support of Bourbon rule. In a letter to José de Grimaldo y Gutiérrez de Solórzano, the Secretary of the *Despacho de*

Guerra y Hacienda (Office of War and Finance), the Archbishop of Zaragoza Antonio Ibáñez de la Riva Herrera remarked that the seditious did not look at the war as a typical one of "fire and blood" but instead inspired people to move against the government through "suggestions and persuasions that they introduce through various means."[28] With a focus on municipalities throughout the *audiencia* jurisdictions of Mexico, Guatemala, Nueva Galicia, and the province of Nueva Vizcaya, this is a study of the counter "suggestions and persuasions" used to channel loyalty to Felipe V and solidify attachment to the empire (Figure I.1).

In municipalities throughout New Spain, officials and ecclesiastics appropriated a myriad of popular symbols and metaphors for exalting Spain's Habsburg monarchs but applied these to its first Bourbon king and promoted an idea that Spain would be reborn. When examined together, New Spain's seemingly disparate commemorations and sermons in support of Bourbon rule communicated a unifying and redeeming message. Indeed, with Felipe V at its helm, the Spanish Empire would enter a golden age marked by fecundity, prosperity, and religious uniformity. This, I suggest, is the beginning of a mythology of Bourbon rule in New Spain, a mythology built firmly on ideas of sacred kingship and the symbols and metaphors used to describe Felipe V's Habsburg predecessors.

By focusing on representations of the Bourbon dynasty in printed propaganda, spectacle, and oratory in municipalities throughout New Spain, I interpret the system of signs that structured Spain's political-religious culture at the end of the long seventeenth century and examine how contemporaries deployed messages regarding sacred kingship and dynastic succession to legitimize Bourbon rule and to create a sense of belonging that spanned the Atlantic Ocean. In this period predating the modern nation-state, I argue that Bourbon influencers sought to affirm and shape an "imagined community" of empire understood through the metaphor of the king's body: the *cuerpo del rey*. As Antonio Feros has recently reminded us, subjects throughout Spain's early modern empire expressed imagined ethnic and political identities long before the development of the nation-state, and these articulations of belonging often emerged during times of crisis.[29] Furthermore, ecclesiastics and writers consistently reaffirmed a Spanish imperial identity through celebrations of the monarchy's evangelization efforts and the heroic acts of its pious subjects and religious corporations in spreading the faith.[30] During the War of the Spanish Succession, articulations of Spanish imperial identity remained linked to the idea of a sacred king. By analyzing reoccurring messages deployed through multivalent symbols and metaphors, I show

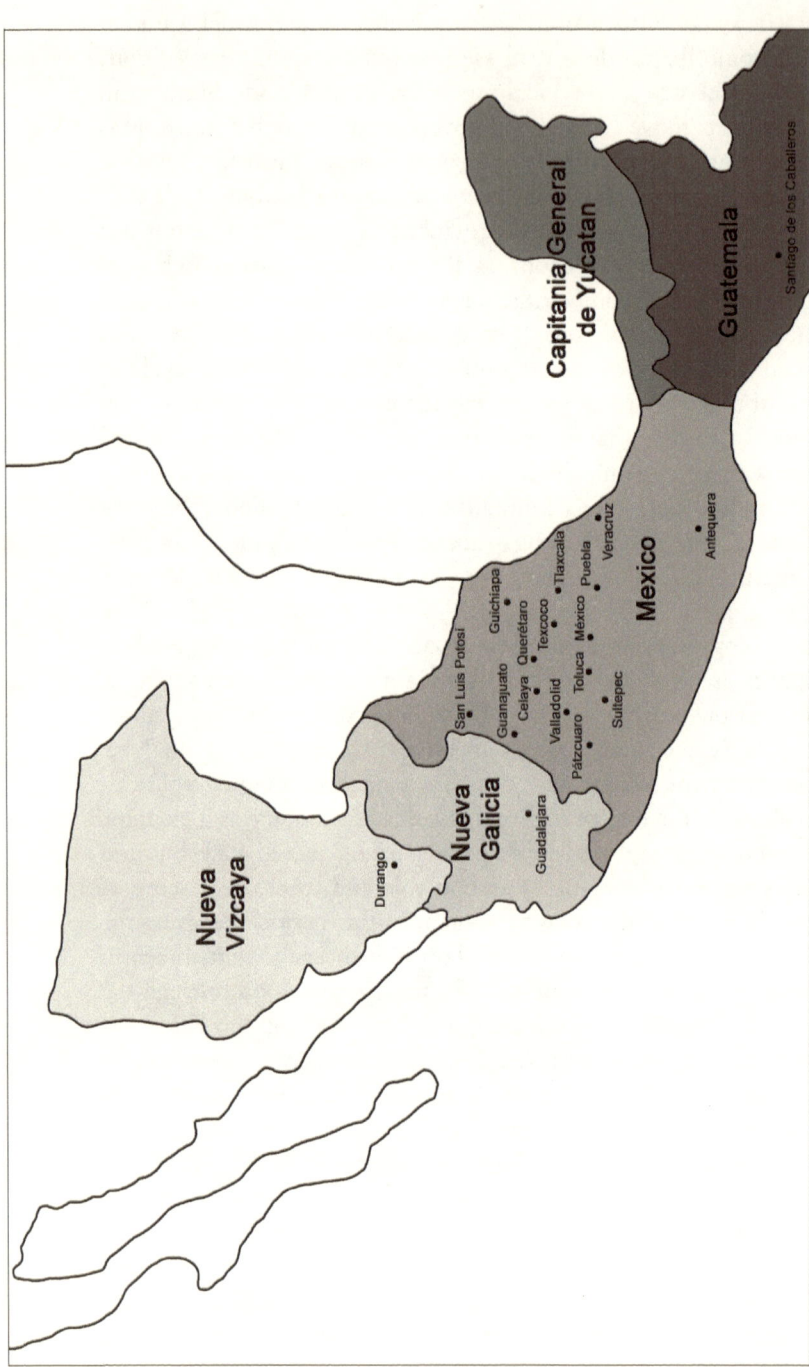

FIGURE 1.1 Map of early eighteenth-century New Spain, highlighting municipalities that hosted royal ceremonies. This map illustrates the geographic distribution of municipalities across New Spain that organized public ceremonies or religious observances in honor of royal events – such as oath ceremonies or military victories – and subsequently published commemorative sermons or descriptions of events.
Map created by the University of South Florida's Institute for Digital Exploration (IDEx).

how bureaucrats and priests invested the viceroyalty in the outcome of the war and in the future of the Spanish Empire.

STUDYING THE SUCCESSION CRISIS IN NEW SPAIN

Historians of early modern Spain have paid a great deal of attention to the War of the Spanish Succession, not only because it was the first full-scale war to take place on Spanish soil since the Reconquest (711–1492) but also because, after some significant attempts under Felipe IV and Carlos II, Bourbon administrators managed to embark on a relatively vigorous program of administrative, fiscal, and cultural reform aimed at ending the political culture of the *Monarquía Hispánica* (Spanish Monarchy), the system of "composite monarchies" that typified the Habsburg era.[31] Although governance of the *Monarquía Hispánica* centered on the king and his tribunals in Madrid, under the Habsburgs, the kingdoms within the Crown of Aragon enjoyed great fiscal and political autonomy through their *fueros*, or privileges, while distant "kingdoms," like New Spain, experienced autonomy through "benign neglect."[32] To punish the Crown of Aragon for largely siding with Austria during the war, Felipe V issued the *Nueva Planta* (the "New Foundation" decrees), a series of measures signed between 1707 and 1716 abolishing legal distinctions between Castilian and Aragonese subjects.[33] This proved to be the first of many policies directed toward making the empire more uniform, efficient, and profitable. At bottom, the reforms would help to channel resources toward a slew of imperial wars.[34]

The "Bourbon reforms" have evolved into a veritable subfield within the historiography of the early modern Spanish Empire, and scholars have shown keen interest in how specific reforms effected the political culture of different municipalities, kingdoms, and viceroyalties. By the reign of Carlos III (1759–1788), bureaucrats in New Spain had taken to representing the king in pageantry, oratory, and artwork as an absolutist leader. Looking at Mexico City and Puebla, respectively, Linda Curcio-Nagy and I have analyzed how monarchical ceremonies became more elaborate and grander in size throughout the course of the eighteenth century, thereby reflecting the growing power of the absolutist king.[35] However, less attention has been paid to early representations of Bourbon rule in the viceroyalty and the ways contemporaries explained the ascension of a new ruling dynasty.

In the 1970s and 1980s, Analola Borges and Luis Navarro García published on suspected disloyalty in Caracas and Mexico City, and

Pedro Emilio Pérez-Mallaína Bueno studied the role of French maritime forces in the defense of the Americas, underscoring the precarious and contingent nature of early Bourbon rule. But while a Bourbon victory was no foregone conclusion, early modern Spanish Americanists have generally glossed over the dynastic transition – although interest has increased notably over the past few decades.[36] Historians, for example, have made significant inroads into how patronage solidified loyalty to the Bourbon Crown. Luis Navarro García, Alfredo Morena Cebrián, Nuria Sala i Vila, Francisco Andújar Castillo, and Christoph Rosenmüller have all examined the sale of appointments in Spanish America during the years of the war and have emphasized the dominance of Creoles in these acquisitions.[37] Recently, Aaron Alejandro Olivas studied the economic and political interests shaping the loyalty and disloyalty of subjects in the province of Venezuela, mainland New Spain, and the Philippines. Focusing on New Spain exclusively, Rosenmüller detangled networks of patronage and corruption within the administration of the Duke of Alburquerque (1702–1710),[38] while Iván Escamilla González examined how the war impacted the relationship between the viceroy and New Spain's merchant guild, or *consulado*.[39]

Despite these contributions, Spanish Americanists have generally not associated the early Bourbon period with concrete reforms, let alone the reformist spirit that typified the reign of Carlos III. Instead, scholars have traditionally analyzed the experience of the American viceroyalties as something apart from the Spanish kingdoms of Iberia and have generally correlated a cohesive vision of reform in the Americas with the post-1762 period; following the British occupation of Havana during the Seven Years' War, the Crown aggressively sought resources to fund a professional standing army, intensifying the pace of reforms. But as scholarly interest in the early Bourbon period has increased, many have come to acknowledge that reformism – as a spirit that defined the political culture of the age – began under the Habsburgs, with significant reforms inaugurated during the succession war itself. Whereas Storrs and others have emphasized the reformist inclinations of Carlos II's administration, Adrian Pearce, Francisco Eissa-Barrosa, Allan J. Kuethe, and Kenneth J. Andrien have also called for a revised timeline of the so-called Bourbon reforms, situating commercial and administrative innovations under Felipe V within a cohesive eighteenth-century vision intent on generating more resources for imperial war. A consensus, therefore, has begun to emerge; rather than representing a period of unprecedented Enlightened innovation, the late eighteenth-century reforms of Carlos III represented the culmination of a spirit of reform that began to take root in the seventeenth century. Upon Felipe V's ascension, Bourbon influencers reinvigorated the reform project and claimed it as theirs.

As this study illustrates, supporters of Bourbon rule did this in a way that might appear contradictory. In selling the populace an enticing vision of the future, they characterized Felipe V and his lineage as sacred rulers in the style of their Habsburg predecessors, poised to end suffering and usher in a golden age. Although early supporters of Bourbon rule embarked on an unprecedented influence campaign that circulated printed material throughout the empire, the cultural dimension of Spain's dynastic transition has only recently captured the curiosity of scholars. In 1966, María Teresa Pérez Picazo produced a foundational study of how print propaganda disseminated by both the Grand Alliance and Franco-Spanish forces targeted would-be supporters in the Spanish kingdoms, but additional studies would not appear for several decades.[40] In the early 2000s, David González Cruz produced a series of essays and books on the pro-Bourbon and pro-Habsburg propaganda that circulated throughout the empire during the War of the Spanish Succession, and argued that both sides framed the struggle as a "holy war."[41] As we will see, the incorporation of Protestant troops within the Grand Alliance allowed Bourbon supporters to frame the war as a defense of Catholicism. But, while González Cruz incorporated a small corpus of printed literature produced in New Spain into his analysis, the *Rebirth of the Spanish Empire* focuses exclusively on the viceroyalty, placing the large corpus of pro-Bourbon material that circulated throughout New Spain within its unique political and cultural contexts.

Utilizing this material, this study then focuses on how subjects imagined their place within the empire at the end of the long seventeenth century and, relatedly, how they processed the end of Habsburg rule. Throughout the seventeenth century, municipalities held succession ceremonies, litanies in support of the Spanish Crown, celebrations of military victories, and commemorations of royal births. However, during the years of the war, these types of public ceremonies occurred in rapid succession within a condensed timeframe, overwhelming the public sphere but also providing an entryway into the dispositions and understandings of everyday subjects. Like the playwrights of seventeenth-century Spain who catered to the tastes and sensibilities of their audiences, all Bourbon propagandists, whether painters, craftsmen, pamphleteers, or orators, sought to connect with subjects, building on what would have been (at least on some level) shared understandings to confirm what people already "knew."[42]

Propagandists understood how to trigger memories and stir emotions and deliberately selected or underscored specific messages rooted in the viceroyalty's political culture. Furthermore, viceregal orators reinforced preexisting understandings based in a shared religious culture: a Spanish one, to be sure, but one rooted in New Spain's unique history.

Recently, several specialists have shifted their attention more concertedly toward the large corpus of sermons given during the War of the Spanish Succession. Iván Escamilla González, Bernarda Urrejola Davanzo, and I independently confirmed that at different moments during the conflict, orators in New Spain characterized Felipe V as a Habsburg, thereby promising continuity to his potentially mistrustful subjects.[43] More recently, Escamilla Gónzalez and I examined the importance of visual imagery and descriptions of the king's corporeality in pro-Bourbon spectacle and oratory.[44] Building from this previous work, and from a sensitive review of the large corpus of propaganda that circulated in the viceroyalty during the war, *The Rebirth of the Spanish Empire* unravels the interrelated symbols and metaphors used in New Spain's pro-Bourbon oratory and ceremony, uncovering a cohesive message regarding Bourbon ascension. In New Spain, prelates, artisans, and intellectuals regarded their audiences as belonging to an empire understood as a body politic, an extension of the king's mystical body. During the War of the Spanish Succession, this metaphorical understanding of the *Monarquía Hispánica* as a body lent itself to explaining Bourbon ascension; the metaphor of a Christ-like body being "reborn" or renewed spoke to the moment. Whether through references to the sun, the Eucharist, or to the literal body of Christ, propagandists promised ascension, resurrection, and renewal. In municipalities throughout New Spain, pro-Bourbon priests reminded subjects that they belonged to the *cuerpo de Cristo* (body of Christ) and the *cuerpo del rey* (body of the king), and communicated similar messages based in millenarian thought, ideas rooted in Spain's collective religious and political history, as well as the specific religious culture of New Spain. Borrowing from what might be perceived as an eclectic, and therefore fragmented collection of biblical passages, symbols, origin stories, and visual tropes, bureaucratic and ecclesiastic leaders created a shared narrative of sacred kingship, redemption, and revitalization.

METHOD AND ORGANIZATION

Throughout the War of the Spanish Succession, administrators in New Spain feared an enemy invasion and the development of homegrown conspiracies against Bourbon rule. To forestall dissent, Crown officials utilized a variety of tactics, including inundating the region with imprints and ordering the mounting of a series of public ceremonies in support of the new dynasty. Although *The Rebirth of the Spanish Empire* is not tightly organized by chronology, a series of developments triggered this type of semiotic activity and provide the temporal and developmental scaffolding for this study.

Military developments and dynastic milestones occasioned the creation and dissemination of pro-Bourbon propaganda in the form of imprints and engravings produced in Spain and the viceroyalty, elaborate public ceremonies held in viceregal municipalities, and the corresponding oratory performed in cathedrals, parishes, and convents. The funerary honors for Carlos II and the oath ceremony for Felipe V in 1701 marked the end of the Habsburg era, and municipalities throughout the viceroyalty marked the transition with lavish spectacles, as we will see. In 1705, Barcelona proclaimed its loyalty to the Archduke Charles of the Holy Roman Empire, acclaiming him Carlos III of Spain, and in 1706, Allied forces occupied Madrid. In April 1707, Bourbon forces defeated the Grand Alliance at the Battle of Almansa, and this occasioned the Crown to appropriate the annual masses previously established by Carlos II for the souls of deceased soldiers.[45] Also in 1707, royal bureaucrats and prelates interpreted the pregnancy of Queen-consort María Luisa Gabriela de Saboya and the birth of Spain's first Bourbon crown prince as a sign that, after many decades of infertility in the Spanish royal house, God showed his preference for Bourbon rule.[46] This happy development occasioned sermons of supplication and thanksgiving following Luis Fernando's birth, succeeded a couple of years later with oaths of loyalty to Luis I (1707–1724). With the defeat of the enemy at the pivotal battles of Brihuega and Villaviciosa in 1710, the Bourbon Crown ordered municipalities and religious jurisdictions throughout the empire to hold celebrations and masses of gratitude. Then, in 1711, in response to reports of sacrilege and iconoclasm by the Protestant forces aligned with Austria, the Crown ordered communities to implement an annual *Fiesta de Desagravios al Santísimo Sacramento* (Feast Day to Make Amends to the Most Holy Sacrament), which occasioned its own inaugural commemorations.[47] Although these represented pivotal moments in the Bourbon influence campaign, bureaucrats in Spain flooded the viceroyalty with pamphlets, as well as newspapers (*gazetas*) throughout the entirety of the conflict. Orators, moreover, expressed the viceroyalty's collective loyalty to Felipe V on a myriad of other occasions.

In Chapter 1, I introduce the conflict in the Spanish kingdoms and show that the War of the Spanish Succession placed the viceroyalty of New Spain on the defensive, with a heightened concern for, and awareness of, dynastic politics. It absorbed the attention of administrators throughout its duration and impacted every level of society to varying degrees. Mixed-race people and free people of color played key roles in defending the viceroyalty, but they also awakened the mistrust of administrators. Some Creole families experienced negative fallout from the crisis on their bottom lines, but others took advantage of the transition to advance within the royal bureaucracy. The uncertainty awakened by the war contributed to a climate of fear that serves as context for understanding how subjects in New Spain received messages regarding Felipe V's political and religious legitimacy. As we will see, contemporaries rooted these messages in medieval notions of kingship and a millenarian "third stage" of history; that is, the future.

In unraveling these messages, I decode the semiotics of the political culture of the monarchy as communicated and received in the viceroyalty of New Spain; that is, I examine how contemporaries in the viceroyalty understood, and were taught to understand, kingship and empire, and how specific scriptural passages, origin myths, prophecies, and visual symbols reinforced a regenerative and messianic message regarding the future of Spain. As the shared memory of a discrete community, culture is a social phenomenon that involves both remembering and forgetting, as well as degrees of knowing and understanding among individuals and groups. In New Spain, bureaucrats, artists, and prelates embedded the new reality of Bourbon rule within the system of signs traditionally used to understand Habsburg Spain's role in the world, and these condensed a variety of interrelated referents. Leaders in New Spain "translated" Bourbon rule, thereby revealing what they believed Spanish subjects understood regarding early modern Spanish kingship, as well as the role of the Spanish Monarchy in God's eschatological plan.[48] This study, therefore, invites readers to think about the reception of these messages, as they were clearly created with consideration to the emotional and intellectual disposition of the audience.

Subsequent chapters rely on the analysis of extant imprints, overwhelmingly in support of Bourbon rule, that circulated within New Spain, including sermons and descriptions of ceremonies given to commemorate military victories or royal milestones. Many pro-Bourbon imprints traveled from Spain to the viceroyalty, and these included reports of military victories, the uncovering of conspiracies, anonymous satires, and accounts of miracles. Sermons and descriptions of public rituals in support of Bourbon rule printed in New Spain total close to sixty for this period and gesture toward a far larger number of sermons that did not make it to print. They reveal how the War of the Spanish Succession dominated the attention of subjects in New Spain and illuminate the strategies deployed by bureaucrats and orators in translating Bourbon rule.

Spanish subjects in New Spain did not passively receive messages in support of the Bourbon succession. Rather, as I argue in Chapter 2, writers and orators had to compete for their audience's attention. Subjects in New Spain maneuvered within a "Baroque public sphere" where they also processed rumors, conflicting news reports, and fragments of pro-Austrian propaganda. While viceregal administrators tried to prevent the circulation of news or the expression of sentiments in support of the Austrian contender, the Archduke Charles, a series of disloyalty investigations in Mexico City reveal how Habsburg sympathizers sifted critically and reactively through the overwhelmingly pro-Bourbon deluge of information, created and disseminated pro-Austrian propaganda, and sought to forge ties to other Habsburg loyalists. Yet, as this chapter also makes clear, a flood of pro-Bourbon propaganda produced first in Spain overcame the public sphere in New Spain, with orators selecting highly resonant anecdotes from printed accounts known as *relaciones de sucesos* (news pamphlets) and then repeating the information, almost verbatim, in their sermons. The drift of information from metropole to viceroyalty to locality helped to reinforce shared understandings of the conflict and an "imagined community" not of nation, as discussed by Benedict Anderson, but of empire.[49] Subjects reinforced their belonging to an imagined community of empire by engaging with print literature, oratory, spectacle, and gossip—forms of propaganda that affirmed their membership in a transatlantic imperial community helmed by a sacred king.

Digging deeper into pro-Bourbon pamphlets, ceremonies, ephemeral art, portraiture, and sermons, a dominant theme emerges in representations of the royal family at the end of the long seventeenth century: the importance of the literal body and the metaphorical body of the king. As Alejandra B. Osorio has argued, representations of the king's body and commemorations centered on his person served as the foundation of a "cultural grammar" that transcended geography and shaped attachments to empire.[50] As I illustrate in Chapter 3, bureaucrats and ecclesiastics played on interrelated metaphors related to the body to affirm the loyalty of all corporations within the viceroyalty to Felipe V. Cultural leaders activated a multiplicity of symbols that helped people associate the healthy body of the new king with the defense of the body of Christ and the revived body politic under the Bourbons; they encouraged people to see themselves as part of the *cuerpo del rey*. Through references to the corporeal, with the implicit contrast of the bodies of Carlos II and Felipe V, leaders within New Spain promised that the empire would rise again like Lazarus, whom Christ miraculously resurrected, or by unspoken implication, Christ himself. As I show here and in subsequent chapters, pro-Bourbon intellectuals engaged in "condensation" whereby, as explained by anthropologist David Kertzer, "individual symbols represent and unify a diverse array of ideas," creating at a "subconscious, and hence more powerful, level" an association of these ideas in an individual's mind.[51]

Furthermore, as I also show, the *Monarquía Hispánica*'s system of composite monarchy allowed municipal leaders and ecclesiastics in New Spain to reaffirm their Spanish identity while simultaneously expressing their devotion to local cults and to the "kingdom" of New Spain, thereby allowing for, in Osorio's words, a form of "colonial hybridity," or what I imagine as "composite identities."[52] Loyalty to the king, kingdom, and locality all mattered, and subjects in New Spain reaffirmed their membership in overlapping body politics through the same devotion. Viceregal subjects, therefore, condensed symbols and metaphors to express "composite" allegiances.

The collective focus on imperial resurrection and revival in early eighteenth-century New Spain's oratory is, on the surface, understandable. Trained in the same seminaries and universities, many orators shared similar exegetical leanings, often drawing from the same biblical passages, theological texts, and visual tropes to interpret the war.[53] Yet the recurring, interwoven messages found in this body of work reflect more than shared educational experiences: they reveal deeply entrenched and widely held convictions about the king's providential role in the world – convictions likely reinforced by a proliferation of anti-Machiavellian literature that extolled the Spanish monarch's moral responsibilities and the religious foundation of his authority. Catholic political thinkers such as Antonio de Guevara (c. 1481–1545), Pedro de Ribadeneyra (1526–1611), Juan de Mariana (1536–1624), Francisco Suárez (1548–1617), Diego de Saavedra Fajardo (1584–1648), and Juan de Palafox y Mendoza (1600–1659) wrote extensively about the ideal Christian prince. They portrayed him as a moral exemplar who ruled with justice, piety, and humility, and as a guardian of the Catholic faith, whose authority was grounded in divine law and directed toward the spiritual and temporal well-being of his subjects.[54]

Emerging from this tradition, New Spain's most respected orators regularly critiqued and approved one another's work. Both regular and secular clergy belonged to tightly knit communities, and higher clergy were often called upon to deliver panegyric or commemorative sermons. Mendicant orators had to submit their writings for approval by their provincials, and publishing any text in New Spain required multiple licenses. Sometimes, the same *calificador* (a censor for the Inquisition) would review numerous sermons from this period while also producing his own. In Mexico City, figures like Juan Ignacio Castorena y Ursúa – cathedral canon, former rector of the University of Mexico, and member of the Oratory of San Felipe Neri – wrote and published sermons and compiled a lengthy account of the cathedral's pro-Bourbon celebrations. As a *calificador*, he also approved the sermons of other preachers, such as Juan de San Miguel, the Franciscan guardian of the Convent of San Antonio in Durango, and the Jesuit Antonio de Valtierra, a cathedral canon in Guatemala. Although geographically dispersed across the viceroyalty, these priests participated in a shared intellectual culture – a "republic of letters" – that transcended physical boundaries and worked collectively to shape, circulate, and police political and religious ideas.

High-ranking orators, as well as authors of descriptions of ceremonies, generally wanted to have their work printed and sent to Spain to serve as a testament to their loyalty to the Bourbon house; demonstrations of loyalty like this could later help to secure future honors and promotions. These, by extension, also exalted any other corporation associated with the commemoration, such as a municipality's governing council, its cathedral chapter, or one of its convents. Whether sermons or descriptions of ceremonies, authors dedicated these printed texts to high-ranking bureaucrats, courtiers, the crown prince Luis I, or to the king himself. Sermons and ceremonies, therefore, served as tools of propaganda in layered ways. The messages conveyed through pageantry and oratory reached large and eclectic audiences dispersed throughout the urban centers of the viceroyalty in a short-lived, although spectacular, fashion. The printed artifact continued to communicate political messages, as elites, religious corporations, the Council of the Indies, and the monarch all received copies. Printing allowed sermons and accounts of ceremonies to have secondary lives, knitting the empire together; they testified to the loyalty of not only individuals but entire communities.

Chapters 4 and 5 focus on a pervasive theme within New Spain's pro-Bourbon oratory: sacred kingship. Specifically, Chapter 4 examines salient aspects of Western Europe's, and especially medieval Spain's, long tradition of messianic prophecy and its application to monarchical rulers. As I show, orators framed their characterizations of Felipe V in understandings rooted loosely in Joachimite prophecy; that is, prophecy deriving initially from the writings of the Calabrian mystic Joachim de Fiore (1135–1202) regarding the inauguration of a "third stage" of history. What is more, the large number of millenarian references suggests an intellectual tradition autochthonous to New Spain, where some Franciscan friars interpreted the "discovery" and evangelization campaign through a millenarian lens.[55] Both chapters focus on the Old Testament as prophecy, and especially exegesis related to the House of David. David's lineage, that is, the genealogical tree deriving from his father, Jesse, played a central role in Christian eschatology and the monarchical millenarianism associated with Spanish rulers.

Chapter 5 continues the discussion of monarchical prophecy by focusing on the central anxiety of early modern monarchies: succession. Here, I examine the meanings attributed to the conception and birth of the first Bourbon crown prince of Spain: Luis I. Sermons of supplication for a safe and healthy birth, sermons of thanksgiving following the birth of the crown prince, and oath ceremonies in honor of Luis I all emphasized the miracle of fecundity through references to nature, and especially flowers, which simultaneously promised future prosperity and abundance. Visual iconography and oratory remained focused on succession from the ascension of the king in 1701 through the death of María Luisa Gabriela de Saboya, the mother of three surviving male heirs, in 1715. Bourbon influencers encouraged their audiences to see her as a millenarian figure.

In the end, characterizations of the Bourbon dynasty during the War of the Spanish Succession reflect expectations regarding the revitalization of the imperial body politic. To look forward, Bourbon influencers had to look back toward traditional understandings of monarchy and the place of the messianic hero in Spanish imperial imaginings. Luis Weckman, Antonio Rubial García, and David Brading have all observed how the cultural history of New Spain does not necessarily align with standard historical periodization. "Medieval" understandings and practices endured through at least the seventeenth century and so-called baroque beliefs and artistic styles persisted well into the eighteenth century.[56] The supporters of Spain's "modern" monarchy looked to the deep past to legitimize dynastic change. The progressive "Bourbon millennium" rested firmly on a Habsburg foundation.

I

New Spain at War

In 1712, Diego Jiménez, a soldier from Mexico City, wrote to the Council of the Indies asking to receive back pay in consideration of the many services he had performed for the Spanish Crown. While serving in Florida, he had been taken prisoner by the English and held captive for four years, and upon being released, he enlisted in the service of Andrés de Arriola, general of the Armada de Barlovento, the viceroyalty of New Spain's coast guard and convoy responsible for shepherding funds and supplies to presidios throughout the Caribbean. Slated for the future governorship of Florida, Arriola traveled to Florida in 1704 with between 150 and 200 Spanish recruits. At some point, while fighting alongside Frenchmen against the English, Jiménez lost his right arm. After this tragedy, he returned to Mexico City to petition the Crown.[1]

Although dramatic, the difficulties faced by Jiménez did not necessarily set him apart from his contemporaries. Indeed, in New Spain, the succession crisis effected all social groups, and its impact could be felt throughout the administrations of four viceroys: the Count of Moctezuma (December 18, 1696–November 3, 1701), Archbishop Juan Ortega y Montañés (November 4, 1701–November 27, 1702), the Duke of Alburquerque (November 27, 1702–January 14, 1711), and the Duke of Linares (January 15, 1711–August 15, 1716). As the viceroyalty most in contact with the metropole and as the headquarters for supplying presidios throughout the Caribbean, New Spain served an important strategic function, and officials in Castile and the viceroyalty immediately set about strengthening its defenses and tying the region and its people to the Bourbon Crown. The conflict, moreover, impacted people's daily lives in significant ways. As this chapter lays bare, it promoted feelings of fear

21

and anxiety, displaced military personnel like Diego Jiménez, and placed financial pressure on residents at all levels of society.

Even if they wanted to stay removed from events in Europe, the people of New Spain were made heavily aware of the succession crisis and understood its implications to varying degrees. As many confronted challenges to security and trade posed by the conflict, others sought to take advantage of the extraordinary circumstances to gain financially and socially. Taking his cue from his grandfather, on March 6, 1701, Felipe V outlawed the sale of bureaucratic appointments, hoping to end the culture of corruption that many believed typified the administration of the *Monarquía Hispánica*. However, after confronting the immense cost of the war, in 1704 Felipe V's administration opened the sale of appointments at all levels of government; most of these posts were in the Indies, with Creoles serving as the purchasers.[2]

Although the brunt of the fighting happened far from New Spain, the War of the Spanish Succession would remain ever-present in the minds of subjects throughout the viceroyalty. As orators, bureaucrats, and artisans planned elaborate pro-Bourbon ceremonies, communities and individuals faced significant threats resulting from the war, and these, of course, shaped how they received and interpreted messages regarding Felipe V and Bourbon forces. Furthermore, onerous policies and taxes designed to meet the exigencies of war contributed to feelings of uncertainty and vulnerability.

Although mainland New Spain never saw battle resulting directly from the succession crisis, it impacted the lives of people throughout the region. Spaniards and Creoles, *castas* (mixed-raced people), and indigenous people all experienced the tumult of the crisis to varying degrees. People from all social stations became involved in preempting enemy attacks and were also expected to help fund the war in Spain and the defense of the viceroyalty. Despite the vast distance that separated Spain from the Americas, the people of New Spain felt the impact of the War of the Spanish Succession on their daily lives.

WAR IN THE SPANISH KINGDOMS

The War of the Spanish Succession involved conflict throughout Europe, North America, and the Philippines, but developments in the Spanish theater naturally triggered the most reverberations throughout mainland New Spain. With the onset of war in Spain, viceregal officials and ecclesiastical leaders responded with demonstrations of support for Felipe V, and, as we will see in the following chapter, subjects shared news emanating from the frontlines. Through *gazetas* and official communications, subjects throughout New Spain learned about recent developments, or at least what officials in Spain wanted them to know.

Carlos II died on November 1, 1700, and by November 12, Louis XIV had received a copy of the testament naming his grandson the sole heir of the Spanish Monarchy. At just seventeen, the recently acclaimed Felipe V entered the Palace of Buen Retiro on February 19, 1701, and then stopped at the shrine of Our Lady of Atocha before entering Madrid for the *jura del rey* (royal oath ceremony), a ritual demonstration that would then be repeated in municipalities throughout the empire. On September 11, Felipe V married María Gabriela Luisa de Saboya, the daughter of the Duke of Savoy, a valued ally of his paternal grandfather, through proxy, but he had little time to settle into his position, let alone married life. Between 1701 and 1704, Habsburg Austria, Prussia, England, the Low Countries, Portugal, and even Savoy would gradually forge a Grand Alliance against France and Spain, leaving the Bourbons with the support of only Bavaria and Cologne. Although Carlos II's will prohibited the union of France and Spain as grounds for nullifying Felipe V's inheritance, the Grand Alliance collectively sought to forestall any possibility of this by placing the Archduke Charles, the second son of Holy Roman Emperor Leopold I, on the Spanish throne. France, England, and the Netherlands, moreover, all used the conflict to seek trading advantages in the Indies.[3]

In September 1701, Felipe V traveled to Catalonia to swear an oath to uphold its constitution, to preside over the Cortes in Barcelona, and to meet his new wife for the first time. Six months later, the king would depart to fight in northern Italy, where conflict had already broken out. Then, on May 15, 1702, the Grand Alliance formally declared war on France and Spain, and would soon invade the kingdoms of Aragon and Castile. In August and September, English and Dutch maritime forces laid siege to both Cádiz and the Port of Santa María, and in October, they pursued New Spain's *flota*, or merchant fleet, attacking it just as it sought safe harbor in the Port of Vigo in Galicia. In December, Felipe V returned to Spain, but the Bourbon Crown immediately confronted a series of provocations. On September 12, 1703, Vienna acclaimed the Archduke Charles "Carlos III of Spain."[4]

Portugal formally joined the Grand Alliance in 1703, and by March 1704, the Archduke Charles had arrived in Lisbon with over 6,000 soldiers, ready to merge with a purported 20,000 more. This provoked Felipe V to briefly invade Portugal, and the forces of the

Archduke Charles breached Spain before being pushed back to Lisbon.[5] These early escalations alarmed people throughout the empire. In July 1703, the Minister General of the Franciscan Order, Alonso Diez, ordered all provincials, superiors, and abbesses under his authority to devote time on the Sundays and feast days during an entire month to a solemn procession throughout their cloisters, and he ordered that they hold daily prayer with mortification in support of Felipe V. This was then signed and ordered by the head of New Spain's Franciscan Provincia del Santo Evangelio (Province of the Holy Gospel).[6]

War in Spain initially concentrated into two zones of combat: land war along the western Portuguese front and maritime battle along the southern and eastern coast. In August 1704, George Rooke's forces continued to attack port cities and, significantly, claimed Gibraltar for Queen Anne; Franco-Spanish forces sought to recoup the site multiple times, but to no avail. In September 1704, French soldiers finally arrived to help shore up the Portuguese front, but while in 1705 Franco-Spanish forces fought key battles in Extremadura, the kingdoms comprising the Crown of Aragon devolved into what can be characterized as political rebellion on one extreme, and civil war on the other. In October, Felipe V lost Barcelona to the Archduke Charles, who would soon take up residence in the city.[7]

Aragon's wavering loyalty lay in decades of conflict with Madrid over the quartering of soldiers in private homes, as well as real and perceived threats to the political and economic autonomy of the Crown of Aragon and its own composite polities. When Spain joined the Nine Years' War (1688–1697) against France, it led to the swelling of troops in the Crown of Aragon and the reigniting of the decades-old conflict regarding the garrisoning of soldiers. Indeed, there would be widespread resistance to impositions from Madrid, with Barcelona even refusing to pay the *donativo*, or voluntary donation, to the Crown. Then, in 1697, the French navy laid siege to Barcelona. These stressors, along with the fierce autonomy of the Crown of Aragon and its polities, would sow antipathy toward the French and fuel resistance to Bourbon rule.[8]

The two-month siege of Barcelona resulted in around 12,000 Catalan deaths. Significantly, the Duke of Vendôme, the future commander of the French military in Spain, directed the siege while Prince George Louis of Hessen-Darmstadt (1669–1705), a Field Marshal in the Austrian Army, defended Barcelona. Hessen-Darmstadt would then serve as Viceroy of Catalonia between 1698 and 1701, endear himself to Barcelona's elite, and lead the Austrian army in Spain during the War of the Spanish Succession (1701–1705).[9] Finally, many subjects in Aragon viewed

French artisans and merchants who resided in the region as economic threats. Tension often erupted in anti-French violence, with incidences increasing in number during the second half of the seventeenth century. Valencia saw two significant anti-French riots in 1678 and 1691, triggered by the constant state of war and the bombardment of the port city.[10]

Franco-Spanish forces faced their most difficult year to date in 1706, with Felipe V leading a siege of Barcelona against an army now set upon returning the Habsburg dynasty to Spain. The Allied forces in Portugal entered Castile in January and gradually pushed all the way to Madrid. Felipe V, however, could not meet the threat in Castile. Anglo-Dutch auxiliary forces and a hostile Aragonese population compelled him to retreat into France on May 9. He did not enter Navarre until June and made it to Madrid just in time to transfer the court to Burgos. On June 27, the Archduke made a triumphal entrance into Madrid, but according to numerous accounts, most *madrileños* remained loyal to Felipe V. Nevertheless, during the Grand Alliance's roughly two-month occupation, many grandees and other high-level functionaries defected to the Habsburg side. Felipe V did not enter Madrid again until October 4.[11]

Several key developments revitalized the Bourbon cause the following year. In February, the Crown made the unprecedented move of announcing the queen's first pregnancy, which prompted widespread rejoicing and boosted morale. Confidence in the dynasty rose again after the Franco-Spanish victory at Almansa on April 25, which helped return the kingdom of Valencia to Felipe V. In June, the monarch punished the rebellious Crown of Aragon by issuing the first of the decrees known as the *Nueva Planta*, abolishing the autonomous laws and governing institutions of the kingdoms of Aragon and Valencia. Then, on August 25, exactly four months after Almansa, the queen-consort gave birth to the first Bourbon crown prince of Spain. Finally, in October, Bourbon forces captured the important city of Lérida.[12]

Despite these positive developments, the Bourbons would face bleak prospects over the next two years. Fighting in the kingdoms of Spain slowed in 1708, with decisive confrontations elsewhere in Europe, but in 1709, Spain and France experienced freezing temperatures, famine, epidemics, and popular unrest, with France much harder hit. This, combined with the financial drain of war, led Louis XIV to send his Secretary of State, the Marquis of Torcy, to the Hague to negotiate an acceptable peace.[13] In June, Louis XIV pulled most of his soldiers out of Spain, and in November, Felipe V broke off all diplomatic relations with Pope Clement XI (1649–1721), who had recently recognized "Carlos III" under intense pressure from the Holy Roman Emperor Joseph I, the successor of Leopold I, who had died in 1705.[14] Then, in 1710, Dutch representatives at the Hague tried to compel the French king to use his army against his own grandson to force his surrender. Instead, Louis XIV sent the Duke of Vendôme to Spain to aid Felipe V, who, along with General Villars, kept fighting the enemy led by Austrian General Guido Starhemberg (1657–1737) and English General James Stanhope (1673–1721). In July, the alliance defeated Spanish forces at Zaragoza, and then in September, the Archduke Charles occupied Madrid for a second time.[15]

All seemed close to lost, but the tide of war soon turned unexpectedly in favor of Felipe V. On October 30, General Vendôme, leading troops of Spanish soldiers, forced the Archduke Charles to flee to Barcelona, defeating his rear guard in Brihuega on December 8. Then, on December 11, General Vendôme and Felipe V routed the remaining force in Villaviciosa. The Crown announced the victories throughout the empire and ordered religious acts of thanksgiving and other "customary" celebrations.[16] Only four months later, another development hastened the conclusion of the war. On April 17, the Holy Roman Emperor Joseph I passed away. Now, the Archduke Charles would succeed his brother, making members of the Grand Alliance wary of supporting Charles's sovereignty over Spain. In September, the newly acclaimed Charles IV left for Vienna, never to return to Aragon. Fighting officially concluded on August 11, 1712, but Barcelona refused to surrender until September 12, 1714.[17]

So far removed from Europe, and yet so tethered to Spain, New Spain felt administrative, military, and economic reverberations from all these developments. As will be examined in depth later, from 1700 to 1714 people throughout New Spain commemorated a series of important milestones related to the succession crisis, and news circulated in the form of imprints and gossip throughout the *audiencia* districts of Mexico, Guatemala, and New Galicia. However, the war also affected people's sense of security, threatened their economic stability, and impacted their social mobility, for better or worse. It could take anywhere from sixty to eighty days for a ship departing from Cádiz to reach New Spain during the war. But, as Sylvia Sellers-Garcia reminds us, compared to the duration of travel to other less prioritized locations in the empire, Veracruz and Mexico City seemed relatively "close" to the metropole from a contemporary perspective.[18] Regardless of its distance from the frontlines, the conflict over the succession had an immediate and sometimes intimate effect on life in New Spain.

DEFENDING THE VICEROYALTY

In the two decades preceding the death of Carlos II, New Spain experienced negative fallout from various imperial contests. In 1683, a group of over 900 buccaneers led by the Dutch pirate Laurent le Graaf (or Lorencillo) raided Veracruz in the middle of the night. The mob terrorized the population and pillaged more than 6 million *reales* (750,000 *pesos*) worth of specie and goods. While this enormous sum – equivalent in its purchasing power to between US$45 and US$75 million – underscores the economic devastation of the raid, four hundred men and women also died because of the attack.[19] Furthermore, the buccaneers kidnapped 3,000 people and held them on the Isla de Sacrificios at the entrance of Veracruz, with free and enslaved blacks representing a third of those abducted. Some died of starvation, and after the pirates received 1.2 million *reales* worth of ransom, they absconded with at least 1,000 free and enslaved blacks, roughly one-sixth of Veracruz's permanent population. The buccaneers then sold these people throughout the Caribbean, regardless of whether they were legally free.[20] Two years later, Lorencillo's crew attacked New Spain again, but this time the port of Campeche. Considering the continuous foreign threat along the coast, in 1700 the viceroy, the Count of Moctezuma, sought to fortify the Isla de Sacrificios.[21]

The years immediately preceding the death of Carlos II should have primed the viceroyalty for war. In 1697, twenty-five French ships descended upon Cartagena at the tail end of the Nine Years' War, resulting in its ransacking and the loss of around 20 million pesos from the royal coffers and from the homes and businesses of individuals and families. The ease with which the city fell led many to suspect its governor of conspiring with the French, prompting an investigation by the *audiencia* of Quito. Then, between 1698 and 1699, the Company of Scotland for Trading with Africa and the Indies attempted to create a colony in Darien right near Portobelo, where the treasure galleons collected the bullion mined in Peru. In response, the Crown ordered the viceroy of New Spain to send money and provisions to Portobelo on March 2, 1700. Significantly, the papacy also granted the Crown permission to use onetenth of ecclesiastical salaries (and up to 1,000,000 gold *escudos*) to pay for the defense of Darien against the Protestant heretics.[22]

The threat of a possible attack became compounded by the presence of foreign pirates, smugglers, loggers, and their African slaves in the Laguna de Términos, a large tidal lagoon in the province of Tabasco between Campeche and Veracruz, rich in the lucrative dyewood *palo de tinte*;

English and Dutch interlopers had long peppered the area with small logging settlements and even military forts equipped with weapons.[23] After the death of Carlos II in 1700, the Spanish Crown, the French Crown, and the French sailors sent to Spanish America to protect the ports and the treasure fleets repeatedly warned New Spain's viceroy of a possible enemy invasion, and in May 1701 the Count of Moctezuma asked again to fortify the Isla de Sacrificios, citing the lingering fear experienced by the residents of Veracruz as a result of Lorencillo's attack.[24] Past trauma, therefore, conditioned how people responded to impending war.

Having received word of the presence of eighty English ships near New Spain, the Count of Moctezuma sent thousands of soldiers to protect Veracruz, the viceroyalty's principal port.[25] Unsettling reports, moreover, also arrived from Venezuela, which quickly became a hotbed of disloyalty. In 1701, an ambassador from Vienna, Don Bartolomé de Capocelato, the Count of Antería, arrived in Caracas via Curaçao, and Captain General Nicolás Eugenio de Ponte y Hoyo, as well as other military officials, several members of the *cabildo*, and many religious reportedly joined him in an ad hoc oath ceremony for "Carlos III." Bishop Diego Baños y Sotomayor raised soldiers against the disloyal and arrested Capocelato. Caracas, a center for illicit trade with Dutch merchants and slave traders, took years to settle down.[26] Then, in February 1702, the viceroy learned that nineteen English war vessels had been spotted off the coast of Jamaica, while the next month, a French admiral sent word from Havana that forty Dutch and English ships circled the island with the goal of taking the fleet that was soon to depart from Veracruz.[27] Intelligence of this kind terrified New Spain's residents, especially in port cities. In May 1703, the Mexico City diarist Antonio de Robles described how fearing an enemy attack, the residents of Veracruz vacated the city with their families and property.[28] Soon, the king would commission engineers throughout the viceroyalty to strengthen coastal presidios. Even as late as 1711, Felipe V advised New Spain's viceroy to fortify the ports of Veracruz, Campeche, and Tabasco, and to send aid to Cuba and Florida.[29]

Fear of the enemy proved well-founded, and subjects from all walks of life became involved in the defense of the viceroyalty. When in 1701 the Count of Moctezuma and his Council of War decided to fortify the Isla de Sacrificios, they did so with the aid of black and mulatto militiamen. Meanwhile, the viceroy sent an additional 100 veteran soldiers, composed of the palace guard, to the port, along with 100 forced recruits (*forzados*) from Mexico City and Puebla. The viceroy, moreover, also requested soldiers and cavalry from the towns of Puebla, Tlaxcala, Huejotzingo, and Tepeaca in the central part of the viceroyalty, and sent instructions to all port cities so that they could prepare for a possible invasion.[30] Although viceregal officials had tried to excise the English from the Laguna de Términos long before formal war broke out in May 1702, the changing context of war with England made dislodging them a priority, especially given reports that between forty and fifty English ships filled the lagoon. In Yucatán, Governor Martín de Urzúa y Arizmendi sought to protect the ports along the coast and famously opened a trail from Campeche to Petén to "reconquer" the Itza people, who he believed vulnerable to foreign influence.[31]

Officials in Campeche and Tabasco directed the effort to force out the English, as these areas proved most threatened by the foreign presence in the lagoon. After two Irishmen who had escaped from the lagoon due to poor treatment by the English arrived in Campeche in 1701, they provided officials with intelligence used to launch an expedition; officials loaded a French sailing ship with 170 men to drive them out, and two Spaniards lost their lives in the ensuing maritime skirmish.[32] Another expedition to the lagoon in November 1701 led to the capture of yet another Irishman, who reported that the English planned on sacking Tabasco, which resulted in another failed expedition from Campeche to the lagoon the following year involving 235 armed men; the captain of the mission, Francisco Fernández, suffered a gunshot wound.[33] Meanwhile, Spanish subjects in Tabasco feared having the enemy in their midst and the following year organized a relatively successful expedition involving 128 volunteers, and in 1703, a maritime expedition of 100 men tried to stop the English from stationing themselves inland to raid and steal.[34] Nevertheless, a group of English buccaneers still managed to move up the Tecolutla River and seize the pueblo of Jalpan, whose residents had to flee into the surrounding area. An expedition of eighty men from Villa Hermosa soon arrived to weed out the foreigners who had taken refuge in the church. With the help of the residents of Jalpan, the expedition arrested 108 men.[35]

People throughout the southeast became involved in frequent efforts to remove the English and Dutch, who continued sailing into the lagoon from Jamaica, Curaçao, and the nearby Isla del Carmen. Groups of Mayan Indians from Yucatán at times worked with the buccaneers and loggers, and at other times resisted them. The English buccaneer William Dampier described how raiding parties enslaved and presumably raped women and sold the men off to different locations in the Caribbean. At times, however, indigenous men and women worked as day laborers for the English, leading to fears of an alliance of the English and Indians against the Spaniards.[36]

In 1704, officials in the viceroyalty convened a Council of War to decide the best method for driving out the foreign dyewood cutters, settling on dual expeditions; ships and soldiers attacked the lagoon from Campeche, whereas an overland campaign of approximately 100 militiamen arrived from Tabasco. After this campaign, the lagoon remained free of foreigners for approximately two years, although in 1705, sailors from Jamaica stole three small ships right from the port of Campeche.[37] Nevertheless, the situation remained relatively peaceful with the help of a coast guard consisting of two galleons funded by Campeche and Tabasco.[38] However, by 1709, the English and Dutch wood cutters returned to the region, and in 1711, 200 men departed on another campaign against the interlopers; approximately half the force served in the infantry of the presidio of Campeche, while the other half consisted of forces associated with the coast guard, as well as volunteers.[39] Not until 1717 did Spanish forces finally consolidate their control over the lagoon, and communities along the Atlantic coast remained vulnerable throughout the course of the war.

While the war provoked a great deal of disruption and anxiety along the coast of New Spain, the viceroyalty also had the obligation of supplying Caribbean presidios with the customary *situado* (the periodic arrival of funds for their maintenance), as well as weapons, munitions, and recruits. Urgency for this kind of support came shortly after the formal declaration of war when a large contingent of English soldiers and Yamasee warriors from Port Royal (Carolinas) raided the Guale and Timucua missions in what is now eastern Georgia before proceeding to San Agustín, where the English laid siege upon the presidio of San Marcos with approximately 1,500 Spanish subjects inside. Word soon reached Mexico City about how the English tortured, disfigured, and burned people alive, and also sold indigenous captives as slaves, and how they planned on striking at the heart of the viceroyalty of New Spain, Mexico City.[40] Meanwhile, General Jean-Baptiste du Casse traveled to New Spain with the new viceroy, the Duke of Alburquerque, and 2,000 soldiers from Galicia for distribution to vulnerable locations throughout the Caribbean; one hundred of these men were destined for Florida.[41] In 1703, the king warned the viceroy, the Duke of Alburquerque, that the enemy, bound for Havana, would try to take ports throughout the Gulf Coast of New

Spain. He again ordered the viceroy to assist all the ports in the Caribbean with defense, which included supplying soldiers.[42]

With horror stories circulating and officials desperate to organize a defense, recruiting soldiers proved difficult, and various contemporaries complained about the high rate of desertion among unpaid soldiers.[43] In 1703, the Duke of Albuquerque complained about the difficulties recruiting soldiers, and the Crown advised him to enlist from the "idle and lazy," something officials in Mexico City already did.[44] On April 1, 1702, the diarist Antonio de Robles reported on how ninety-six men, three women, and seven children were forcibly sent from Mexico City to a ship departing for Pensacola. Seemingly disturbed, he emphasized that many of the people were drafted for the slightest infractions, or even for no reason at all. Later, on November 29, 1703, he reported that twenty-four men were forcibly taken to different presidios throughout New Spain.[45]

Efforts to expel the English and Dutch permanently from the lagoon and protect ports throughout the Caribbean involved indigenous people and free blacks, as well as Spaniards and mixed-race people from different municipalities. In 1701, the same year that the Count of Moctezuma mobilized thousands of soldiers to protect the port city of Veracruz, indigenous leadership from Cunduacán, Tabasco, informed the acting viceroy about their community's observance of the oath of loyalty for Felipe V. In this delicate moment of war and dynastic crisis, the community astutely complained about how the Spanish *alcaldes mayores*, or Crown-appointed heads of municipal councils, forced indigenous people to sell native textiles and European goods in the system known as *repartimiento*. Seeking assistance, Cunduacán's leaders appealed to the Crown at a moment when it was especially eager to secure support in the Tabasco region. Significantly, they claimed that exploitation *forced* native people to flee into Chiapas or, worse, toward the Laguna de Términos to work alongside the English. While asking that the Spanish *alcaldes mayores* be removed from the region, they reported on how the English had looted Villa Hermosa and, notably, how the indigenous communities frequently sent expeditions to drive the English out of the lagoon and connected rivers.[46] Cunduacán, therefore, tried to benefit from the Bourbon Crown's vulnerability and gain concessions in exchange for loyalty.

A dual expedition forced the foreign dyewood cutters out of lagoon in 1704 for at least two years, but English ships eventually returned, and in 1709, indigenous sentinels spotted them off the Chiltepec River.[47] Later, free blacks from Veracruz assisted in driving the English and Dutch from the lagoon, as reported by Manuel de Landaeta in 1712. As Captain General of San Miguel de la Antigua Veracruz, Landaeta stood at the head of one hundred militiamen of color; he and his men reportedly observed the ocean and sent warnings about the presence of enemy ships to the Port of Veracruz and all the way to Mexico City, where they circulated and heightened alarm. Landaeta, moreover, reportedly traveled to Laguna de Términos to excise the smugglers, loggers, and their large number of slaves.[48] Like many others, including Diego Jiménez, Landaeta also traveled with a group of soldiers to Florida to fight the British. On his return to New Spain, he fell ill and was forced to convalesce on the nearby island of Cuba for eight months.[49]

Royal bureaucrats continued to recruit from diverse pools of would-be soldiers. Perhaps the best examples come from 1706, when contending with rumors of a planned invasion of Cartagena and Veracruz, the viceroy, the Duke of Alburquerque, ordered that a chain be placed at the entrance of the port, and convened a Council of War composed of all *alcaldes mayores* with military experience back in Europe to advise him. He then formed two companies of cavalry and two companies of infantry to help guard the castle at San Juan de Ulúa. He also sent the palace guard from Mexico City to Veracruz.[50]

By this time, the situation in both Spain and New Spain had become precarious. Word reached the viceroyalty that Felipe V failed to retake Barcelona and had been forced to transfer his court to Burgos. News regarding enemy attempts to turn Seville to the Archduke's side, as well as a copy of a letter that Felipe V wrote to Louis XIV, arrived in Mexico City around this same time; concerned about the state of the war in Iberia, Felipe V asked his grandfather to send an additional 80,000 soldiers across the Pyrenees.[51] Furthermore, a Spanish sailor who had been taken prisoner in Jamaica for three months, and two English captains captured by French forces all reported that between fifteen and seventeen English naval ships were docked in Jamaica.[52]

The viceroy's Council of War responded quickly with plans to acquire more arms and to recruit more soldiers. Commenting a mere fourteen years after Mexico City experienced its largest and most destructive uprising in history, led by its *casta* population, the advisors also clarified that the viceroyalty needed to defend itself from internal, as well as external, enemies, and that the capital needed to remain protected at all costs. In a collective statement, the committee expressed fear of the indigenous people's supposed propensity toward vice but admitted that they had been easy to dominate and identified the *casta* population as the

New Spain at War   33

viceroyalty's biggest threat. Still, no group escaped the committee's contempt. It decried the laziness of Creoles and even expressed fear of the many Spaniards who escaped Spain, fleeing "infamous" crimes, only to arrive and associate with the *castas*.[53] The committee ordered a volunteer company of merchant militiamen to remain in the capital along with the volunteer militia companies composed of guilds, including those of the bakers, pulque makers, and pork butchers.[54]

The Spanish advisors to the viceroy did not regard Indians, blacks, mixed-race people, Creoles, or even Spaniards as trustworthy but still recruited from all these groups except the Indians. The council took a census of all eligible men fourteen years old and older and jotted down their number of arms and horses. While the capital's *pardo*, or free black, militia was sent to Veracruz, other municipalities like Córdoba and Tepeaca gathered men and arms as well. In Córdoba all the draftees who failed to show up for military service were to be fined 10 pesos and serve eight days in jail.[55]

New Spain remained in a state of readiness through the conclusion of the war, but the flurry of activity of 1706 would not be repeated. Rather, it seems that officials succeeded in maintaining an adequate state of preparedness from that point on, with the viceroy even traveling to Veracruz to presumably check on the defenses of New Spain's most important port. Nevertheless, the threat to New Spain lasted through the duration of the war, with officials seeking to mobilize support for its defense from a cross-section of royal subjects. In 1709, word arrived in New Spain that the English planned on attacking from Jamaica, and in 1711 the Crown warned the viceroy that the enemy intended to conduct surprise invasions on specific port cities and ordered officials in Veracruz, Campeche, and Tabasco to be on the defense. Significantly, the Crown instructed that Indians from surrounding areas be ordered to help with defense, and that aid be sent immediately to Havana and Florida.[56]

FINANCING WAR AND NEGOTIATING LOYALTY

New Spain carried a heavy financial burden during the War of the Spanish Succession. Treasure fleets from Peru did not arrive in Spain during most of the war, and in 1708, when a treasure fleet attempted to travel to Spain from Portobelo, a British squadron prevented its passage, sinking one of its primary ships, the San José, and capturing another. But, while Peruvian silver did not arrive in Spain through official channels until 1711, New Spain provided a steady stream of bullion. In 1702, the

Crown acquired its largest injection of silver from New Spain right as the conflict began. When enemy ships forced New Spain's treasure fleet to the port of Vigo, Felipe V collected the largest amount of bullion from one fleet in Spain's history, made possible by confiscating silver earmarked for Dutch and English merchants. In total, the Crown collected 13,639,230 pesos worth of silver, with 7,000,000 going directly into royal coffers.[57]

While access to Peru's resources remained restricted, royal officials continued to rely financially on New Spain. Although no fleet arrived from Veracruz between 1700 and 1706, four fleets arrived between 1706 and 1715. Furthermore, the *capitana*, or headship, of New Spain's coast guard, the Armada de Barlovento, crossed the Atlantic in 1705, 1707, and 1711 with more than a million pesos total.[58] These hauls, gathered from the royal fifth on silver, the sale of mercury, indigenous tribute, a variety of taxes, donations, loans, and other extraordinary schemes, helped finance the war. According to Stanley and Barbara Stein, after Louis XIV withdrew troops from Spain in 1709, the arrival of around 1 million pesos worth of silver in 1710 provided the resources for Felipe V to continue fighting.[59] Still, New Spain's treasury also had to pay for the overhauling of the presidio of San Juan de Ulúa and the fortifying of garrisons in Havana, Puerto Rico, Cartagena, Portobelo, and Manila.

Defense of the region demanded heavy resources. In 1701, for example, the Count of Moctezuma sent Havana 103,000 pesos and another 30,000 to other ports in Cuba. Santo Domingo, meanwhile, received 80,000 pesos, Florida 62,000 pesos, Puerto Rico 50,000 pesos, and Cumana 20,000 pesos; port officials, moreover, received a selection of weapons, as well as grain.[60] However, after the disastrous attack on the Timucuan mission and a siege of the presidio of San Agustín by British forces in 1704, the Crown sent a letter to the viceroy condemning the fact that the presidio had not been paid the *situado* for a number of years and transferred responsibility for the presidios in Florida to the superintendent of the *alcalaba* tax collection in Puebla, Juan José de Veytia y Linaje. Previously farmed out to the local oligarchy, the sale's tax generated considerable revenue, and the appointment of the tax collector had initially been implemented under Carlos II to improve efficiency and curb corruption. To the annoyance of many within the district of Puebla, Veytia y Linaje proved a zealous tax collector, and in 1708 sent the presidio of San Agustín a *situado* consisting of 98,152 pesos.[61] Meanwhile, the Crown repeatedly complained to the viceroy about not supplying the other presidios in a timely or complete manner, as he often sent less than the requested amount of money or the desired number of arms and ammunition.[62]

Port cities and local bureaucrats had to pitch in to defend the viceroyalty and secure the coast, a process complicated by the paltry number of ships at the disposal of viceregal administrators. Campeche stepped up in 1705 with the construction of two galleons that served as part of a coast guard. Although it is not clear how the community financed the ships, the *alcalde mayor* of Tabasco personally paid for the construction of another that lasted until 1709, when it was replaced by four smaller ships. In 1711, Felipe V communicated his intention to the current viceroy, the Duke of Linares, of restoring the Armada de Barlovento to the number of ships and personnel in which it was founded; this would have meant that it would be restored to fifty ships.[63] One year later, the flagship vessel of the armada sank near the island of Cuba; sixty people drowned, but officials managed to save the 500,000 pesos in bullion that it carried for the "urgencies" of the war. Later, a French ship carried the treasure to the Port of San Luis in France.[64]

Clearly, the Bourbon Crown had to improvise at all levels to deal with the increasing challenge of funding a war. To make ends meet, the Crown implemented a series of extraordinary measures that impacted people's daily lives. In 1702, a decree ordered the collection of 5 percent of all bureaucratic salaries to be used for the war against the Grand Alliance.[65] Although the Crown originally stated the measure would last only one year, the order continued to be reissued, rising to 10 percent of salaries by 1709.[66] In 1703, the Crown availed itself for two years of a tax on *encomiendas*, or groups of indigenous tributaries; this policy extended throughout Spanish America.[67] Finally, in addition to these extraordinary measures, the Crown created a special junta within the Council of the Indies to impose heavy fines on those engaging in contraband trade. To avoid a scandal and place perpetual silence on the matter, those accused often made a sizeable "donation" to the Crown.[68]

To pay for the war, Felipe V and his advisors appropriated funds earmarked for holy war and religious causes. In 1701, the Crown allowed funds collected through the periodic publication of the Bula de la Santa Cruzada (Bull of the Holy Crusade) to be used for the defense of the viceroyalty, and the Count of Moctezuma immediately availed himself of 27,800 pesos from the collection.[69] In this same year, Felipe V cited the papal edict issued for the defense of Darien and ordered that 10 percent of the salaries of regular and secular clergy be used for the defense of the viceroyalty, given the "very probable news that the English and Dutch plan to invade and conquer the Indies." The Crown justified using the ecclesiastical donations designated for the defense of the viceroyalty by arguing that they were the same project: "the war against enemy heretics of the Crown and of religion."[70]

Requests for donations put pressure on people from all levels of society and made the urgency of the war palpable in New Spain. In 1701, the interim viceroy Ortega Montañés replaced the current viceroy, the Count of Moctezuma, who returned to Castile to preside over the Council of the Indies. Shortly thereafter, a royal order arrived instructing the interim viceroy to gather donations for the Crown, and Ortega Montañés responded by dispatching directives to the *alcalde mayores* of other municipalities to gather donations from all social groups, excepting blacks. Although municipal magistrates often coerced residents to give more than they wished, the interim viceroy put off requesting donations from the capital's wealthiest citizens until the arrival of his successor.[71] In October 1702, the Duke of Alburquerque fulfilled orders from the Crown to send back 350,000 pesos immediately to Spain, an amount that he exceeded by 25,631 pesos.[72] Then, in 1705, the viceroy sent 95,194 pesos to Spain, and in 1710, he dispatched an additional 75,944 pesos.[73]

In the early years of the war, several elite corporations hesitated in sending aid to the Bourbon Crown, perhaps concerned about investing their money in the losing side. Possibly, however, some elites may have sought to defend their corporate privileges. The cathedral chapters of Mexico and Puebla initially donated to the Crown for the defense of Darien, but after the expulsion of the foreigners, they doubted that the same papal decree applied to the War of the Spanish Succession. In October 1703, Mexico City's cathedral chapter and archbishop clashed over the collection, with the chapter arguing that "tributes" could not be imposed on ecclesiastics under penalty of excommunication. One month later, the cathedral chapter of Puebla made clear that they also resented the extension of the papal edict.[74] While the papal edict approved the collection of up to 1,000,000 gold *escudos*, by 1709, the Crown complained of having received only 60,648 silver *pesos* from the entire archbishopric of New Spain.[75]

While New Spain's higher clergy publicly rallied behind the Bourbon Crown, their loyalty varied and was far from monolithic. In Puebla, there is evidence that suggests some well-connected clergy favored the Habsburg side. In 1699, Carlos II named Diego de Gorospe e Irala (1649–1715), ex-prior of the city's convent of San Domingo, Bishop of

New Segovia, but in 1703 he still refused to depart for the Philippines, pleading outstanding debts and lack of funds. According to several witnesses, when the bishop finally assumed his post in 1704, he placed an engraving of the Archduke Charles being crowned by angels in the episcopal palace, and reportedly made controversial statements indicating his favor for the Habsburg dynasty.[76] Significantly, he would deny these claims and respond with a sermon in honor of Manila's oath of loyalty to Luis I. The new governor of the Philippines, Martín de Ursúa y Arizmendi, sponsored its publication.[77]

Similarly, in 1711, an anonymous accuser claimed that the archdeacon and vicar of the cathedral chapter of Puebla, Juan de Jáuregui y Bárcena, had expressed disloyalty toward Felipe V. Although appointed to the bishopric of Caracas in 1709, Jáuregui y Bárcena delayed his departure, supposedly stating that he could not risk his position in Puebla if the Archduke won the war. The archdeacon denied ever saying this and blamed his family's political enemy, the *alcalde mayor*, Superintendent of the *Alcabala* (royal sale's tax), and Commissioner of the Philippine Trade, Juan José de Veytia y Linaje.[78]

Some members of the ecclesiastical elite may have felt torn in their allegiance, but so did Mexico City's *consulado*, or merchant guild. This purportedly surprised the Duke of Alburquerque, who, shortly after arriving in New Spain, consulted with his advisor, who cautioned against alienating the viceroyalty's wealthiest citizens with a "forced" donation. Instead, the advisor suggested suspending the annual *situado* so that the money could be sent directly to Spain.[79] Given the hovering threat of a possible English or Dutch invasion and the need to fortify ports, Alburquerque balked at the suggestion but temporarily paused the collection, nonetheless.

The Crown had traditionally counted on the aid of Mexico City's *consulado* and naturally assumed that the viceroyalty's richest family – the extended Sánchez Tagle clan – would rush to make a generous donation. Luis Sánchez Tagle and Pedro Sánchez Tagle headed Mexico City's *consulado* during the first few years of Felipe V's reign. The family had long helped finance the mining industry and had even lent money to the viceroy to buy mercury. Another branch of the Tagle family had become heavily entangled in the Philippine trade. Furthermore, the Sánchez Tagles loaned well over a million pesos to the Crown over the past two decades.[80]

All signs indicated that the loyalty of the family and their powerful network would transfer from the Habsburgs to the Bourbons. *Consulado* merchants even led a cavalcade during the capital's *jura* for Felipe V; they all donned French attire, signaling to everyone their loyalty.[81] However, in pursuing his own self-interest, the Duke of Alburquerque quickly alienated the network by plotting with rival merchants. In a strike against the power of the Sánchez Tagle family, the viceroy accused Luis's nephew, Juan Domingo Ruiz de Tagle, the general of the *Nao de China*, of smuggling unregistered goods and silver back and forth from Manila. The viceroy even jailed Ruiz de Tagle and obstructed his wedding to the daughter of the governor of the Philippines, Fausto Cruzat; with the death of her father, Ignacia Cruzat's brothers wanted her to marry an *oidor*. In 1704, the poor woman died of typhus while awaiting her fate in a Mexico City convent.[82]

But, whether the accusations of contraband were true (and they surely were), the viceroy also engaged in contraband, primarily with French sailors, thus making his visit to "inspect" defenses in Veracruz suspect. However, while his crimes would be confirmed by a secret investigation toward the end of his term, his illicit dealings would have been obvious at the time. In one purported scheme, he placed price ceilings on specific goods, undercutting the profits of powerful merchants. Then, he hoarded goods and released them only after lifting the ceilings.[83]

By 1706, the viceroy had launched full force into collecting for the Crown and, in 1707, sent a special shipment of 1 million pesos to Spain, most of which consisted of donations and loans from the viceroyalty's wealthy wholesale merchants. But what might seem like an improbable ability to forgive can be explained by the Sánchez Tagle network's instinct for self-preservation. As Guillermina del Valle Pavón has convincingly argued, the merchants' willingness to aid the Duke of Alburquerque likely derived from ongoing negotiations regarding the collection of the *alcabala* in Mexico City. Between 1694 and 1708, the *consulado* had enjoyed the privilege of collecting the tax in exchange for a yearly sum to the Crown, and this assured the merchants a financial advantage, as well as power and influence over others. In 1706, the viceroy and the merchants had just begun the process of renegotiating the *alcabala* collection, and not coincidentally, after the *consulado* donated the money, it won its bid, and six of its most generous members received military titles.[84]

However, the willingness of the Sánchez Tagle network to support the Crown with donations would also reflect on its nemesis, the Duke of Alburquerque. For his part in arranging the donations, the viceroy received the *Toisón de Oro*, the insignia representing membership in the most prestigious military order in the empire.[85] Although the *consulado*

New Spain at War 39

merchants had little choice but to accommodate to the Duke of Alburquerque, it could not have been easy to work with him. Perhaps not coincidentally, the Sánchez Tagle family had ties to the *consulado* of Seville, the force behind the secret investigation into the Duke of Alburquerque's business dealings.

Indeed, it is likely that merchants on both sides of the Atlantic communicated regarding their weakening control over commerce in the Indies, leading to the eventual investigation into the viceroy. Exactly two months after the death of Carlos II, the Crown sent a decree to New Spain declaring the "close friendship that this Crown has with that of France," and shortly thereafter ordered Spanish American port officials to allow French ships to dock when persecuted by the enemy.[86] Spain was forced to rely on the French navy, given that in 1702, it only had thirteen naval ships and some other frigates compared to the French armada's 300 ships, and by 1710, Spain had only one naval ship for the entire Armada de Barlovento.[87] It had to depend, therefore, almost entirely on France, and French captains had to provide sustenance and salaries to their sailors.

Louis XIV and the Spanish Crown allowed French ships to carry up to 1,500 pounds of "trifles" to trade for food and drink, but despite prohibitions to the contrary, French merchants in Saint-Malo and Rouen loaded up ships with textiles, and ended up flooding Spanish American markets with relatively cheap European cloth. To complicate matters, Seville's *consulado* sent no convoys to New Spain between 1700 and 1705, although five arrived during the subsequent decade.[88] During the years of the war, a reported 103 French ships docked in New Spain compared to seventy-six Spanish vessels. Also, as these figures only account for Veracruz, the number of French ships must have been much higher as many likely sold their wares out of Campeche.[89]

Furthermore, Mexico City's *consulado* members lost practically all their merchandise during the attack at Vigo in 1702. Early concerns about illicit trade and the catastrophic loss of merchandise in 1702 likely contributed to the merchants' reluctance to provide a sizeable donation before 1706. But, perhaps even more significant, the Duke of Alburquerque had begun taking bribes from each French ship loaded with contraband that docked in Veracruz. Unsettled by the flooding of New Spain with contraband, in 1709 Seville's *consulado* convinced the Crown to launch a secret investigation; it revealed the viceroy's involvement in a smuggling scheme with French sailors and port officials that earned him between 30,000 and 60,000 pesos per ship. The Crown determined that it had been defrauded by the viceroy of approximately 3,000,000 pesos and fined him the extraordinary amount of 700,000 pesos on his return to Spain in 1713.[90]

Although intent on weeding out "corruption," Felipe V inherited a system that often relied on secret arrangements, bribes, and rule bending, all practices largely determined by "custom." Because the viceroy's behavior fell so outside the parameters of custom, it had to be dealt with, but both the Habsburg and early Bourbon Crowns tolerated a significant amount of "corruption." Both administrations accepted that people pursued their self-interest through royal service and intensified the sale of bureaucratic appointments as a way of achieving a variety of political ends. As Rosenmüller has illustrated, the administration of Mariana of Austria began selling *beneficios*, or "revocable appointments to noninheritable offices," as a way of undercutting councils, who appointed people based primarily on lineage, and in the case of New Spain, to curtail the ability of viceroys to extend patronage; in other words, rather than existing as an inherently corrupt practice, the regency intended that the sale of appointments would help to reform practices that it perceived as inefficient or, even, "corrupt."[91] In 1692, Carlos II would reverse course and order a reduction in the number of all unnecessary bureaucrats, and then in 1701 Felipe V's administration reissued the order.

Nevertheless, under Carlos II, the Crown continued to sell bureaucratic offices to help fund the Nine Years' War, and Felipe V would do the same to fend off the Grand Alliance. In 1701, Felipe V annulled all purchasable titles and future administrative posts (*futuras*) acquired during the past ten years but would resume selling appointments again three years later through a *Junta de Beneficios*. Purchasers generally disguised payments as "*donativos*" or the like, allowing for the illusion that the person had earned his term appointment through virtue, merit, and "service" to the Crown.[92] Posts at all levels went up for sale, and in all three branches of the Crown: administrative, fiscal, and judicial. Although Felipe V originally nullified the sale of appointments under the advice of Louis XIV, the Sun King would also find himself forced to sell posts and titles to defend his grandson's inheritance.[93]

The Indies provided a large portion of these posts in the form of *beneficios*; although not permanent positions, these provided individuals with appointments for a set number of years and could therefore be sold and purchased multiple times as "*futuras*." Furthermore, the Crown also sold the privilege of the purchaser to substitute someone else in the position, thus creating a secondary market. Many people purchased several appointments as speculative investments. The Crown, moreover, also sold licenses permitting functionaries to marry women from their jurisdictions and sold remarkably high-ranking appointments, including that of captain general and president of the *audiencia* of Guatemala. What is more, the Crown also sold numerous titles of military rank.

In New Spain, the Crown sold positions with sensitive wartime responsibilities. As we saw at the beginning of this chapter, Diego Jiménez traveled to Florida in 1704 with Andrés de Arriola, the Captain of the Armada de Barlovento and the *future* governor of Florida. However, the Crown sold many other positions with strategic importance. For 4,000 pesos, José Muñoz de Estrada bought the position of *alcalde mayor*, *castellano* (military commander), and *capitán a guerra* (captain of war) of Acapulco in 1704. This appointment came with the privilege of residing elsewhere and assigning a lieutenant to work in his stead.[94] Officials often bought multiple *beneficios* to secure their family's status and influence; some resold them, and others gifted them to sons and sons-in-law. Again, many of these positions required vigilance and skill. For example, in 1711, the Crown sold the title of captain general of Yucatán.[95]

Perhaps even more remarkable, the Crown sold positions on the *audiencias*, core institutions of justice, and in this way, facilitated the advancement and entrenchment of numerous Creoles. The priest and mine owner Juan Díez de Bracamonte is a case in point. In 1706, he purchased the position of *audiencia* judge, which he held until 1719. He would end his life and career in Puebla, where he served as archdeacon of the cathedral chapter in 1728.[96] The Crown clearly viewed Bracamonte, who had gained considerable wealth in the 1690s, as someone whose allegiance merited cultivation, whereas Bracamonte clearly understood how to work the system and earn favor. In 1711, he sponsored the publication of a sermon given in honor of the victories at Brihuega and Villaviciosa and dedicated it to the new viceroy, the Duke of Linares.[97]

The Crown sold numerous positions in New Spain, including six other appointments as *oidores*.[98] It also made many redundant, or supernumerary, appointments, and even invented positions for the purpose of sale. In 1707, for example, it sold the position of visitor of haciendas in the *audiencias* of New Galicia and Mexico, with the specification that property owners needed to present their titles to assure their legitimate rights to the land and to specific natural resources. The Council of the Indies, which had been largely cut out of Felipe V's intensive sale of appointments, objected, citing the abuses that would likely occur. So, instead, the

Crown ordered a special *donativo* just for landowners, with specific expectations. Those with large haciendas would pay 100 *pesos*, and more modest landowners would pay 50 *pesos* to avoid an inspection, which could result in heavy fines. The Crown, in turn, collected 131,515 pesos from the scheme, which it put toward the needs of the war.[99]

This example illustrates the creative ways the Crown made subjects in New Spain fund the conflict, and how the cost of war trickled down. Although non-lifetime positions like this one generally sold for considerably less money, these types of appointments moved in far greater numbers, as they could be sold multiple times as *futuras*. Among the many temporary positions that sold, subjects most coveted those that allowed for economic advantage. In 1706, while in the middle of war, the Crown sold the position of governor of Veracruz to an individual whom the Council of the Indies feared lacked experience. Among other objections to the sale, the council cited the past mistake of allowing another inexperienced individual to buy the governorship, which made Veracruz susceptible to Lorencillo's attack in 1683. José de Grimaldo, the de facto prime minister of Spain during the war, ordered that the sale go through.[100]

Of the viceroyalty's most coveted positions, those in the royal treasury fetched the greatest prices, given the potential for illicit profit. The Crown sold the position of *Regente del Tribunal de Cuentas* (President of the Royal Auditing Court) in Mexico City for 300,000 *reales* to someone many characterized as incompetent.[101] The positions of *contadores*, or accountants, of the royal treasury in Veracruz also proved expensive. In 1707, Pedro Carrasco y Aguilar and Francisco San Juan Santa Cruz purchased the positions for 90,000 *reales* a piece. These men would later be implicated in the contraband scheme involving the Duke of Alburquerque and, in 1710, pay a fine of 180,000 *reales* to the Crown.[102]

While allowing the Crown to raise needed revenue, the sale of appointments helped the Bourbon dynasty establish ties of patronage with ambitious individuals and families. Whether through positions held in perpetuity or those of limited term, Creole families used the Bourbon "fire sale" to place themselves on the radar of the new king and to advance their positions and that of their families. Although members of the Sánchez Tagle family had recently fended off attacks on their business practices by the Duke of Alburquerque, they would tie their fate to the success of the Bourbon dynasty. In 1708, Pedro Sánchez Tagle bought the position of *Tallador Mayor de la Casa de Moneda de México* (Chief Engraver of the Mexico City Mint), with the ability to leave it in inheritance or sell it to another. Although he purchased it from another

New Spain at War 43

individual, he paid the Crown an additional 480,000 *reales* for the office.[103] His nephew, Luis Antonio Sánchez Tagle, bought the future position of governor and captain general of the Mariana Islands and the position of *justicia mayor* (chief magistrate) of the port of Cavite. Another nephew, Domingo, bought the title of Marquis of Sierra Nevada for 150,000 *reales*. Finally, Andrés Sánchez Tagle bought a lucrative position that had previously been unavailable for purchase: *alguacil mayor* of the treasury of Durango for 60,000 *reales*.[104]

CONCLUSION

The War of the Spanish Succession reverberated throughout New Spain in a myriad of ways and at all levels of society. Although mainland New Spain did not experience conflict directly resulting from the war, residents of New Spain lived in constant fear of an enemy attack and experienced frequent engagements with pirates and loggers. Although foreigners had long posed a security risk, the succession crisis made expelling them from Laguna de Términos a priority. Viceregal administrators dispersed countless recruits from inland cities to the coast of New Spain and to presidios throughout the Caribbean, while volunteers from Campeche, Tabasco, and Veracruz also worked to keep the enemy at bay. These soldiers came from a variety of backgrounds, as Spanish, Creole, black, and mixed-race individuals could volunteer to serve the Crown or be forcibly impressed to do so. Even indigenous people served in the defense of the viceroyalty, either by acting as sentinels or by being at the ready to defend Campeche and other port cities from an invasion.

But in some ways, it was simpler to defend the viceroyalty from a possible enemy attack than it was to help pay for the viceroyalty's defense and the Crown's battles back in Europe. Of the two American viceroyalties, New Spain carried the heavier financial burden during the war, and support came in a variety of forms. Clearly, the Crown gained the lion's share of American resources from mining, but there were a host of other ways that the Crown gained revenue. This, again, had an impact on people's lives. The Crown tried to force ecclesiastics to give up a tenth of their salaries, while it took a tenth of the salaries of its bureaucrats. Meanwhile, the Crown requested donations from all segments of society, from wealthy merchants to plebeians, and sold countless bureaucratic appointments and titles.

Although far removed from the frontlines, New Spain's population still resided within an empire at war, and people could not forget it, even if they tried. French sailors moved throughout the Caribbean basin, and French textiles destabilized the market to the benefit of consumers. While merchants and high-level functionaries sought to take advantage of the circumstances to profit from illicit trade and the buying of appointments, plebeians faced impressment and forced contributions. Furthermore, as will be explored in Chapter 2, subjects living in municipalities had access to a steady stream of news in the form of imprints, rumors, and sermons, which helped them connect to the frontline.

2

An Early Modern Public Sphere

On March 6, 1701, a *navio de aviso*, or mail ship, approached Veracruz draped in black mourning cloth and firing off military salutes in honor of the passing of Carlos II. The ship contained a crate full of letters and decrees, which included notice of the monarch's death, a copy of his last will and testament, an account of Madrid's oath ceremony for the new monarch, and engravings of the seventeen-year-old Felipe V, as well as a pamphlet reporting the garroting of an *oidor*, or judge, from Madrid's high court, who dared object to Spain's new Bourbon king. Approximately six months later, another ship arrived in Veracruz carrying news that another *oidor* had been exiled permanently to the Philippines for crafting a manifesto in support of Austria and against Bourbon rule. The *aviso* contained additional news regarding the succession crisis, including word that the regent and Archbishop of Toledo, Luis Manuel Fernández Portocarrero, had exiled the Admiral of Castile and others from court for demonstrating disloyalty to Felipe V. These accounts circulated throughout Mexico City, starkly warning of the consequences of disloyalty.[1]

The War of the Spanish Succession, as we have seen, put fiscal and military pressure on the viceroyalty, but royal administrators and ecclesiastics made sure to discourage disloyalty by censoring and shaping narratives emanating from both sides of the Atlantic. As this chapter illustrates, officials, prelates, and other writers in the Spanish kingdoms produced printed material in support of Felipe V, and this material shaped narratives regarding the succession crisis in the viceroyalty. Although there are few copies of propaganda in support of the Archduke Charles in Mexican archives or libraries, this material also circulated, as evidenced by some examples, as well as inquisitorial edicts.

However, most of the printed propaganda that arrived in New Spain proved firmly pro-Bourbon and did not necessarily encourage critical reflection or individual agency, yet it did contribute to a nascent "public sphere" that worked to influence public opinion and even dissent.[2] The public sphere, as first defined by Jürgen Habermas, emerged in the late eighteenth century as a social sphere of activity independent of the state and economy, where individuals and groups could freely share ideas and work toward influencing political actors and institutions. Although various scholars have discussed how print and manuscript literature, as well as rumor, circulated at the court of Felipe III (1598–1621) and other urban centers throughout the century, the Crown had a hand in this dissemination, as well as in the censoring of information.[3] So, while Spanish officials allowed for the circulation of print and manuscript literature and the formation of public opinion aligned with the Crown and the Church, they did not facilitate or condone uninhibited speech. Later, in the early eighteenth century, royal bureaucrats took pains to censor information to the benefit of Felipe V, and a complicated influence campaign developed. While the Bourbon Crown provided constant reminders of the legitimacy of Felipe V and the superiority of Franco-Spanish forces, the continued importance of rumor and the persistent circulation of uncensored information in manuscript form allowed individuals to gain variegated perspectives on a given issue, outside of monarchical or ecclesiastical control, which then allowed for the articulation of countervailing identities to that of Bourbon loyalists. Despite the real threat of repercussions, those who subscribed to a counter-identity often gestured subtly or even outwardly toward it in public places as a way of searching out solidarity with like-minded individuals.

While officials in New Spain worked hard to censor, shape, and distill information to favor the Bourbon house, royal subjects maneuvered within what William Childers has termed the "baroque public sphere," or within a culture in which knowledge is "opaque" and "fragmented," and in which groups and individuals "attain political agency without the transparency of rational debate or any pretense of equal participation."[4] Although Habermas correlated the emergence of the public sphere with the robust reading and writing cultures of the Enlightenment, reflecting on sixteenth- and seventeenth-century Spain, Fernando Bouza has argued for an early modern public sphere based on visual and oral communication, as well as the circulation of both printed and manuscript writings. This public sphere, moreover, depended on literate people reading aloud, sharing information in both private and public gatherings.[5]

By participating in an admittedly stunted, although more broadly conceived, public sphere, the people of New Spain cemented their attachment to an imagined community of empire. As examined in Chapter 3, subjects grounded understandings of empire in corporeal and Eucharistic metaphors, and saw themselves as belonging to the *cuerpo del rey*: the body of the king.

In New Spain's early modern public sphere, priests often shared published pro-Bourbon anecdotes in their sermons. Indeed, ecclesiastics, bureaucrats, and craftsmen worked to guide emotion, and therefore, cognition, through propaganda and ceremony.[6] The Spanish Crown, meanwhile, sought to stifle pro-Austrian sentiment, as evidenced by its cautionary tales of disloyalty and by its censoring of any news related to Austrian military victories. Allowable examples of printed propaganda in the form of state-sanctioned *relaciones de sucesos* traveled to New Spain and made their way to the viceroyalty's many cities. Moreover, a pro-Bourbon narrative of the war also circulated throughout the viceroyalty through newspaper-style publications, like the *gazetas* produced in Madrid, Alcalá, Sevilla, Cádiz, Zaragoza, Salamanca, and Cartagena.[7] Often, pro-Bourbon literature consisted of no more than a couplet or short anonymous tract (sometimes in the form of a "letter") and mentioned no publication information at all. Pervasive throughout Castile and Aragon, this type of propaganda arrived in New Spain, and especially Puebla, New Spain's "second city," which sits between Veracruz and the capital.

Printed material in support of Bourbon rule helped to create an overarching narrative of the succession conflict. It introduced the contest in New Spain and worked to invest royal subjects emotionally in the war by framing it as a struggle between good and evil. Given the difficulty in fully controlling the influx of information into the viceroyalty, creating a master-narrative capable of uniting subjects proved crucial, and so supporters of Felipe V frequently deployed the concept of holy war, with the War of the Spanish Succession largely characterized as occurring between the Catholic forces in support of Felipe V and the Protestant forces incorporated into the Grand Alliance. Bourbon supporters emphasized the religious dimension of the conflict from its very inception, inciting denials of heretical intentions from the Admiral of Castile in 1702 and the Archduke Charles in 1706. Indeed, many Habsburg loyalists regarded this line of argument as a "false flag," and pro-Austrian imprints noted the many times France and Spain had allied with non-Catholics during past conflicts.[8] Furthermore, Bourbon supporters dealt with the refracted nature of communication in the early modern Spanish world as rumors ran rampant, even across the Atlantic Ocean. Bourbon propaganda, therefore, sought to either amplify or preempt rumors while encouraging a sense of proximity to Spain.

Advocates for Felipe V stressed the narrative of holy war and sometimes evoked history to do so. While promoting the view of the War of the Spanish Succession as a religious contest, propagandists sought to quash anti-French sentiment by framing Spain and France as the true bulwarks of the Catholic faith. In this same vein, the propaganda that reached New Spain characterized Felipe V's piety as fundamentally Spanish in nature, thereby emphasizing continuity between his own style of rule and religious devotion and that of his Habsburg predecessors. For this reason, supporters emphasized his devotion to the Virgin Mary, and particularly, the Virgin of Atocha. As this chapter illustrates, during the War of the Spanish Succession, subjects in New Spain participated in an early modern public sphere that, despite the significance of rumor and pro-Habsburg propaganda, helped to legitimize the Bourbon dynasty as defenders of the faith.

THE CIRCULATION OF PRO-AUSTRIAN PROPAGANDA

Bourbon supporters in both Spain and New Spain understood that for their messaging regarding Bourbon legitimacy to take root, they had to prevent the extensive dissemination of pro-Austrian materials, as well as expressions of disloyalty to Felipe V. On June 6, 1707, inquisitors issued an edict for the entire viceroyalty of New Spain forbidding priests from using the confessional to try to persuade people to switch their allegiance from Felipe V to the Archduke Charles. As the tribunal reminded New Spain's faithful, Pope Clement XI (1649–1721) had declared that people who forfeited the oath of loyalty to Felipe V committed a mortal sin, punishable by excommunication. The devout, therefore, had an obligation to turn traitorous priests into the Inquisition.[9] Also in 1707, inquisitors caught word that at least two couplets in support of the Archduke Carlos circulated in New Spain and ordered that those who wrote, copied, or shared these couplets be prosecuted.[10]

In this climate, pro-Austrian writings could not be imported easily into the viceroyalty, but some material did enter convent libraries, such as the three-volume history of the Roman Emperor Trajan (98–117) by Francisco Solanes; full sets made their way into Puebla's Convent of San Francisco and its Convent of San Agustín. Solanes published the first two tomes in Barcelona in 1700, but when he published the last volume in 1706, he made sure that it glorified local patriotism and regional autonomy. Even more incriminating, he dedicated it to "Carlos III of Spain" and referenced the patronage of Anton Florian of Liechtenstein (1656–1721), the Chief Intendant and Prime Minister of the Habsburg Crown, who resided in Barcelona.[11]

The Bourbon Crown's relentless concern with Habsburg propaganda suggests that it remained a significant problem throughout the war. As late as 1710, the Inquisitor General ordered the Holy Tribunal in New Spain to disseminate a papal brief that warned of the "diabolic cunning" of the Protestant enemy that planned on introducing bibles written in the "Mexican language [Nahuatl]" to "poison" the viceroyalty. The brief noted that the Protestants had already introduced an imprint into New Spain titled *Catechismos y liturgias impressos en Londres (Catechisms and Liturgies Printed in London)*.[12]

In addition to keeping seditious imprints out of New Spain, the Crown had to monitor who traveled to the New World, given that anybody could be an agent for the Habsburg side. One of Felipe V's first decrees reaffirmed previous restrictions on foreigners traveling to the New World and then, after Portugal joined the Grand Alliance in 1704, the Crown ordered officials throughout the American viceroyalties to embargo the goods of all Portuguese residents, and this likely served as a deterrent to other foreigners.[13] Administrators particularly feared the arrival of disloyal clergy. Although most religious supported Felipe V, a sizable number in Aragon professed loyalty to the Archduke Charles. In 1703, the Crown warned Spanish American officials that a pair of Trinitarians residing in London, one Spanish and one German, planned on traveling to Spanish America with bales full of pro-Austrian propaganda in the form of "manifestos from the Emperor" to "tempt the loyalty of those vassals."[14] The Duke of Alburquerque then instructed his secretary to write to all the provincials of religious orders to inquire whether any friars had entered New Spain without a license and instructed officials in Veracruz to inform him regarding who arrived on the most recent mail and mercury ships. He requested to remain informed regarding all those arriving in the future without licenses, adding that seditious literature would be confiscated, and all papers would be reviewed for "clauses that look to induce or persuade the spirits inclining them toward the imperial voice."[15]

Royal officials did not just fear propaganda produced in Europe, but within the Americas as well. The English governor of Jamaica sent letters to the governors of Santo Domingo, Cartagena, and Havana to try to lure them over to the Austrian side. In 1706 in Caracas, the same city that witnessed a spontaneous oath of loyalty to "Carlos III" in 1702, the governor investigated the introduction of "seditious papers in favor of the Archduke." He arrested three Portuguese men for disseminating copies of imprints and decrees from the Archduke from nearby Curaçao, as well as newspapers and manifestos from the Holy Roman Emperor and the Admiral of Castile.[16] Officials in Caracas shipped the three men off to New Spain, but the fear that they would influence others in favor of the Archduke proved so acute, instead of jailing them in Veracruz where they could spread their seditious thoughts *a la voz del agua* (through word of mouth), the Duke of Alburquerque chose to imprison them inland in Puebla before sending them to Seville to be prosecuted.[17] Perhaps viceregal authorities felt that Puebla proved the safest place, given that in 1706, the *alcalde mayor* of the city declared that anyone who uttered disparaging remarks about Felipe V would have their right ear cut off.[18]

Even the victories at the decisive battles of Brihuega and Villaviciosa in 1710 did not ease concerns over pro-Habsburg propaganda. In 1711, the Crown warned the viceroy, the Duke of Linares, about the enemy's desire to introduce "the contagious seed of disaffection" through books, pamphlets, and other papers regardless of the "true intelligence of the favorable progress that the divine Majesty has dignified to grant me." Because the viceroy's jurisdiction was so large, the monarch advised placing the task of searching for pro-Austrian propaganda in his most trusted provincial officials. Fearing that the enemy would attempt to spread the "plague of disaffection" among the religious, he ordered enquiries to be made with the leaders of all the viceroyalty's religious communities.[19]

Viceregal authorities clearly regarded (and were instructed to regard) pro-Austrian propaganda and sentiment as a form of contagion. After an expedition from Tabasco caught a Spaniard in Laguna de Términos with a copy of the Archduke's manifesto, the governor quickly dispatched him to Spain.[20] In 1706, Franco-Spanish forces faced a series of setbacks, including the temporary occupation of Madrid by enemy forces and Felipe V's failure to recapture Barcelona, which had been lost in 1705. Rumors soon began circulating that Felipe V had abandoned Spain altogether. Significantly, at the end of a letter detailing the unfortunate events of 1706, Felipe V asked officials in New Spain and Peru to ferret out agitators spreading pro-Austrian propaganda.[21]

Viceregal authorities in Mexico City took this directive seriously. After preparing for the rumor of a planned invasion of Veracruz, officials arrested roughly two dozen men for being *desafectos* (disaffected) toward Felipe V. The subsequent witness interrogations exposed a broad network of individuals who, if not outrightly disloyal, engaged actively in the "baroque public sphere" by gossiping about the war and circulating pro-Austrian imprints and manuscripts. For example, Salvador Mañer, one of the men accused of disloyalty, insisted on his innocence but admitted to hearing men gossip inside a gambling house. The men reportedly discussed the defense of the Admiral of Castile's allegiance to the Archduke, written by the Jesuit Juan Álvaro Cienfuegos. Copies of the Admiral of Castile's manifesto, moreover, had also reportedly made their way to New Spain.[22] In their investigation, viceregal investigators also determined that a Portuguese leather tanner in Mexico City named Manuel de Sousa y Prado owned two pro-Austrian pamphlets published in Valencia and Barcelona. These accused the French of planting positive stories about Bourbon successes to inspire faith in Felipe V.[23]

The wave of arrests in 1706 and 1707 in Mexico City over supposed disloyalty to the king involved several people with personal and professional rivalries, and the witness testimony taken as part of the investigation reveals how written propaganda sowed curiosity, incredulity, and even ambivalence regarding Bourbon rule. In 1706, Bernardo López Lovato, a spice merchant who worked in the capital's main plaza with his brother, a royal accountant, testified about a web of gossip that had ensnared many merchants and artisans whose stands stood nearby. Indeed, he claimed that several men had taken to gossiping about the war in the main plaza, and that they often uttered disloyal remarks that he castigated. As a result, the men had taken to calling López Lovato "the judge." Rosenmüller has illustrated that the two brothers proved tightly allied to the viceroy, and that their accusations of disloyalty, especially against a Galician wholesale merchant named Gregorio Gasco, served to bolster the position of contrabandists, including the viceroy himself, whose agents engaged in illicit trade with French sailors.[24]

The witness testimony in Gasco's case indicates that heightened French involvement in illicit trade provoked a group of merchants to express their distrust of pro-Bourbon literature and to search for like-minded associates by publicly suggesting support for a Habsburg succession. While gossiping about recent developments in Gasco's home, the locksmith Juan López Camaño noticed that Gasco did not refer to Felipe V as the monarch but only as the Duke of Anjou, whereas he referred to the

Archduke Charles as Carlos III. Gasco likely intended this to serve as a subtle clue as to his pro-Austrian leanings. Another witness who claimed to have conversations with Gasco "long ago" remembered vaguely that he seemed to doubt good news regarding Franco-Spanish victories and repeatedly noted the strength of enemy forces.[25]

Doubting good news regarding Franco-Spanish victories served as a clear indicator to pro-Bourbon officials that an individual favored a Habsburg succession. Among the men arrested in 1706 and 1707, royal officials also learned of the potentially disloyal murmurings of a group of provincial bureaucrats who resided in Mexico City while awaiting licenses from the viceroy to assume their posts. In November 1707, Luis Pérez de Tamara accused the freshly appointed *alcalde mayor* of Tepeaca and Tecali, Antonio de Rada, of stating that the "Austrian eagles will always predominate and that our king should be the one that has more [military] forces," and of murmuring "irreverently of the successes" of the Bourbon Crown.[26] Through a lengthy investigation that eventually cleared Rada, officials discovered that not only did Pérez de Tamara have a serious gambling problem but that he resented Rada, whom he had attached himself to while both men resided in Mexico City.

Ironically, Pérez de Tamara had himself been accused of disloyalty back in Spain for supplying George Rooke's forces with supplies during the 1702 siege of Cádiz and Santa María. Then, after fleeing to New Spain and befriending Rada, Pérez de Tamara told the owners of a gambling den in Puebla that the *alcalde mayor* would cover a large debt, but Rada refused. While waiting for his license, Rada gathered frequently with other bureaucrats in the luxury market off the *Calle de los Mercaderes* (Street of the Merchants) to discuss the war. Despite claims that he sometimes doubted the veracity of good news in front of his fellow bureaucrats, the governor-elect of the Province of Maracaibo testified that when bad news arrived in 1706, Rada admonished that it should not be believed, because of the many *gazetas* published in Spain with "many things that are not true."[27] The incoming *alcalde mayor* of Sonora testified that while discussing the occupation of Madrid by Allied forces, Rada had stated that "whoever had the most forces was the victor," which seemed to indicate ambivalence about the outcome of the war. If true, Rada could have been hoping to bait like-minded individuals. Nevertheless, when pressed about who he meant, Rada responded that "the Most Christian King [Louis XIV]" of course.[28] Although never convicted, the owner of a house in Seville where Rada lodged for four months in 1711 described him as "notably without affection" for Felipe V.[29]

Disloyal individuals like Rada sometimes made their positions overtly known or, as this example indicates, used subtleties to draw like-minded people into conversation and create a sense of solidarity. Rada had initially bought the *corregimiento* (indigenous jurisdiction) of Aymaraes, a wealthy district in the viceroyalty of Peru, in 1698, before Felipe V suppressed the sale of bureaucratic appointments. After Felipe V resumed the sale, Rada purchased the position in Tepeaca and Tecalí, but, as Aaron Olivas has suggested, he may have experienced lingering resentment.[30] Rada, moreover, may have sought to clue associates as to his true feelings. Pérez de Tamara reported hearing Rada state that he had a "coat with two linings" under the *portales* (arches) on the Street of the Merchants. When asked about the comment, Rada admitted to uttering it but stated that he just meant that he was awarded a bureaucratic position by both Carlos II and Felipe V. Viceregal authorities believed that it suggested ambivalence regarding the outcome of the war.[31]

In a similar approach to Rada, Benito Cartagena, a merchant and the first person arrested in 1706, reportedly waved a napkin made of *alemanisca* (huckaback cloth) at a dinner party and expressed a desire for "this flag" to fly over New Spain.[32] Possibly because of the name of the cloth, with its incorporation of "alemán" or "German," "servilletero" or "napkin ring," became synonymous with Austrian sympathizer. Significantly, at least two broadsides arrived in New Spain that used the term *servilleteros* for Austrian sympathizers, and Cartagena's dinner companions clearly understood what he was alluding to with his waving of the napkin.[33] Don Manuel de Sousa y Prado, a Portuguese tanner and shoemaker, reportedly demonstrated happiness upon hearing bad news about Franco-Spanish forces. A few days before his arrest in Mexico City, he claimed publicly that all of Spain had sworn fidelity to the Archduke. Also, on two different occasions, he bet publicly 50 pesos that the Archduke would take Badajoz and keep Barcelona. Finally, he falsely claimed that an English squadron waited off the coast of Veracruz for the viceroyalty to swear its allegiance to the Archduke Charles.[34]

Searching for confidantes and doubting official reports often went hand in hand. In 1705, Joaquín Puyol, a cloth merchant in Parral, informed Gasco in a letter that he had shared his disposition for a Habsburg succession with residents in his community. After Puyol refuted the veracity of recent accounts of Bourbon victories, a Portuguese neighbor (whose goods had been embargoed) reportedly rejoiced. Puyol added that sharing his preference for Austria made him "many friends" and that all the region's military captains invited him to eat, drink, and lodge at the presidio over three days.³⁵ Significantly, another associate of Gasco, Pedro Collazo de Soto, was arrested for toasting to the Archduke Charles. After his arrest, Collazo explained that when people had conversations at *cacahuaterías* (small street shops specializing in peanuts and snacks) and gatherings throughout Mexico City, "they told me that Barcelona was restored, I don't believe it; that Portugal was won, I don't believe it, because I have reasons for saying this ... and I do not fear prison."³⁶

Spanish subjects deployed rumor and refuted news favorable to Franco-Spanish forces to carve out their identities as Habsburg loyalists or, at the very least, as ambivalent regarding the outcome of the war. But, in this public sphere of refracted information, people also used handwritten forms of propaganda to bypass censorship. Although the Inquisition issued several edicts prohibiting pro-Austrian imprints, Habsburg sympathizers sometimes copied prohibited pamphlets in their own hand or wrote their own original pieces. Officials arrested Gasco's confessor, Lorenzo González Figueroa, on November 30, 1706, and found incriminating letters in his possession. In one letter, the priest referred to the *Bula de la Santa Cruzada* (Bull of the Holy Crusade) and criticized the archbishop for levying a tenth of church income for the king when this capital likely ended up in the hands of British merchants. Even more significant, the priest had pro-Austrian propaganda in his possession and even admitted to copying a letter mocking Felipe V by referring to him as the Duke of Ajo (garlic) instead of the Duke of Anjou. Although he admitted to only being amused, not *desafecto*, the ecclesiastical court exiled him from Mexico City for two years. Because pro-Habsburg priests sometimes tried to sway people in the confessional, the ecclesiastical court also stripped González Figueroa of his license to hear the sacrament of confession.³⁷

The case of Salvador Mañer, the overseer of an hacienda in Toluca, underscores the importance that early modern Spanish officials attributed to political writings, and the ease with which uncensored tracts circulated in New Spain. Mañer was first arrested for publicly betting that all of Spain would eventually support the Archduke and for having visited Venezuela and remaining in contact with an uncle in Caracas. As noted, he reported that while visiting a gambling house, he overheard several men discussing a book in defense of the Admiral of Castile's loyalty to the Archduke Charles.³⁸ Significantly, he added that while incarcerated in the Mexico City jail, he witnessed a vendor dropping off books for Pedro Collazo de Soto, who then used the material to take "notes" on the disputed succession. Collazo also reportedly developed a "response" to two imprints that had arrived from Spain, called "*De mojiganga de mojiganga*" ("From Farce to Farce") (copies of which also circulated in Puebla) and *Luzifer en audiencia* ("Lucifer in Court"), and asked Mañer to transcribe these in tiny print. Set to travel to Spain on a French vessel, Mañer did not want to risk being caught with pro-Austrian materials. He intended to fold the documents into a sealed letter addressed to an associate. Eventually, viceregal officials deported Mañer to Spain, where in 1711, he escaped from Seville's *Casa de Contratación* (House of Trade). When recaught, Mañer carried papers in support of the Archduke, which he also claimed to be recopying for others.[39]

THE CIRCULATION OF PRO-BOURBON PROPAGANDA

The wave of arrests in 1706 and 1707 exposed networks of gossip and the circulation of pro-Austrian imprints and manuscripts, but mainland New Spain remained relatively loyal compared to other regions like Venezuela. Part of the reason behind the region's tenuous adherence to Bourbon rule likely derived from the influence of pro-Bourbon imprints. Although these imprints touched on a variety of themes related to Felipe V's political legitimacy and Franco-Spanish military victories, they fundamentally worked to unite the metropole and viceroyalty in a shared vision of Felipe V as the defender of the faith.

High-ranking officials in Madrid, ecclesiastics in the provinces, and even anonymous authors from cities all over Spain produced literature in support of Bourbon rule. Official imprints related to Felipe V's right to the Crown and Franco-Spanish victories came from the monarch's principal office, the *Despacho Universal* (Universal Dispatch Office), where Felipe V gathered a cohort of ministers to advise him. In the last years of his life, Carlos II had also ruled mainly through the *Despacho Universal*, where his secretary, Antonio de Ubilla y Medina, summarized information from the government councils and dictated or even crafted orders on behalf of the king. Ubilla remained secretary of the *Despacho Universal* through 1703, and during that time helped produce texts in support of Bourbon rule, including a massive chronicle describing Felipe V's arrival in Spain and his exploits fighting in Italy in 1702 and 1703. Ubilla justified Felipe V's claim to the throne largely through the monarch's willingness to lead troops into battle, a theme that, as we will see, resonated strongly in New Spain, where at least three copies of the chronicle arrived.[40]

Then, in 1705, Felipe V promoted José de Grimaldo to Secretary of the *Despacho de Guerra y Hacienda* (Secretariat of War and Finance), and he would order the dissemination of pro-Bourbon imprints and the mounting of commemorations through the end of the conflict. After the decisive battles of Brihuega and Villaviciosa in 1710, for example, Grimaldo instructed Francisco Ronquillo, the President of the Council of Castile, to share news of the Bourbon victory through correspondence, broadsides, newspapers, and public ceremonies. He also instructed Ronquillo to make sure that official descriptions of the victories emphasized the imprisonment of James Stanhope, the commander of the British contingent of the Grand Alliance.[41]

Although most printed propaganda did not note an author, specific ecclesiastics contributed instrumentally to the creation of a pro-Bourbon narrative capable of bridging the Atlantic. After the English attacked Cádiz and the port of Santa María in 1702, occupied Gibraltar in 1704, and occupied Barcelona in 1705, news spread regarding the sacrilege committed by English and Dutch forces, which emboldened pro-Bourbon ecclesiastics in Spain to declare the conflict a holy war. In 1706, Inquisitor General Ibáñez de la Riva dismissed doubts regarding the legality of Felipe V's ascension by arguing that it served as a mere pretext to sow civil war and introduce heresy into Spain. He emphasized that those Spaniards who refused to defend their king committed the crime of *lesa majestad*, or treason against the sovereign.[42]

Similarly, in 1706, the Bishop of Cartagena, Luis Belluga y Moncada, started characterizing the conflict as a religious war. In a pastoral letter directed to his diocese's humble residents, he decried the disloyal priests who tried to persuade people to support the Archduke Charles through private conversations and even in the confessional. He said that all the *cabezas* (or principal towns) of the Spanish kingdoms had sworn an oath of loyalty to Felipe V, and by virtue of this, individual citizens had professed their loyalty as well; going back on this oath was an affront to God, a position later upheld by Clement XI. Most significant, however, was his claim that England's real intention was to spread the Protestant heresy, as evidenced by enemy forces using churches as stables for horses, preaching their heretical beliefs from pulpits, and feasting on holy wafers. By providing aid to the Grand Alliance, individuals committed an "abominable sin" punishable by excommunication.[43] Belluga raised money for the Bourbon cause and even designed military strategy for the defense of Murcia. His loyalty would lead Felipe V to name him viceroy and captain general of Valencia and Murcia in 1707, and his equation of the War of the Spanish Succession to a holy war would echo throughout Spain and across the Atlantic Ocean.[44]

Printed propaganda kept subjects in New Spain informed about the major players and abreast of significant developments in the war. The king, of course, enjoyed primacy in descriptions of events, and as will be explored in depth in Chapter 3, municipal leaders and priests in New Spain also displayed portraits of members of the Bourbon dynasty in commemorations of royal milestones and Bourbon victories. By visually introducing the royal family, Bourbon loyalists sought to make the Bourbon house literally and figuratively "present." Descriptions of the monarch's activities, moreover, also countered anti-French sentiment by emphasizing Felipe V's dedication to Marian shrines in both Castile and Aragon. Priests throughout the viceroyalty cited from *relaciones de sucesos* testifying to this in their sermons and thereby helped to encourage familiarity with the king and a sense of proximity to events in Spain.

Pro-Bourbon officials exported newspapers, books, and imprints legitimizing the succession, and the war failed to impede their arrival. *Navios de aviso* (dispatch ships) sailed ahead of the fleet that periodically carried European goods to Veracruz, but mail also arrived during periods when the fleet did not depart from Spain. Between 1695 and 1718, Seville's *consulado* (the corporation primarily responsible for *navios de aviso*) sent fifty-four mail ships to the New World, although Spain lost six of these ships to inclement weather or maritime attacks. During the War of the Spanish Succession, one or two *navios de aviso* made it to Veracruz each year, except in 1706, 1708, and 1712. However, mail continued to arrive with no significant interruption, as the Spanish Crown licensed French ships to begin carrying mail to the New World in 1705. The ships left from Cádiz, the Canary Islands, or French ports, and sometimes, Spanish *navios de aviso* would transfer correspondence to French ships to ensure that monarchical orders and news arrived safe and sound. Between 1705 and 1712, the Crown dispatched eighteen French ships carrying Spanish mail to Veracruz.[45]

Important news made it to New Spain post haste, but not necessarily through direct channels. After Franco-Spanish forces defeated the Grand Alliance at the Battle of Almansa on April 25, 1707, the Crown sent the printed *relación* to New Spain with a French *navio de aviso* that would be forced to dump its mail overboard during a corsair attack. By the time the official *relación* arrived in New Spain, the Duke of Alburquerque had already learned the news from several sources of information, including the Governor of the Canary Islands. In his letter acknowledging receipt of the *relación* along with notice of the birth of the first Bourbon crown prince of Spain, the Duke of Alburquerque acknowledged that news from

Spain served as a "great consolation" in "places so distant from the Royal presence of Your Majesty."[46]

After a news report arrived in New Spain, viceregal authorities sometimes took measures to amplify it. When the last will and testament of Carlos II arrived in 1701, New Spain's interim viceroy, Archbishop Ortega y Montañes, had it reprinted in Mexico City for broad circulation.[47] Newspapers also arrived, describing the first inklings of impending war and introducing some of the main contenders in the conflict. Immediately after the death of the last Habsburg monarch, the Spanish Crown sent an extraordinary delegation to Versailles, a description of which arrived in New Spain. It referred to the partition treaties that would have led to the dismembering of the Spanish Empire and explained that the Archduke Charles had delayed in deciding about war until he knew what the Duke of Savoy, an enemy of Louis XIV, intended to do. The Duchy of Savoy would become a key member of the Grand Alliance.[48]

While helping American subjects to vicariously experience the war, imprints served to bolster support for Felipe V and discourage disloyalty. After the Portuguese front opened in 1704, the Crown created *relaciones de sucesos,* exaggerating Bourbon military achievements, and these arrived in Puebla.[49] Along with providing word of Franco-Spanish victories, imprints warned about the consequences of disloyalty, as reflected in the accounts of the punishments suffered by the two disloyal *oidores* at the beginning of this chapter. Another imprint that arrived in New Spain described the quashing of an attempted uprising in Granada in 1705, which reportedly involved a diversity of people, including priests, shoemakers, silversmiths, carpenters, and masons. Apparently, a rumor circulated that British ships waited off the coast of Málaga for a general uprising to occur during Corpus Christ; the enemy reportedly intended to take advantage of the chaos of a popular uprising to invade southern Spain. The imprint describing the failed uprising noted that pro-Bourbon officials hanged many traitors.[50] Later, after the Grand Alliance temporarily occupied Madrid in 1706, a rumor circulated throughout the Spanish kingdoms that the Archduke Charles had died. Hoping to discourage Habsburg supporters, provincial newspapers amplified the rumor. Through *gazetas,* the rumor reached New Spain.[51]

But, while some rumors could help the Bourbon cause, the Crown understood that it needed to get ahead of others that could jeopardize Felipe V. After the enemy forced Felipe V to flee Madrid in 1706, he immediately sent a letter to New Spain and the rest of the Spanish kingdoms to dispel the rumor started by the enemy that he intended to abandon the throne.⁵² Although many grandees defected to the Austrian side during that year's occupation of Madrid, a *relación de sucesos* printed in Seville emphasized the continued loyalty of the capital, even describing the oath ceremony for the Archduke Charles as akin to a funeral.⁵³ Just days before he fled Madrid, Felipe V sent the Duke of Alburquerque a letter warning him to only honor orders signed directly by him or his secretaries. Learning that many members of the Council of the Indies defected during the occupation, he warned the viceroy of New Spain to ignore all communications from the council between July 11, 1706 (the king's departure from court) and his reinstatement.⁵⁴ Although the occupation only lasted forty days, the idea that decrees could have been sent to New Spain by the "fake" Council of the Indies alarmed the Bourbon Crown.

After the decisive victory in Almansa the following year, the Bourbon Crown sent a detailed description of the battle, with lists of the enemy dead, the imprisoned, and the weapons and pennants collected after the battle, to New Spain. The account declared that God had assured the triumph of a wise and pious king.⁵⁵ Despite this, rumors regarding the disloyalty of the grandees continued to sow ambivalence and doubt. In 1707, for example, a witness reported that Pedro Collazo de Soto, the Galician merchant and associate of Gasco, spoke publicly about the monarch's problems with the grandees, and other witnesses reported that Salvador Mañer gossiped about Felipe V's preference for the French nobles who followed him to the Spanish court and the subsequent alienation of the Spanish grandees. During public conversations, Mañer reportedly claimed that "those called traitors now will be considered the most loyal later" after a Habsburg victory.⁵⁶

Hope for a Bourbon victory seemed almost extinguished after Louis XIV withdrew his ambassadors and troops from Spain in 1709. Given the ambivalence or even outright disloyalty of many nobles, pro-Bourbon bureaucrats sought to reassure the populace regarding the steadfastness of the empire's most powerful. In the fall of 1710, the Duke of Alba traveled to Versailles and presented Louis XIV with a letter signed by thirty-two grandees. In addition to asking the French king to send aid to his grandson, it reassured him regarding the "firmness" and "constancy" of the Spanish nobility. The Crown had an imprint of the letter sent to New Spain, where the viceroy then had it reprinted for broad circulation.⁵⁷

After Bourbon forces defeated the Grand Alliance in Brihuega and Villaviciosa in 1710, the Crown sent copies of a detailed *relación* to New Spain, which the viceroy also had reprinted.⁵⁸ As previously mentioned, Secretary of War Grimaldo had insisted that the imprints and commemorations in honor of the victories emphasize the arrest of the English General Stanhope, likely recognizing the political utility of characterizing the victories as a triumph of Catholicism over Protestantism. Priests throughout New Spain grasped the importance of framing the contest as a holy war and emphasized the threat to religious orthodoxy. Cathedral canon Juan Ignacio de Castorena y Ursúa gave the sermon commemorating the victories at the University of Mexico. In emphasizing the legitimacy of Bourbon rule, he warned his audience that England intended to keep the Indies for itself. This likely terrified viceregal audiences, for which orators frequently raised the specter of Martin Luther.[59] Echoing Belluga, he claimed that Lutheranism and Calvinism would be proselytized in churches if this came to pass and asked what would happen to the Virgen de Guadalupe, given that Lutherans "erase, burn, [and] destroy all images"?[60] He noted that the Protestant enemy had profaned against seventy-two different churches in Spain but that the victories at Brihuega and Villaviciosa brought James Stanhope and other enemy leaders to their knees.[61]

While reinforcing the narrative of holy war, propaganda glossed over recent history and argued that France and Spain had always partnered in the defense of the faith. Antipathy for the French seemed ingrained in Spaniards, as many believed at the time. When arrested in 1707, viceregal authorities accused the Catalan cloth merchant Joaquin Puyol of stating publicly that things would go badly for Felipe V because Spaniards never get along with the French.[62] To quash this type of thinking, some Spanish authors, like the Cistercian monk and royal chronicler Pablo Yáñez de Áviles, promoted a vision of the past emphasizing cooperation and commonalities between the people of France and Spain. His *España-Francia, union, y amistad de las dos naciones* arrived in Puebla, and Yáñez de Áviles described how French and Spanish ecclesiastics and nobles worked to eradicate specific heresies as early as the seventh century. It emphasized that the kingdoms of both regions shared relics and opened their pilgrimage sites to the devout from both lands, and asked readers to remember the many times Spain and France formed alliances to advance the faith.[63] The text exalted France and Spain as the bulwarks of Catholicism and likely encountered a receptive audience among Puebla's large community of religious.

Another pamphlet that arrived in Puebla also sought to address the decades of hostility that had existed between France and Spain. Written as a letter from someone at the Spanish court to a friend in Andalusia, it acknowledged recent conflict between the two empires but argued that when one looks back in history, one can see that the two polities enjoyed a special relationship. To make this argument, the author reached back to the Reconquest, providing as an example the famous Battle of the Navas de Tolosa (1212). The author stressed French aid in this battle and reminded readers that the Grand Alliance intended to dismember the empire. Like the claim made by Castorena y Ursúa in his sermon, the author declared that England and the Netherlands would get the Indies.[64]

Pro-Bourbon pamphlets pushed the narrative that the current war represented a defense of Catholicism and underscored the involvement of miraculous forces. One specific imprint from 1705 arrived in Puebla, and it described events as supposedly experienced by the Inquisitor of Murcia. The Inquisitor reported on statements by a "holy man" visiting a family in the community who tried to convince people that God wanted the Archduke Charles recognized as king. However, the Inquisitor explained that after undergoing an exorcism, the man confessed to being a trouble-making demon.[65] This account circulated broadly. The Inquisitor sent a copy of the same account to the nuncio of Spain, who then sent it to Cardinal Fabrizio Paolucci, Secretary of State of the Vatican.[66]

Given the document's provenance, Bishop Belluga likely influenced the account, but a copy of what is arguably the bishop's most famous pastoral letter arrived in Puebla as well. Written in 1706, it described a miracle that took place in Monteagudo, where a sculpture of Our Lady sweated and wept over the course of two days while Franco-Spanish forces fought the English, a seemingly Godless enemy that entered churches, decapitated sacred images, and even disinterred two holy women while searching for jewels. Belluga named this manifestation of the Virgin Mary Nuestra Señora de las Lágrimas (Our Lady of Tears) and dedicated various sermons to her, including one in commemoration of the birth of the first Bourbon crown prince, Luis I.[67] His exhortation, which later arrived in Puebla, implored parishioners to help fight Spain's "holy war" by fasting for three days the following week, and ordered all churches in his diocese to display the Host. Finally, he awarded forty days of indulgences for every time a parishioner prayed to the Holy Sacrament for the triumph of Felipe V.[68]

The reported iconoclasm and sacrilege committed by enemy forces allowed officials in Spain to label the conflict a holy war, and this would become a pervasive theme in many imprints that arrived in New Spain.[69] One anonymous account of the occupation of Madrid in 1710 expanded on the acts of sacrilege committed by Protestant soldiers.[70] Another pamphlet found in Puebla even played on the fear of Judaism. It relayed the story of a four- or five-year-old boy in Cádiz whom neighbors discovered badly beaten, circumcised, and barely alive. A priest then reportedly prayed over the dying child and requested that once in Heaven, he ask God to protect Felipe V, the defender of the faith.[71]

Some pamphlets addressed the legality of the succession, even while characterizing an Austrian victory as an existential threat to Catholicism. In 1660, María Teresa renounced her claim to the Spanish throne for herself and any future children upon her marriage to Louis XIV, and many believed that this invalidated Felipe V's succession. A related line of argument had an impact on subjects in New Spain. According to testimony by Antonio Freire, a merchant with a stand in the main plaza in Mexico City, Pedro Collazo de Soto, and the priest Lorenzo Sánchez did not believe that Felipe V could inherit the throne because of Salic Law, which prohibited women from succeeding to the French throne.[72] In Bishop Belluga's pastoral letter directed toward "humble" people, he argued that his mother María Teresa's renunciation of her claim to the throne was illegitimate because it ignored Spanish custom and the long tradition of succession based on maternal lineage. Many, however, still used María Teresa's renunciation to argue that Felipe V had no legal claim to the throne. As a counter to this argument, a pamphlet arrived in Puebla declaring that no legal argument is valid when the Catholic religion is under attack, and no legitimate king would permit the kind of sacrilege taking place throughout the Spanish kingdoms.[73]

The Crown embraced this line of argument in its official communications with New Spain. On July 4, 1709, during the hardest period for Felipe V in the war – soon after France, England, and Holland debated the future of the Spanish Empire at the Hague – Spain's monarch sent a letter to all municipal councils, dioceses, and religious houses in which he responded to Dutch demands for a general peace. According to the monarch, the Dutch made clear that they would not accept Bourbon rule and believed that they should retain the Spanish Netherlands, while Portugal should be offered most of the Spanish kingdoms, including Extremadura, Castile, Galicia, and the Indies. Felipe V then added with biting sarcasm that, since every enemy of Spain and the "true Religion" had already been granted a share of the empire, the only thing left was to hand over land to the Moors. Finally, he claimed that because the Archduke Charles married a Protestant, it cast suspicion over his piety and his motivations for invading Spain.[74]

An Early Modern Public Sphere 63

Spanish subjects in New Spain did not necessarily have to read or listen to a reading of an imprint to receive messages regarding the "holy war," as priests often cited from specific publications in their sermons. In 1711, in a sermon commemorating the victories in Brihuega and Villaviciosa in the sanctuary of the Virgen de Guadalupe outside Mexico City, the Franciscan Manuel de Argüello referred to several *relaciones* that relayed reports of miracles that took place in the period surrounding the victories.[75] Similarly, in a sermon given in Patzcuaro's main parish, the Jesuit José Brabo also mentioned the miracles that had transpired, noting that the Bourbon forces were "few" while the enemy had "thousands" of soldiers and that this had been reported in *gazetas* throughout Spain.[76] In a sermon given in Real de Minas de Sultepec, Bernardo Unibárbia cited directly from a *relación* by Bishop Belluga that described a vision shared by more than thirty witnesses. Shortly before the battles of Brihuega and Villaviciosa, a large group of people witnessed an army charging on horseback from Castile to Catalonia "made up of men of horrible figures, with colored, blue and yellow dress, who were raised from the ground about two *varas*," and that startled everyone with their "terrible roar." He saw the demons fleeing from Castile as evidence of the fervent loyalty of the kingdom to Felipe V.[77] Citing from the same imprint for a sermon given in Mexico City, the Franciscan Pedro Dañon also commented on the army of demons that fled from Castile while "raised from the ground."[78]

HOLY WAR AND HISPANIZATION: FROM *PIETAS AUSTRIACA* TO *PIETAS BORBÓNICA*

Sermons, therefore, relayed anecdotes described in Spanish imprints and helped to shape a narrative of the conflict that spanned the Atlantic Ocean. While alluding to the religious implications of the war, this literature stressed continuity between the Habsburg and Bourbon monarchies by characterizing Felipe V's religious sensibility as unmistakably "Spanish" and as a continuation of the *pietas austriaca*, or the piety of the House of Austria. Many, for example, stressed the love and devotion that Felipe V and his queen María Luisa Gabriela de Saboya felt for the Virgin Mary. Commonly characterized as a warrior who crushed the snake in Genesis, the virgin blessed and defended Catholic monarchs since at least the thirteenth century, when she aided Alonso XIII of Castile in the battle of the Navas de Tolosa. Although the Austrian Habsburgs focused their devotion primarily on the Holy Sacrament and the cross, she developed into a second pillar of faith for the Spanish Habsburgs. As Anna Coreth noted, the first Habsburg monarch of Spain, Holy Roman Emperor Carlos V (1500–1558), visited the Virgin of Montserrat in Catalonia eleven times during his reign, including before his conquest of Tunis in 1535. In 1571, Our Lady of the Rosary famously aided Spanish forces at the Battle of Lepanto. As an act of gratitude, Felipe II (1527–1598) sent one of the enemy flags seized from an Ottoman ship after the battle to the shrine of the Virgen de la Atocha outside of Madrid.[79]

The latter devotion would eventually become inextricably tied to the Spanish Habsburgs. After the establishment of a permanent court in Madrid in 1561, Spain's Habsburg monarchs traveled far less than they used to and transferred their most fervent devotion from dispersed advocations of the virgin, like the Virgen de Guadalupe in Extremadura and the Virgen del Pilar in Aragon, to local cults like the Virgen de Atocha: a sculpture of the virgin and the Christ-child dating from the twelfth or thirteenth centuries but rumored to have been sculpted by Saint Luke. In 1602, Felipe III named the church a *capilla real*, or royal chapel, and she transformed into a patroness of the Spanish Habsburgs, with the royal family paying frequent visits to the shrine, especially when staying at the nearby Palace of Buen Retiro. Felipe III placed his coat-of-arms inside the chapel, and according to a chronicle of the shrine written in 1670, Felipe IV visited the church of Nuestra Señora de Atocha thousands of times.[80] Given the virgin's special relationship with the Spanish Habsburgs, it is no coincidence that while waiting for Felipe V's arrival at court in 1701, officials organized a mass for his seventeenth birthday at the royal chapel of Atocha.[81] Then, according to an edition of the *Gazeta de Madrid*, a copy of which later arrived in New Spain, the freshly acclaimed king gave thanks personally at Atocha, where, as had also occurred on his birthday, attendees sang the traditional hymn of thanksgiving, the *Te Deum Laudamus*.[82] Later, before taking her place at court, María Luisa Gabriela de Saboya gave thanks before Nuestra Señora de Atocha, an event that Antonio de Ubilla described in an imprint that arrived in New Spain.[83]

Bourbon influencers gave the Virgen de Atocha a central place in the war, which is not to say that the Crown did not acknowledge other shrines within the composite monarchy. When Felipe V traveled to Aragon to swear to honor its *fueros* in Zaragoza, he also visited Nuestra Señora del Pilar. After he departed from Barcelona for the campaign in Italy, his wife honored the monarchy's compact with the virgin by leaving jewels for Nuestra Señora del Pilar and for Nuestra

Señora de Montserrat; these acts of reciprocity at iconic Spanish shrines were all relayed by Antonio de Ubilla in his chronicle. However, throughout the seventeenth century, the Virgin of Atocha transformed into a bulwark for the Spanish Habsburg dynasty and became closely associated with the well-being of the empire. During the Revolt of the Catalans (1640–1652), the Virgen de Atocha emerged as the central Marian devotion of the Habsburg Crown. Felipe IV's primary advisor, the Count-Duke of Olivares, declared the Union of Arms to be able to conscript soldiers from all over Spain, but the Catalans refused and allied with France. Like the Protestant soldiers during the War of the Spanish Succession, the French soldiers aiding Aragon reportedly committed acts of iconoclasm, and during both conflicts, Spain's monarchs sought the aid of the Virgen de Atocha.[84] Later, as the War of the Spanish Succession developed into a supposed war against heresy, both the Habsburg and Bourbon sides tried to control the shrine and gain the virgin's favor. Bourbon victories involved the taking of weapons and pennants from the enemy, which Felipe V then ordered deposited in Atocha.

Reports about the king's devotion to principal Marian images within the Spanish monarchy, and particularly his love for the Virgen de Atocha, surely resonated in New Spain. People throughout the empire customarily prayed for the royal family before important images of the Virgin Mary, and in 1706 two witnesses for Benito Cartagena claimed that after learning about recent Habsburg victories, they accompanied Cartagena to pray for the king at the shrine of the Virgen de Guadalupe.[85] Furthermore, many people residing in New Spain would have been familiar with Nuestra Señora de Atocha and the Habsburg dynasty's devotion to the cult. Members of the royal family prayed privately in their chapel at the shrine, but they also authorized and helped choreograph elaborate spectacles for the virgin as acts of thanksgiving, such as a cavalcade to the convent and a celebratory mass following the end of the Ottoman siege of Vienna in 1683.[86] Starting in 1633, the Council of the Indies began participating in the annual feast day of the Presentation of the Virgin (November 21) at the shrine. During the ceremony, the Council of the Indies placed all the territories within its jurisdiction and all the vessels that traveled to the Americas under her protection. In 1636, the Council of the Indies transformed Nuestra Señora de Atocha into a special patroness by vowing to honor the feast day at the shrine in perpetuity.[87]

After the temporary occupation of Madrid by the Grand Alliance and the decisive Bourbon victories at Brihuega and Villaviciosa in 1710, the Crown had a detailed *relación* disseminated throughout the empire, including New Spain. It noted that the pennants captured after Felipe V's victory at Luzzara in northern Italy in 1702 and at the important Bourbon victory at Almansa in 1707 had been placed before Nuestra Señora de Atocha and described how these were shamefully removed from the shrine by the enemy during the Archduke's occupation of Madrid in 1710. Before making his triumphal entrance into the city, the Archduke had heard mass at Atocha, which the imprint characterized as hypocrisy, given the amount of sacrilege later committed by the 2,500 soldiers that accompanied him. Indeed, the account described how Protestant soldiers sacked churches and killed people who had sought refuge inside. Significantly, it also recounted how Protestants stole Eucharist wafers and hurled them to the ground. A priest who collected the wafers reportedly took them to the Archduke, demanding justice in God's name. The Archduke then reportedly sent the priest to talk to General Stanhope, who brushed him off by sending him to speak with the Supreme Commander of Austrian forces in Spain, Guido Starhemberg. Angered by the disinterest, the priest resolved to wait for divine retribution. Given that Bourbon forces would soon defeat the Grand Alliance almost definitively at the battles of Brihuega and Villaviciosa, the imprint made clear that God answered his prayer.[88]

Other imprints that arrived after the battles emphasized the struggle for control over the shrine, treating it like a metaphor for the entire war.[89] An account printed in Madrid but that later arrived in New Spain decried the disloyalty of priests who sought to sway parishioners to the Austrian side and refused to absolve Bourbon loyalists in the confessional. It described how, during the fifty-day occupation of Madrid, priests initiated the singing of the *Te Deum Laudamus* in the Archduke's presence but emphasized that this was out of fear, and how before leaving for battle, Felipe V and the Bourbon commander, the Duke of Vendôme, prayed before Nuestra Señora de Atocha.[90]

Pamphlets recorded the anecdote regarding the monarch's visit to Atocha before the pivotal battles of Brihuega and Villaviciosa, and several priests in New Spain recounted the episode in their sermons. A sermon given in Celaya made use of the archetype of the "virgin as warrior" and described how Felipe V abandoned court in 1710 to "arm" himself by prostrating himself before the virgin in Atocha. It also decried the Protestant desire to destroy the Inquisition, permit priests to marry, and profess Lutheranism and Calvinism from the pulpits.[91] Bernardo Unibárbia of Real de Minas de Sultepec gave a sermon that described the same heretical acts mentioned by Castorena y Ursúa, including the

An Early Modern Public Sphere 67

desecration of seventy-two churches. Citing none other than Bishop Belluga, he described how Felipe V left his crown before Our Lady at Atocha before leaving for the pivotal battles of Brihuega and Villaviciosa.[92] The virgin, a symbol long associated with war and Spanish piety, assured Felipe V's victory.

CONCLUSION

During the War of the Spanish Succession, New Spain's residents had access to refracted information, which they then processed through their own biases and ambitions. Many of the two dozen men accused of disloyalty in 1706 and 1707 were either merchants or bureaucrats who experienced negative professional consequences from the transition from Habsburg to Bourbon rule. They proved skeptical of accounts of Franco-Spanish military victories and with good reason, as the Bourbon Crown censored information assiduously and warned viceregal officials that pro-Austrian agents and propaganda might arrive in the Americas. Despite this, many people shared pro-Austrian imprints and manuscripts that filtered into the viceroyalty, and some even transcribed them for further distribution or generated their own pro-Austrian tracts. People shared rumors and even gestured toward their true loyalties in public places as a way of finding like-minded confidantes. Most of the propaganda that arrived in New Spain, however, sympathized with the Bourbon dynasty, but the political culture that developed still rested heavily on rumor. Imprints that arrived in New Spain tried to address rumors that could prove detrimental to the Bourbon cause, and viceregal authorities even had some of these imprints reprinted within the viceroyalty for wide distribution.

Pro-Bourbon bureaucrats and inquisitors engaged in a concerted effort to curb the circulation of pro-Austrian information in the viceroyalty. Although New Spain had a circumscribed and stunted public sphere, bureaucrats sought to inundate the viceroyalty with pro-Bourbon imprints whose contents priests later shared in sermons. High-placed ecclesiastics in Spain helped to establish the interpretative framework of the conflict as a holy war, and imprints helped take this message to New Spain to then be amplified by bureaucrats and orators. Although pro-Bourbon propaganda could not prevent gossip or stamp out persistent loyalty for the Austrian side, it characterized the Bourbon Crown's position as righteous. This propaganda, moreover, addressed rumors questioning the commitment of Felipe V to the Crown of Spain and the loyalty of Spain's grandees, but overall, the deluge of pro-Bourbon material successfully framed the conflict as a holy war. In this way, pro-Bourbon imprints and sermons inspired the piety of individuals and played on fears of heterodoxy to assuage critical thinking. They, in essence, contributed to an imagined community of empire, one based on piety and a perceived, and continuously reinforced, connection to the metropole. Furthermore, while discouraging Francophobia, addressing criticisms regarding the legality of Bourbon rule, and promising continuity in the piety of the ruling monarchy, imprints worked to "Hispanicize" Felipe V.

Bourbon loyalists used the concept of holy war to frame Felipe V as a defender of the faith against Spain's heretical invaders. But, while Bourbon influencers pushed this framework, subjects in New Spain deepened the discussion, playing on the importance of the body of the king to Spain's political culture. Indeed, as explored in Chapter 3, in subtle and overt ways, orators and organizers of royal ceremonies in New Spain repeatedly referenced the long-held notion that the king's body reflected the broader body politic and even reflected the body of Christ, the other central focus of the *pietas austriaca* and, by extension, Spanish imperial identity. Through an emphasis on the metaphor of the body, imprints, sermons, and spectacles related to the succession promised continuity, but also regeneration. The elite and commoners of New Spain – "limbs" within the body politic – were all expected to perform their membership in the empire, which was based fundamentally on loyalty to the king and the empire's premier symbol of faith, the body of Christ.

3

The Body Politic and Imperial Resurrection

On April 4, 1701, the day of Mexico City's oath ceremony, or *jura del rey*, for Felipe V, the capital's residents admired a large platform in the main plaza, right next to the entryway to the viceregal palace. Roughly 25 meters long running east to west and almost 13 meters wide, the structure held a canopy comprised of silk cloth, in the center of which artisans embroidered two gold lions. Under the canopy, spectators could see a large gold crown resting atop two globes flanked by two statues: a European woman, representing Castile, and an Indigenous woman, representing the Indies.[1]

Organizers of oath ceremonies customarily placed a throne bearing a full-body portrait of the ascending king upon the event's main platform, but the inauguration of a new ruling dynasty called for something more. So, the Count of Moctezuma decided to place the royal portrait in the most "imminent place," the central balcony of the viceregal palace. Painted by the respected artist Juan Rodríguez Juárez (1675–1728), the full-body portrait of the *Monarquía Hispánica's* new Bourbon king depicted him dressed in the Spanish style, with dark vestments and *a la golilla* (wearing a high, stiff collar) and donning the *Toisón de Oro*, signaling his role as the head of Spain's Order of the Golden Fleece. At the young king's feet, spectators could behold a lion offering him the world.[2]

Given that the *jura del rey* occurred just one month after engravings of the king and a detailed description of Madrid's oath ceremony arrived in the viceroyalty, it is probable that Mexico City's organizers took inspiration from Madrid's *jura*, which occurred on November 24, 1700, before Felipe V arrived at the Spanish court. With the new king still absent,

Madrid's organizers chose to place the royal portrait on the principal balcony of the Real Alcázar, hanging over the platform constructed for the oath of loyalty.[3] From an elevated vantage point, "the king" could gaze upon his subjects in both Mexico City and Madrid.

During the War of the Spanish Succession, New Spain commemorated the rites of passage of members of the royal family, Spanish military victories, and litanies in support of Franco-Spanish forces. These occasions provided opportunities to present the Bourbon dynasty, and especially Felipe V, to subjects in New Spain. Textual descriptions of the king's appearance, along with visual likenesses of the monarch and his family, promised the resurrection and revitalization of the empire through a healthy king. Meanwhile, imprints, sermons, and commemorations cloaked the Bourbon dynasty in symbols associated with Habsburg rule.

Messages regarding the resurrection and renewal of the Spanish monarchy depended on metaphors grounded in the body, with interrelated references to the body of the king, the body politic, and the body of Christ. The imagining of the monarchy – and by extension, the empire – as a metaphorical body derived from the spiritual body of Christ is exemplified in Romans: "For as in one body we have many members, and not all the members have the same function, so we, who are many, are one body in Christ, and individually we are members of one of another."[4] The concept, therefore, reflected not just hierarchy, with the king as the "head" of the body politic, but it also justified inequality. Law 5 of the second section of the thirteenth-century Castilian law code *Las Sietes Partidas* reads:

> The king is the head of the kingdom, for just as the senses originate from the head, through which all the members of the body are governed, so too through the command that originates from the king, who is lord and head of all in the kingdom, must they be ruled and guided and be in agreement with him to obey, protect, guard, and set right the kingdom of which he is both soul and head, and they the members.[5]

As a concept, the body politic also reflected the integrated and interdependent nature of the imperial structure, visually reaffirmed in public ceremonies with the involvement of the city's elite, leading tribunals, and corporations referred to interchangeably as either "limbs" or as "*cuerpos*," or bodies themselves. These corporeal imaginings of monarchy persisted through the seventeenth century when the leading Jesuit thinker Juan Eusebio Nieremberg (1595–1658) described the king as the soul of a "mystical body."[6]

During public ceremonies, municipalities, urban elites, and local corporations all demonstrated their loyalty to the king and their membership in the body politic, and as we will see, some orators directly referred to the empire as a resurrected body. Ceremony proved crucial in communicating this understanding, as well as clarifying and cementing the relationship between Felipe V's subjects in New Spain and the imperial body politic. Edward Muir has noted how early modern Christian polities faced a "chronic problem" with their political rituals: how to establish and represent "the relationships between the various kinds of political bodies and their parts."[7] This was no simple task in New Spain, given that the *Monarquía Hispánica* represented a "composite monarchy" of separate, semi-autonomous polities, with others nested inside. Stability rested on "a mutual compact between the Crown and the ruling class" of each kingdom, and as evidenced by the slew of anti-Protestant propaganda that circulated throughout New Spain during the war, religion served as a primary mechanism of social cohesion, as did loyalty to the king.[8]

The imperial body politic had other political bodies nested inside it, and these all shared the same basic structure and ceremonial culture. The Crown of Aragon, for example, incorporated the largely autonomous kingdoms of Aragon, Valencia, Sardinia, Mallorca, Sicily, and Naples, as well as the Principality of Catalonia. Although New Spain functioned as a viceroyalty, officials also understood it as a *reino* or kingdom, and it incorporated other *reinos* inside its jurisdiction. These included the kingdoms of México, New Galicia, and Guatemala, which all enjoyed a limited degree of autonomy through their *audiencias*, or tribunals, but the southern kingdom of Yucatán functioned as a military district, and the northern kingdom of New Vizcaya represented a relative frontier. At the foundation of this administrative structure rested the *cabildos*, or municipal councils, the most basic and necessary political units within the *Monarquía Hispánica*. Kings, viceroys, governors, and *alcalde mayores* were all referred to as the *cabezas*, or "heads" of their respective body politics, and ceremonies of etiquette observed with the king were also observed with viceroys and *alcaldes mayores* in New Spain. When the king experienced a death in the family, for example, delegations from municipalities throughout the viceroyalty paid the viceroy, the surrogate king, a visit to express their condolences.[9] This reaffirmed the jurisdiction's relationship to the king, as well as the imagined unity of king and kingdom.

Ceremonies held in municipalities throughout New Spain during the succession crisis worked to reaffirm this unity during an unprecedented dynastic crisis. While transmitting messages regarding the resurrection of the body politic and its revitalization, public ceremonies demanded the involvement of not just political and ecclesiastical elites but also various religious institutions and corporations, integrating all members of society within a hierarchical framework. In New Spain, municipal leaders borrowed from symbols of monarchy used throughout the Spanish Empire, but they also made sure to ground messages within their local contexts. Regardless, political rituals tended to transform or mask differences into one, unified identity, or political and cultural body.[10]

The metaphor of the body helped urban elites communicate a variety of interrelated messages. While municipalities and corporations performed their membership in the body politic, the death of any monarch – let alone a whole ruling dynasty – jeopardized stability. Organizers in New Spain astutely channeled disgust toward the iconoclastic Grand Alliance and rallied support for Catholic Spain. To do this, supporters of Felipe V appropriated one of the central mysteries of the Catholic faith: the body of Christ in the consecrated host. The Habsburg dynasty had been founded on an origin story of devotion to the Holy Sacrament, which then became a defining characteristic of Spanish Habsburg piety and, by extension, Spanish imperial identity. With sacrilege against the sacrament increasing throughout the course of the war, the Spanish Bourbons positioned themselves as defenders of the cult, something orators in New Spain emphasized. What is more, the king, the Eucharist, and the body politic all reflected one another, and through visual likenesses, the king reproduced himself throughout his empire, just as Christ reproduced himself in the Eucharist. Like the sun – another symbol for the Eucharist – the king sustained his subjects wherever they resided. Furthermore, just as Christ rose again after death, orators assured New Spain's faithful that the Spanish monarchy would do so as well.

THE BODY OF THE KING AND THE BODY POLITIC

The king's body and, by extension, the body politic, served as the defining metaphor of the *Monarquía Hispánica*. While organizing large public rituals during the war, organizers in New Spain made repeated references to the interrelated body politics and, by extension, the *cuerpos eclesiásticos* and *cuerpos municipales* nested inside the empire. Indeed, the corporeal metaphor extended to every sphere of government, with head towns of Nahua city-states, or *altepetl*, becoming known as *cabezas* after the conquest. Different "bodies" performed their membership within the *cuerpo del rey* during ceremonies ordered by the Crown, and local leaders made these events priorities of government. They reaffirmed that the Spanish Empire functioned as an "empire of towns," and bureaucrats and ecclesiastics regarded demonstrations, sermons, and imprints as opportunities to also exalt their *patrias* (homelands) and position them for royal favor.

For urban leaders navigating the delicate transition from Habsburg to Bourbon rule, declaring their community's loyalty to Felipe V took priority. In 1701, Mexico City's municipal council found itself unable to pay for the *jura* due to its massive debt, which had even precipitated the viceroy to place the *cabildo*'s spending under the control of Miguel Calderón, the most senior *oidor*, or judge, on the *audiencia*. But noting the importance of the event, the viceroy instructed Calderón to release funds.[11] The Mexico City *cabildo* spent a reported 5,000 pesos on the *jura*, but it was likely far more, given that many councilmen contributed to the festivities with their own money.[12] Meanwhile, Mexico City's cathedral chapter organized six different commemorations during the war (three with novenas) for roughly 6,836 pesos.[13] These were elaborate events, marked by ornate decorations, candles, costumes, ephemeral art, music, refreshments, and fireworks.

Royal ceremonies usually featured visual representations of the king, and sermons referred to the king's beauty and physicality, as people of the early modern Spanish World generally paid attention to what their kings looked like for clues as to their characteristics as a ruler. In the early modern period, the appearance of people or things revealed their essence, and perception was, therefore, "analogical," as people searched for hidden "meanings."[14] From the perspective of early modern Spanish Catholics, everything that occurred in the world was interconnected, and the physical health of the Spanish king reflected upon his empire. For example, with the death of Carlos II, the *Gazeta de Madrid* alluded to the monarch's sterility and then noted that during the embalming process, his heart appeared dry and consumed, and his liver, intestines, and lungs "*cancerados*" (cancer-ridden).[15] During the funerary sermon given in Mexico City's Franciscan convent, Blas de Pulgar relayed the same anecdote regarding the king's dry and consumed heart, claiming that this proved that while he was not a god, he was more than a man, asking what "man" could survive with no blood pumping through his heart? Then, alluding to the unity of the king and his kingdom, he stated that the king holds the people (*"el pueblo"*) in his hand and that he is *"la respiración con que vivimos*," or the "breath that allows us to live."[16] For San Luis Potosi's funerary sermon in honor of Carlos II, the Franciscan Juan de San Miguel cited the same anecdote and argued that the dehydrated nature of the monarch's insides resulted from the "weight" of his crown.[17]

Subjects may have recognized a relationship between the state of the king's body and conditions in two epicenters of the empire. The Iberian Peninsula experienced bad harvests in 1697 and 1698, and a related uprising in Madrid forced the President of the Council of Castile, the Count of Oropesa, to renounce his position. In Mexico City, bad harvests and the ineptitude of officials led to a popular uprising in 1692, resulting in the burning down of half the viceregal palace, followed in 1696 with a devastating epidemic.[18] Toward the end of 1698, the fleet that carried news regarding the ratification of the Peace of Ryswick between France, England, Holland, and Austria also brought orders to hold rogations on behalf of the monarchy, which unleashed rumors that the king had died. This coincided with a plague of "*chahuistle*" (a fungal disease) on wheat plants in central Mexico, which threatened to provoke another food shortage. In response, Mexico City's municipal council named the French saint Bernardo de Claraval (Bernard of Clairvaux) a patron against plagues and for the "health of our king," two phenomena that contemporaries clearly regarded as related.[19]

It was within this context that the *Gazeta de Madrid* published its first official description of Felipe V on December 21, 1700, seventeen days after he departed from Versailles for the Court of Madrid. Citing letters by "trustworthy" sources in Paris, the author described the new king as charming in his appearance, as well as "very gallant and very Spanish in his air." It described his hair as "very blonde, and curly *a la mode*," and elaborated upon his wide forehead, arched eyebrows, large eyes, and slightly elevated lower lip, which carries "hints of Austrian [heritage]." Overall, it described his countenance as "benign" and commented on his inordinate strength, specifying how he could bend a silver tray "without much exertion."[20]

This description promptly made its way to New Spain, as evidenced by a sermon given by cathedral canon Miguel Núñez de Godoy in commemoration of the oath ceremony for Felipe V in Guadalajara. Núñez de Godoy compared Felipe V to the biblical King David, the seventh son of Isai, who had been chosen by King Saul to rule Israel, noting that both Felipe V and David did not rise to their respective thrones through direct descent. Significantly, the cathedral canon also noted that just as David had been young, blonde, and attractive when he became King of Israel, so was Felipe V, and he repeated the same story published in the *Gazeta de Madrid* about the silver plate, thereby underscoring the king's strength and virility.[21] An account of Guadalajara's oath ceremony by *audiencia* chancellor Miguel de Amescua described the king as physically "beautiful," something also noted in pamphlets in Spain, and significantly, one of the paintings that graced the *jura* platform referenced the *Gazeta de Madrid*'s description of Felipe V; it depicted him holding a silver plate with both hands.[22]

From the onset of the succession crisis, officials in the metropole and bureaucrats and ecclesiastics in the viceroyalty worked to communicate that a new, healthy king from a foreign dynasty would renew the monarchy. The strong and attractive Felipe V served as a stark contrast to the sickly and less attractive Carlos II, particularly during the last decade of his life. Foreign ambassadors to Spain commented on Carlos II's unhealthy pallor, general weakness, and the protracted shape of his jaw, which he carried in the Habsburg bloodline.[23] In contrast, Felipe V's overall health promised to end decades of infertility within Spain's ruling dynasty, something that will be explored in more depth later. Yet, the young king's ascension also promised renewed vitality. Indeed, contemporaries understood that the king and the empire mirrored one another, and so the *Gazeta de Madrid*'s description also elaborated on the intellectual and physical vitality of the king, discussing his study of Latin, Spanish, history, writing, and fencing.[24]

Realizing the political utility of his grandson's appearance, Louis XIV attempted to flood New Spain with images of Spain's new Bourbon king. According to an account of Mexico City's oath ceremony for Felipe V, the *navío de aviso* that arrived in New Spain in March 1701, containing the last will and testament of Carlos II, also carried the new king, "if not in the original, in his royal copy." This, according to the account, consisted of fine engravings of Spain's new monarch.[25] Although these were but a first introduction to the seventeen-year-old, they fulfilled the objectives of Louis XIV and the Marquis of Torcy, his minister of foreign affairs, who ordered that engravings be sent along to the Indies with copies of Carlos II's testament.[26] The King of France understood the importance of representation to the cementing of royal power, and also understood the need to stress continuity between Habsburg and Bourbon rule, something gestured toward in the *Gazeta de Madrid*'s mention of Felipe V's "Austrian" lower lip.

After receiving and accepting the contents of Carlos II's testament, Louis XIV commissioned court painter Hyacinthe Rigaud to create a full-body portrait of Felipe V dressed in the Spanish style and adorned with two insignias: the *cordon bleu du Saint-Esprit* and the *Toisón de Oro*. The first designated him as a member of the chivalric order presided over by his paternal grandfather as the Sovereign Grand Master. The collar for the Order of the Golden Fleece, which was far more visible in the portrait, also designated him as Grand Master of Spain's ancient Burgundian Order, the most exclusive military order in the world. As Martha Sandoval Villegas has noted, Luis XIV advised Felipe V to eschew French fashion at the beginning of his reign and, for this reason, he entered Madrid for the first time wearing Spanish vestments.[27]

In 1700, Joseph Vivien also created a portrait of Felipe V, and this became the basis for a fine engraving by Cornelius Vermeulen, which in turn served as the inspiration for engravings reproduced and shipped throughout the Indies (Figure 3.1).[28] The engraving, as well as others modeled after it, resembles the description of Felipe V contained in the *Gazeta de Madrid* and proved an effective mechanism by which to introduce the king in overseas territory. In the engravings modeled after Vivien's full-body portrait of the king in military armor, artisans added the collar of the Order of the Golden Fleece, while his lower lip remained enlarged, thereby highlighting his Austrian heritage.

In municipalities throughout New Spain, organizers had to carefully consider how to portray the king in oath ceremony portraits. Mexico City's portrait depicted the king according to the Habsburg tradition; that is, Juan Rodríguez Juárez depicted him dressed in traditional Spanish dress. Additionally, he also presented him as a Habsburg and a sacred king. The Salón de Espejos (Hall of Mirrors), the principal ceremonial space within Madrid's Real Alcázar, contained six buffet tables sustained by twelve bronze lions supported by globes, and Rodríguez Juárez painted a lion resting at the king's feet.[29] As Mínguez has argued, lions not only commonly represented strength and majesty but also alluded to the mythical link between the House of Austria and King Solomon. Indeed, the throne of Solomon featured six steps decorated with twelve lions ascending toward a throne, sustained by two more lions.[30] As a reminder, the canopy of Mexico City's oath ceremony platform included two lions embroidered in gold thread. Along with the lion in the portrait, these likened Felipe V to two iconic figures: Christ the "lion of Judah" referred to in the Book of Revelation, and King Solomon. Given the Bourbon position that the War of the Spanish Succession represented a

FIGURE 3.1 Philip V, King of Spain, 1701. Engraving by Cornelius Martinus Vermeulen after Joseph Vivien. Chalcographic print. Biblioteca Nacional de España.

holy war, the inclusion of lions made political and religious sense. Furthermore, the depiction of Felipe V in Spanish dress and the inclusion of the *Toisón de Oro* promised continuity.

But despite the overriding emphasis on continuity, some of the organizers of other succession ceremonies throughout New Spain chose to depict the king as a Frenchman and, in so doing, foretold renewal. In Mexico City, the viceroy ordered the *Compañía de Milicias del Comercio*, or the voluntary militia company of *consulado* merchants, to parade in honor of the oath ceremony. The powerful and wealthy merchants chose to forego traditional-style dress and to proclaim their loyalty by opting for French-style clothing.[31] Although Carlos II's funerary honors in Puebla emphasized continuity as well as renewal, the portrait included in the city's oath ceremony did not feature the king dressed in Spanish garments. The royal standard bearer, who sponsored most of the event, had the monarch represented in a crimson French-style costume, while he himself wore the exact same color. The painting, which stood atop the platform during the oath of loyalty, likely depicted the king's entire body. After the ceremony, militiamen moved it from the platform to the main balcony of the municipal palace, where militiamen continued to guard it as if the monarch were embodied in the portrait.[32] During the oath ceremony in Guadalajara, the municipal council commissioned an enormous allegorical painting, which featured the goddess Pallas painting a full-body portrait of the king in a blue French-style costume. As in Puebla, Guadalajara's standard bearer wore the exact same color.[33]

As various scholars have argued, full-body portraits proved crucial to royal ceremonies throughout the early modern Spanish World because, according to seventeenth-century artistic theories, life-size portraits allowed for a better capturing of reality, permitting the monarch to become "present" in his likeness.[34] Organizers of commemorations in New Spain made sure to make the king "present" throughout the entirety of the war, but these representations proved especially important during oath ceremonies when subjects "met" their king for the first time. Indeed, contemporaries recognized similarities between a well-executed royal portrait and Christ as embodied in the Eucharist. Just as the Eucharist wafer embodied Christ, subjects believed that royal portraits embodied the king and allowed him to become present in a multitude of locations at the same time.[35]

During the celebrations in honor of the victories at Brihuega and Villaviciosa in 1710, corporations and individuals commissioned various paintings of members of the Bourbon dynasty, making sure to emphasize that credit for the salvation and eventual renewal of the empire belonged to them. In 1711, the cathedral of Valladolid celebrated the victories, and as part of a long period of celebration, it also decided to commemorate the birthday of the monarch on December 19 with a celebration in the first salon of the palace of the Cathedral's dean. The decorations consisted of a throne draped in crimson cloth, atop which rested three portraits: one of crown prince Luis I, another of the queen-consort, and another, of course, of the victorious Bourbon monarch, Felipe V.[36]

Commemorations in Mexico City for the victories took place over the course of three months, and the University of Mexico celebrated with a cavalcade of students on horseback and a mass of thanksgiving in the university chapel. Organizers draped the walls of the antechapel with Turkish cloth and placed a throne in the middle of the room holding a portrait of Felipe V on horseback. The antechapel housed another two thrones with two other portraits on top: one of Pope Clement XI and the other of Felipe V, who enjoyed royal patronage over the Church. On the wall of the entrance to the chapel, organizers hung another portrait of the king, and at each side, two other portraits: one of Luis XIV and the other of the Grand Dauphin, the Duke of Burgundy. Inside, organizers placed a portrait of the king and a portrait of the queen on each side of the main altar, along with statues of the French monarch and the Spanish monarch, who became "saints": Louis IX of France (1214–1215) and Ferdinand III of Castile (c. 1199–1252).[37] Not coincidentally, these were also the namesakes of crown prince Luis Fernando, on whose birthday the university held its thanksgiving mass.

BODIES AND LIMBS IN NEW SPAIN

Orators, bureaucrats, and other educated contemporaries imagined the king as the head of the metaphorical body politic, but conceptions of Spain's composite empire (with other semi-autonomous body politics nested inside it) often blurred the line between metaphor and reality. Indeed, just as the king could become physically present through his royal portrait, his physical body became inextricably enmeshed with the overall notion of the body politic. The king's portrait remained veiled in a "sacramentary mystery" that encouraged subjects to seek union with the imperial body, just as the Holy Sacrament allowed for union with the body of Christ.[38]

Under the gaze of the king as embodied in his royal portrait, subjects in New Spain often performed their membership in the body politic, reenacting ceremonies performed with the king in Madrid or with the viceroy in Mexico City. The American viceroyalties functioned as discrete political bodies nested within the empire, and these had their own "kingdoms" and municipalities, with public squares and churches acting as primary stages for royal spectacles. Ceremonies ordered by the Crown required the participation of municipalities throughout the region, and once orders arrived from Spain, Mexico City's *cuerpo de ciudad* or municipal council went first, with the additional leadership of the viceroy and cathedral chapter. After the *cabeza* of New Spain held its funerary honors, other cities usually followed in loose order of importance. The Count of Moctezuma paid for the funerary honors held for Carlos II in Mexico City on April 26 and 27, which were followed by those of other institutions within the capital, such as the Royal Convent of N.P.S Francisco, which held its funerary honors on May 13, 1701.[39] Tlaxcala held an unusual double ceremony – funerary honors and a *jura del rey* or royal oath ceremony – on May 1, two days before the feast day of Saint Felipe the Apostle. Meanwhile, Puebla held its funerary honors on May 8, but Querétaro did not hold its honors until June 21.[40] Outside the capital, *cabildos* proved primarily responsible for the choreography of rituals ordered by the Crown and started planning the 1701 succession rituals soon after receiving a copy of the clause of Carlos II's testament announcing Felipe V as heir; these were sent to municipal governments and cathedral chapters throughout the viceroyalty.

Municipalities served as semi-autonomous body politics, and with the rise of a new ruling dynasty, local elites used royal rituals to educate the Bourbon king regarding their *patrias*. In 1708, a sermon given in Puebla's Franciscan convent in honor of the birth of the first Bourbon crown prince began: "Most fortunate a thousand times [over] illustrious *patria* of the Angels. Ancient and noble land of loyal heroes! A city included among the most excellent of America."[41] Similarly, an account of how Durango, the *cabeza* of the kingdom (or province) of New Vizcaya, celebrated the oath ceremony for Luis Fernando began with a short history of its settlement. It celebrated the sixteenth-century "heroes" who overcame a "barbarous terrain" and a multitude of idolaters to settle the farthest region of the viceroyalty and how, in gratitude, Carlos V awarded the people of New Vizcaya special *fueros*. It informed the king that the region had provided the Crown with so much silver, it would be impossible to count, and how Durango is filled with loyal and noble subjects.[42]

Before municipalities could go ahead with their ceremonies, the court of Mexico usually proceeded with a ceremony in which the viceroy, as the *cabeza*, aligned himself with the king. The Count of Moctezuma's, the Duke of Alburquerque's, and the Duke of Linares' performance in royal rituals served as an example to elites and commoners and may have helped to safeguard their positions. After the death of Carlos II, French officials received intelligence that the Count of Moctezuma had been engaged in illegal trade with the English and Dutch, and Bourbon officials therefore suspected him of ambivalence regarding Bourbon rule and called him back to Spain in November 1701. His performance of loyalty during the royal funerary honors and *jura*, during which he waved the royal standard while acclaiming the king, may have helped to address these suspicions. In 1703, the Crown promoted him to the Council of the Indies, and in 1705, he became its president.[43]

Viceroys continued to support the new Bourbon monarch in public commemorations held throughout the course of the war and, in this way, benefitted by associating themselves with the king. Key among these public commemorations were funerary honors for fallen soldiers, which New Spain's viceroy first celebrated in Mexico City in 1694, two years after the viceregal capital experienced the largest urban riot in its history and while Spain fought against France during the Nine Years' War.[44] The ceremony remained on the annual calendar of the Jesuit's La Casa Profesa, but after 1696, ten years went by before a member of the capital's elite chose to sponsor another publication of a sermon related to the honors. Because sermons cost a great deal to print, elites usually reserved their publication for extraordinary years, like 1707.

That year, the Crown ordered the Duke of Alburquerque to hold elaborate funerary honors for Spanish soldiers after two tumultuous years, which included the enemy's temporary occupation of Madrid, followed by the seemingly miraculous victory at Almansa. High-ranking officials in Madrid lost no time in sharing the good news with Mexico City and ordered the Duke of Alburquerque to hold annual funerary honors for Spain's fallen soldiers.[45] These rituals – solemn, symbolic, and state-sponsored – anticipated the patriotic ceremonies at the tombs of unknown soldiers that served as hallmarks of twentieth-century nation-building projects.[46]

While helping subjects to imagine themselves as part of an imperial community, the funerary honors bolstered the position of the king and his ministers. In 1707, the Duke of Alburquerque found himself in a contentious struggle with the capital's *consulado* merchants. As previously discussed in Chapter 1, the viceroy profited from contraband trade, setting himself up against New Spain's powerful network of commercial families. Also, while pondering the fragile state of Caracas and a series of internal threats, in 1706 and 1707, the viceroy had to manage threatening intelligence reports that enemy forces planned on attacking Veracruz. In this tense climate, the funerary honors for fallen soldiers would reflect the viceroy's growing concerns. While listening to the sermon, attendees gazed upon a large catafalque, of which there is unfortunately no detailed description. Yet, the sermon by famed orator Juan de Goikoetxea condensed messages regarding Felipe V's leadership and legitimacy and, consequently, the loyalty owed to his simulacrum, the viceroy. After extensive comparisons between the king and the biblical hero King David, he referred directly to the viceroy as "prince of his militia and captain general."[47]

As the head of the viceregal body politic, the viceroy played a leading role in most royal ceremonies held in Mexico City, including funerary honors. However, custom and law determined that local *cabezas* also perform their relationship to the king during public rituals. In Guadalajara, the governor of New Galicia, the *audiencia*, and the *cabildo* sat upon the main stage of their city's oath ceremony, and on another stage immediately adjacent sat the wives of the *oidores*, on a platform decorated with "Plus Ultra," the Latin motto used by Carlos V to signify his expansion of the limits of the known world.[48]

Public rituals like these helped tether the elite of the viceroyalty to the empire, and printed descriptions of royal celebrations typically noted the effort made by the locality's elite in demonstrating their loyalty to the Crown. The *alférez real*, or royal standard bearer, for example, played a key role in New Spain's succession rites. *Las siete partidas* identified the king as the "head" of the body politic and primary officials as important "limbs" of his "body," making no distinction between the king and an abstract state. Because the *alférez real* carried the royal banner into battle and led armies when the monarch could not, he functioned as one of the most important limbs, and *Las siete partidas* mandated that the *alférez real* carry a sword to demonstrate his authority as "supreme judge." By the sixteenth century, the *alcaldes mayores* became the king's primary representatives in municipalities throughout the empire, but the position of *alférez real* remained important. In Mexico City, the honor of serving as royal standard bearer in royal ceremonies befell the most senior councilmen, but in Puebla, elites could purchase the prestigious position,

The Body Politic and Imperial Resurrection 83

which came with the distinction of sitting to the right side of the *alcalde mayor* and carrying a sword into *cabildo* meetings.⁴⁹

For *juras del rey*, the *alférez real* sponsored most of the event, and carried the royal pennant onto the main platform, where waving it, he gave the oath of loyalty on behalf of his city. In both Mexico City and Guadalajara, the *alférez real* performed his role with the assistance of a *padrino*, or godfather, but in the viceregal capital, the godfather mainly helped by passing out silver coins after the oath. In Guadalajara, on the other hand, the *alférez real* Juan Bautista Panduro and the *padrino* Don José de Robles Porres worked closely together; both rose to the platform at the same time, and at the commencement of the oath, Robles Porres handed Bautista Panduro the pennant. The *alférez* then started reciting "Castile, Castile. New Galicia, New Galicia for Felipe King of Castile and Leon" while handing the pennant over to the president of the *audiencia*, Don Alonso de Cevallos Villagutierre.⁵⁰

The municipal council of Guadalajara and *audiencia* of New Galicia had a long history of contentiousness, and, for this reason, the ceremony likely made a point of underscoring the roles of the *alférez*, a councilmember, and Alonso de Cevallos Villagutierre, the president of the *audiencia* and governor of New Galicia, who, by this time, had held the position for a remarkable twenty-two years.⁵¹ In Guadalajara, moreover, the oath ceremony platform contained numerous paintings of not just the king, which was to be expected, but also of local leaders. On the platform rested a scepter and a crown, objects that, along with the royal standard and portrait, embodied the essence of monarchy. However, right below the throne, organizers placed a portrait of Villagutierre, which visually announced his role as a proxy for the king. On the left side of the platform, and again "under the 'king'" as the description reads, attendees could view portraits of six members of the *cabildo*: Don Juan Bautista Panduro, Don José de Robles y Porres, the two *alcaldes ordinarios* (annually elected magistrates), and two councilmen.⁵²

In Puebla, the oath ceremony and royal funerary honors also underscored the power of the local oligarchy. The Marquis of Altamira, who had purchased the position of *alférez real* four years previously, became the first titled noble in New Spain's history ever to lead succession ceremonies. As the person who waved the royal standard at the time of the oath, the standard bearer acted as the king's champion. Altamira personally spent a combined total of 13,000 pesos for the 1701 *jura* and the 1710 oath ceremony for crown prince Luis I.⁵³

Rituals related to monarchical succession usually featured the main bureaucrats within a locality. Yet, other corporations throughout New Spain played important roles in a variety of public rituals held during the war, beginning with the publication of the six-month period of mourning following the death of Carlos II. At 10:30 AM on March 16, 1701, Mexico City's *alcalde mayor*, along with other important members of the municipal government, left the municipal palace in a cavalcade that consisted of an assortment of musicians on foot, followed by the municipal council's mace bearers and then the magistrates and members of the *cabildo* on horseback. All wore mourning attire, and even the musical instruments and maces were draped in black cloth. The committee proceeded to the viceregal palace, where the councilmen met with the viceroy and expressed their sorrow over the death of the king. The *cabildo* then accompanied the town crier outside to publicize the order, after which the cathedral started tolling its bells. As the committee traveled in front of the Episcopal Palace and the Tribunal of the Inquisition to repeat the order, the tolling continued until 4:30 in the afternoon, with seventy-one religious institutions joining in. Then, on March 22, members of different tribunals in order of antiquity visited the viceroy to give their condolences. These included the *audiencia*, the Royal University, the *cabildo* (again), the *consulado*, and the *protomedicato* (Royal Medical Tribunal), all dressed in mourning.[54]

New Spain's convents also worked to legitimize Spain's new ruling dynasty, giving distinct funerary masses in cathedral chapels in diocesan sees. On the morning of the king's funerary honors in Mexico City, the religious orders held sung masses inside the various side chapels, and held distinct masses and sermons in their own convents throughout the viceroyalty. Several years later, New Spain's convents hosted litanies in support of a healthy birth and sermons of thanksgiving after the crown prince arrived. In Puebla, the city's Dominican and Franciscan convents hosted thanksgiving masses, along with the cathedral.[55] In Durango, the cathedral and *cabildo* sponsored masses of thanksgiving in the cathedral, while local magistrates hosted a mass in the Convent of San Antonio.[56]

Later in 1710 during the celebrations held in Mexico City in honor of the victories in Brihuega and Villaviciosa, the viceroy led a procession to the cathedral for a mass of thanksgiving, which included many of the viceregal court's most important corporations, such as the Royal Treasury, the *cabildo*, the *consulado*, the *protomedicato*, and the city's confraternities, as well as individual clergymen and religious officials. The capital's celebrations also included masses hosted by other institutions, including the University of Mexico, the Sanctuary of the Virgen de Guadalupe, the Sanctuary of the Virgen de los Remedios, the Franciscan Convent, the Royal College of San Juan Letrán, the Seminary of San Pedro and San Pablo, the Hospital of the Immaculate Conception, and the Convent of Jesús María.[57]

While featuring governing elites and bureaucratic and religious corporations, ceremonies held throughout the war showcased different segments of the viceroyalty's social hierarchy. In Tlaxcala, four militia squadrons took part in the oath ceremony for Felipe V: two from Tlaxcala, one from the nearby indigenous town of San Felipe, and another from the indigenous town of Huamantla.[58] Royal ceremonies, therefore, required the participation of people throughout New Spain's social and spatial hierarchy. The printed description of Guadalajara's oath ceremony emphasized the participation of two indigenous militia battalions, as well as Spanish infantry. Although one battalion of indigenous soldiers dressed in the Spanish style, the other dressed in traditional clothing. The city's indigenous community also helped to entertain the populace through the creation of firework displays, as well as a large *navio*, or ship, carrying animals; indigenous men moved the *navio* through the crowd and, at the precise moment of the *jura*, released the animals into the main plaza to the delight of spectators.[59]

Because Tlaxcala enjoyed special privileges awarded for supporting the Spanish monarch during and after the conquest of Tenochtitlan, its municipal government remained in the hands of the locality's traditional native elite. Tlaxcala's indigenous *cabildo* represented its four *altepetls*, or ethnically based political units. Its Spanish governor helped to organize and pay for the oath ceremony and its printed account, which the author and militia captain Antonio Carlos de Castañeda dedicated to him. However, the account stressed the participation of the indigenous *principales*, or leaders, as the author sought to educate Felipe V about the longstanding loyalty of the city's indigenous community. It described Tlaxcala's obedience to Hernán Cortés in the conquest of the "bloodthirsty" Mexica, and the nobility's almost immediate declaration of loyalty to Carlos V. The platform for the *jura* featured paintings of the four indigenous leaders who initially allied with the Spaniards. Then, in the middle of these paintings, spectators could admire another painting of an indigenous female *principal*, with a sign connected to her mouth declaring "Viva Filippo Quinto, Viva, Viva." Indigenous *principales* from the four altepetls, moreover, sat upon the platform throughout the entire oath ceremony.[60]

Although Tlaxcala's native leadership literally took centerstage during its *jura*, New Spain's royal ceremonies generally featured indigenous people in different capacities as a way of declaring the loyalty of New Spain's two "republics": the republic of the Spaniards and the Republic of the Indians. In 1701, the governor and indigenous magistrates of the *"pueblo y cabeza"* of Coatepec held costly funerary honors for Carlos II, replete with a large catafalque. In recognition of its "obvious" loyalty and the exorbitant costs associated with this ceremony, the community asked the Council of the Indies for a six-year moratorium on tribute to be able to rebuild its church. Coatepec also requested that its Spanish governor, Don Manuel de Castro y Romero, be allowed to continue in the position with all the prerogatives and exemptions that are enjoyed by governors of *cabezas*, or head towns.[61] Although Coatepec attempted to benefit in a targeted way from its demonstration of loyalty, all municipalities featured actual indigenous people or representations of indigenous people. For the oath of loyalty that Durango held for Luis I in 1711, two squadrons of Indians from neighboring towns paraded with their banners and bows and arrows, and eighty men rode around on horseback.[62]

RESURRECTION THROUGH BOURBON RULE

The governing corporations and bureaucracies of New Spain engaged in a form of cultural mimesis in a context in which the structure of the viceroyalty and the municipalities mirrored that of the empire. Indeed, the political and social organization of the empire consisted of bodies inside other bodies (administrative units and corporations), with "heads" and "limbs." Contemporaries imagined these parts of the body politic as integral to the body of the king. Although the *Monarquía Hispánica* functioned as a composite monarchy, the sameness of the rituals performed in geographically dispersed locations helped to tether it together. Although the adhesion of elites to the body politic proved most important from the perspective of the Crown, all members of New Spain's complex social hierarchy were expected to play roles, either by participating in public rituals or by merely attending them.

Orators commemorating different events throughout the war invited listeners to make variegated associations between different "bodies" and the king. Still, the metaphor of the body derived its potency mainly from its connection to the figurative body of Christ (as in the Church) and the literal body of Christ (as in the Eucharist). The Spanish Habsburgs had a special devotion to the Eucharist, which, as we will see, became synonymous with Spanish identity. The War of the Spanish Succession, with its reports of sacrilege committed against the Holy Sacrament, provided an opportunity for Spain's new ruling dynasty to assume guardianship over the cult.

The Austrian and Spanish Habsburg dynasties traced their origin to Rudolf I (1218-1291) of the Holy Roman Empire, who, according to the dynasty's foundation myth, lent his horse to a priest carrying the viaticum to a dying man shortly before his coronation; the Habsburg dynasty's support for the mystery of the Eucharist created an almost contractual relationship with the divine, which only intensified after the Council of Trent (1545-1563) declared the mystery of Christ's presence in the consecrated host to be dogma.[63] Since the reign of Carlos V, all of Spain's monarchs have reenacted the Habsburg ritual of origin by giving up their horses or carriages to the viaticum or by simply kneeling when they encountered it in public. In 1685, Carlos II gave up his coach to a priest carrying the viaticum, inspiring several printed accounts of how the king humbled himself before the Host.[64] With the example set by Spain's monarchs, kneeling before the viaticum while en route became common practice throughout the empire. This included Mexico City, where even as late as the nineteenth century people commonly knelt before the viaticum on public streets.[65]

On the eve of the War of the Spanish Succession, priests in New Spain noted the devotion of Carlos II to the mystery of transubstantiation, sharing the account of how he gave up his coach in their sermons.[66] In 1701, the organizers of Puebla's succession ceremonies also chose to emphasize the contract between God and Spain, cemented by the monarchy's devotion to the Holy Sacrament. When the *alférez* entered the cathedral for mass on the day of the *jura*, he moved immediately to the main altar and lowered the standard three times before the Host, suggesting that Felipe V would continue to earn divine favor for Spain. Cathedral canon Gómez de la Parra explicitly addressed the foundation myth of the Habsburg dynasty in his eulogy. He recounted, for example, God's pact with Rudolph I and described how Carlos II reaffirmed his commitment to the Holy Sacrament by asking the Pope's permission to display the Host in the Royal Chapel.[67]

After the second occupation of Madrid by enemy forces in 1710, imprints arrived in New Spain recounting how Protestants within the Grand Alliance entered churches at court and hurled holy wafers to the ground, while Catholic officials serving the Archduke Charles did nothing.[68] Orators in New Spain partially attributed the Bourbon victories in

Brihuega and Villaviciosa to the Bourbon army's defense of the Holy Sacrament, as well as the Immaculate Conception, on whose octave Spaniards achieved victory. These represented the central devotions of the *pietas austriaca*, or the devotions of the Habsburg ruling lines, and helped to envelope Spain's monarchs in an air of sacred legitimacy.[69] Nevertheless, reports of iconoclasm during the war, as well as the creative oratory of priests, helped to transfer the devotions, which were already synonymous with Spanish piety, to Spain's Bourbon dynasty.

By the turn of the eighteenth century, Spaniards had come to see the two central cults of the famous *pietas austriaca* as central to Spanish identity. In a sermon in honor of the victories in Brihuega and Villaviciosa in Santiago de Querétaro, the Franciscan Juan de Guevara reflected on the "horrible news" that arrived on August 20, 1710, of the loss of Zaragoza and how heretical troops had then sacked Madrid, dismembering images of the Virgin Mary and hurling holy waters to the ground or selling them for the price of a sheep. He recounted how, when priests tried to resist, soldiers attacked them, even lighting one priest on fire. Guevara, therefore, set about praising both the mystery of the Immaculate Conception and the Eucharist for securing Spain's victory.[70] Preaching in Celaya in 1711, the Augustinian Francisco de Aguilera Izaguirre recalled how people sought the aid of the Archduke Charles in preventing sacrilege against the Holy Sacrament, and how he delegated this important task to apathetic subordinates. The priest explained that this inaction did not surprise him because "it was not the first time that the Heretics state, that the Most Holy Sacrament of the altar *Is God only of the Spaniards, and not theirs*" (emphasis his).[71]

Orators made subtle and sometimes direct equations between the body of the king, the body politic, and the body of Christ. The monstrance for the Eucharist resembled a sunburst, and not coincidentally, when discussing the king, orators referenced the multiplicity of meanings listeners might have attributed to the sun. Throughout the Spanish Empire, the monarch was often represented as the sun, an essential source of warmth and life that sets only to rise again, just like Jesus Christ died only to rise again. As a reminder, the entire emblematic design of the Count of Moctezuma's funerary honors for Charles II in 1701 centered on the equation of the king and the sun, eclipsed before reaching its zenith.[72] However, the sun and monarchy did not remain eclipsed. As part of the celebrations in honor of the victories in Brihuega and Villaviciosa in 1710, one of the decorative emblems inside the Church of the Virgen de Guadalupe featured the sun with the motto *Nunca muere*, signifying how the sun never sets on the Spanish Empire. For the commemoration's sermon, the Franciscan Manuel de Argüello equated Felipe V to the Host, and said that just like heretics deny the presence of God in the wafer, disloyal Spaniards deny the presence of the king in his kingdom.[73] For erudite observers of the war, the monarch and the body politic were one, a sacred entity similar to the Holy Sacrament in its transcendence and power. Like the body of Christ and the sun, the king and kingdom rise again through succession.

At different points throughout the war, orators invited listeners to imagine the empire as a body. In a sermon celebrating the victories at Brihuega and Villaviciosa, cathedral canon Juan Ignacio de Castorena y Ursúa compared the Grand Alliance's plans to partition the Spanish Empire to the Judgement of Solomon – the Old Testament account of when two women, both claiming to be an infant's mother, asked Solomon to intervene; the monarch proposed that if both women insisted the child was theirs, there would be no choice but to cut him in two. One of the women immediately renounced her claim, prompting Solomon to declare her the true mother. Castorena y Ursúa recalled — falsely – that while the Holy Roman Empire wished to partition the *Monarquía Hispánica*, France refused and asked listeners to recognize France (the Bourbon dynasty) as its true mother.[74]

In the imagination of contemporaries, the Spanish imperial body politic could be reborn, and this understanding, and the traditional way it had been expressed, spoke to the moment. During Veracruz's funerary sermon for Carlos II, the Franciscan Antonio de Posada remarked how his subjects had observed the monarch "sick for such a long time," suggesting that the empire had also been suffering, although especially so after his death. However, Posada consoled his audience, reminding them that the friends of God "die well," and resurrect like Lazarus. Given the unity of monarch and kingdom, he seemed to suggest that the empire would also rise again, especially since Carlos II charged his successor with supporting the mysteries of the Immaculate Conception and the Eucharist. He reminded listeners how during services for Corpus Christi, the Spanish Crown's premier religious holiday, a priest utters the statement: "as we do with the Sacrament, God will do with us."[75] A sermon given in honor of the birth of Luis Fernando in Durango in 1707 associated the arrival of the prince to Samson, whose name means sun, and compared the birth to the sun rising. The orator declared that the glories of Carlos V would rise again with the prince and added that the empire would also rise again through his birth, just as Israel rose again with the birth of Samson.[76]

Similarly, in 1707, while preaching in the sanctuary of *Nuestra Señora de la Soledad* in Antequera de Oaxaca, Bishop Ángel de Maldonado stated that the loyal supporters of Felipe V still experience fear, despite their faith in him, and speculated that Lazarus must have also experienced fear, waiting for Christ to resurrect him.[77] Later, Maldonado would be less subtle in his comparisons. While commemorating the health of the king and the achievements of the monarchy in 1713, the bishop equated the Spanish Empire to Lazarus, and by implication, Felipe V to Jesus. With Felipe's aid, the empire rose again.[78]

The Crown instructed bureaucratic and religious institutions throughout the empire to honor the Holy Sacrament and the Immaculate Conception for the victories in Brihuega and Villaviciosa, but in 1712, it also established a *Fiesta de Desagravios al Santísimo Sacramento*, or Feast Day to Make Amends to the Most Holy Sacrament, cementing the Bourbon Crown's patronage over the mystery, a patronage transferred over to Felipe V by his great uncle, Carlos II. On June 19, 1711, the Crown ordered the viceroys of New Spain and Peru, as well as governors, archbishops, bishops, and municipal governments in both kingdoms, to establish an annual mass and sermon to the Most Holy Sacrament, thereby inscribing an association between the Crown and the mystery on the collective memories of Spanish subjects in far-flung regions; the decree stated the Crown's expectation that this "memory will be celebrated in future centuries," and acknowledged the variety of iconoclastic behavior committed by Protestant soldiers, such as the dismembering of images of the Virgin Mary. However, it highlighted what Felipe V considered the most painful and sacrilegious act: the desecration of the Host. To make amends to God for this behavior, the monarch ordered cities, towns, and villages throughout his kingdoms to hold an annual mass and sermon To Make Amends to the Most Holy Sacrament in front of the visible Host on the Sunday immediately following the feast day of the Immaculate Conception.[79]

In their inaugural sermons for the annual commemoration, various orators recognized the ties that bound the Holy Sacrament and the Spanish Monarchy, and promised listeners that God's protection over Spain would continue under the Bourbons. For the inaugural mass and sermon in Pátzcuaro, the Jesuit José Brabo compared the Eucharist in its monstrance desecrated by the enemy to the sun eclipsed by "aborted enemies of the shadows." As an antidote to this sacrilege, he recalled how Carlos II came across the viaticum, dismounted his horse, and knelt before it, only to then accompany it to its destination. He stated that in establishing the annual feast day, Felipe V proved devout like his uncle.

The Body Politic and Imperial Resurrection 91

Speaking directly to the kings of Spain, Brabo declared, "God has chosen you, for his worship, for his defense, for his reparation."[80] In the inaugural sermon given in the cathedral of Guadalajara, cathedral canon Miguel Núñez de Godoy spent considerable time unraveling Felipe V's genealogical ties to the Spanish Habsburgs before declaring that if devotion to the Holy Sacrament ensured the Spanish throne for descendants of Rudolph I, the throne remained secure in Felipe V, a descendant of Rudolph I who remained devoted to the Eucharist.[81]

CONCLUSION

In choreographing and scripting the transition from Habsburg to Bourbon rule in New Spain, supporters of Felipe V relied heavily on metaphors associated with the human body, as physically making the king present in New Spain proved a priority, especially given the messages of regeneration embedded in public ceremonies held throughout the war. Supporters of Bourbon rule displayed the king's attractive figure and face whenever they could, signaling to all a healthy future for the Spanish Empire. Priests and bureaucrats incorporated full-body images of the monarch in public ceremonies and signaled the almost miraculous presence of the king in his image, mirrored in the presence of Jesus Christ in the central devotion of the monarchy, the Eucharist. During public rituals, religious and bureaucratic corporations performed their relationship to the monarch and, by extension, the empire. All these imaginings and public performances of loyalty gained their potency from the metaphor of the spiritual body of Christ and its embodiment in the Eucharist. Given the importance of the Holy Sacrament to Spanish identity, Spain's Bourbon Crown quickly sought to appropriate devotion to the Eucharist, something long associated with the founding of the Habsburg dynasty.

Bourbon influencers encouraged subjects in the viceroyalty to see themselves as part of the body of the king. Indeed, the metaphor of the body allowed people to reaffirm their loyalty to the king and empire during an uncertain transition prolonged by war. But, as reflected in the symbol of the sun rising and falling, or in the "resurrected" body of Christ, the narrative of the transition from Habsburg to Bourbon rule centered on destruction and regeneration or challenge and renewal. While this is clearly seen in some of the associations listeners potentially drew from the metaphor of the body, it also served as the central thread uniting prophecies associated with Spain, the monarchical succession, and a future "golden age."

4

Prophecy and the Bourbon Succession

On November 17, 1706, viceregal officials in Mexico City interviewed Basque general Juan de Garikoetxea as part of a broad investigation into a possible anti-Bourbon conspiracy. A contrabandist who facilitated the Duke of Alburquerque's illegal trade with the French, Garikoetxea frequently conducted business with merchants and artisans in the capital's *plaza mayor*; so, the investigators asked, specifically, if the general had any information about the disloyal inclinations of master blacksmith Juan López Camaño, a one-time friend of Gregorio Gasco, a Galician merchant and avid supporter of a Habsburg succession (see Chapter 2). In describing the questionable loyalty of Camaño and the rest of Gasco's cohort, the general described the lot as "Sebastianistas," or people who held the millenarian belief foretelling the arrival of a warrior-king who would restore Portugal to a "golden age."[1]

The labeling of Gregorio Gasco and his associates as Sebastianistas seems, on the surface, absurd. Why would a general accuse a group of Spanish subjects of being Sebastianistas? Only one member of Gasco's circle, his confessor Don Lorenzo Sánchez de Figueroa, came from Portugal; of all the men interviewed regarding rumored disloyalty, he best fit the profile of a Sebastianista. In addition to transcribing satires mocking Felipe V, Sánchez de Figueroa at one point declared publicly that the King of Portugal should rule over Castile, in addition to other nationalist sentiments.[2] While many of Gasco's associates made statements in support of Habsburg rule, no one else declared support for Portuguese nationalism.

Despite the seeming misalignment between the use of the term "Sebastianista" and its meaning, observers of the war bandied it about

Prophecy and the Bourbon Succession 93

with little reflection. The concept of Sebastianism dates to the years immediately following the Portuguese defeat by Muslim forces on August 4, 1578, at the Battle of Alcácer Quibir in northern Africa, but it possibly dates back further, to the idea of the "Hidden" or "Sleeping King" exemplified in Iberia by the fourteenth-century prophecy that Fernando III de Castilla and León (1199/1201–1252), the conqueror of Sevilla and Córdoba, would return to lead the conquest of Jerusalem.[3] Inspired by similar myths, crusading legends, and chronicles, King Sebastián set out to conquer Morocco only to lose his life. When his body could not be recuperated until December, it sparked rumors that Sebastián lived on and would someday return to restore and revitalize Portugal. After Felipe II became monarch of Portugal in 1580, the millenarianism unleashed by Sebastián's death conflated with the nationalism inspired by the union of Spain and Portugal.[4]

Portuguese forces joined the Grand Alliance in 1704, and anonymous authors began accusing the Portuguese, as well as the Archduke Charles's Spanish supporters, of being Sebastianistas. One pamphlet that arrived in New Spain described the Spanish supporters of the Archduke as

Malcontents, or Calvinists, because they do not believe in the true news reports, because they are favorable, and conducive to the salvation of the state, and vassals; and others are given the notorious name of Sebastianistas, as an allusion to the foolish hope of the Portuguese, who await their King Sebastián, in detriment to the reigning king, although one hundred and twenty-six years after [his] death in the famous battle of Africa.[5]

Another pamphlet written specifically for circulation in the Indies claimed that Protestant forces committed acts of iconoclasm in Catalonia, something that the "Sebastianistas" refused to believe.[6] Still another pamphlet sent to New Spain following the occupation of Madrid by the Grand Alliance in 1706 complained that the Portuguese squadrons that occupied court were filled with "Sebastianistas."[7]

Although Bourbon loyalists mainly directed accusations of Sebastianism toward the Portuguese who had allied with the Grand Alliance, the wielding of the accusation, whether accurately or not, reveals the importance that contemporaries attributed to Providence in deciding the outcome of the succession crisis. In analyzing the ascension of Felipe V, orators in New Spain appealed specifically to the Spanish kingdoms' centuries-old tradition of monarchical prophecy. As this chapter illustrates, public ceremonies, sermons, and imprints worked to condition subjects in New Spain to perceive the war in terms of a plan of destruction and regeneration, with Felipe V as the main protagonist.

Furthermore, while drawing on well-established monarchical prophecies to characterize Felipe V as a "New David" (a messiah) and to celebrate a collective Spanish victory, some orators in Mexico City positioned New Spain as the New Jerusalem, the central Republic of the millenarian age.

Given the polemics surrounding a Bourbon succession and the framing of the conflict as a holy war (see Chapter 2), it is understandable why some orators sought to characterize Felipe V as a messiah. However, people also responded to this common characterization of Spain's first Bourbon king because of the long history of Spanish orators and chroniclers describing monarchs in messianic or even millenarian terms. In the Spanish kingdoms, monarchical millenarianism developed, for the most part, from the prophecies of the Calabrian abbot Joachim de Fiore (1145–1202) and the application, and expansion, of his prophecies by others (Joachimite prophecy), especially as applied to bolstering the sacred legitimacy of the thirteenth-century Aragonese monarchy. Fiore predicted that history would move through three stages (like the Trinity), culminating in the Age of the Holy Spirit, a golden age preceding the Last Judgement. Also, emboldened by prophecies attributed to Isidoro de Sevilla (c. 560–636), by the fourteenth century, the neo-Gothic messianic tradition in Aragon centered the monarch in a war against "evil" (meaning Judaism and Islam) and used examples from history (chronicles and scripture) to predict the success of different rulers and the return of a Visigothic golden age.[8] Influenced by both Joachimite and neo-Gothic prophecies, Iberian intellectuals began regarding Spanish history as teleological and destined to culminate in a "rebirth."

By the fifteenth, sixteenth, and seventeenth centuries, orators who cited prophecy did not necessarily identify the origin of each one. Instead, as illustrated by numerous sermons given in New Spain during the War of the Spanish Succession, direct and subtle allusions to the Book of Revelation, Sibylline and Joachimite prophecy, and neo-Gothic writings all contributed to a narrative of Bourbon legitimacy and desirability. While orators tended to show restraint in citing prophecy, a narrative of destruction and renovation shaped collective memory and the adoption of millenarian figures and eschatological themes.[9] This is most clearly seen in prophecies related to the Last World Emperor, who in Iberia would be conflated with the Encubierto, or Hidden King, as well as the New David. As will become clear, King David (c. 1010–970 BCE), the Old Testament warrior-king who united Israel and Judea, acted as a mnemonic device in New Spain, conjuring up scriptural references and popular prophecies.

In municipalities throughout New Spain, orators compared the Bourbon king and his heir, Luis Fernando, to a slew of mythological heroes and biblical figures but relied most heavily on King David, the father of Solomon (c. 970–931 BCE), who would lead during a golden age that saw the construction of the First Temple. By comparing Felipe V repeatedly to David, orators promised a new dynastic lineage for Spain that would inaugurate another Solomonic age. Monarchs of this lineage would "save" Spain, convert heretics, unify Christendom, and inaugurate a new stage of history. Some even promised that as the New Jerusalem, Mexico City would play a central role in a Bourbon millennium.

THE MESSIANIC HERITAGE OF THE SPANISH KINGDOMS

Although orators in New Spain struggled to understand the significance of Felipe V to God's plan, they formed part of a transatlantic intellectual community intent on supporting the *Monarquía Hispánica's* first Bourbon king. To reconcile these aims, orators in New Spain drew from a deep and vast pool of messianic writing centered on an eschatological emperor who would preside over a golden age. But, while several strains of prophecy would shape Bourbon messianism, the Book of Revelation (and exegetical commentary related to it) proved the most influential.

After the siege of Judea by Roman soldiers and the destruction of the Second Temple in Jerusalem around 70 AD, John of Patmos sought to make sense of the tragic loss for the Jewish followers of Jesus. He claimed that Jesus, appearing with his face "shining like the sun," announced a final conflict between good and evil. Among other visions, the prophet saw a slaughtered lamb standing next to God's throne before trumpets blared and the four horsemen of the Apocalypse appeared, presaging war, famine, and death. John then witnessed an angel marking the loyal members of the twelve tribes of Israel so that they would be spared from eternal damnation before, up in Heaven, two signs appeared: a pregnant woman laboring to give birth to the messiah and a bright red dragon set to devour the child before it miraculously ascended to Heaven, after which an eagle whisked the Virgin away. Two beasts continued waging war on earth when, eventually, a divine warrior on a white steed appeared, with a sword emanating from his mouth. After this Jesus-figure defeated Satan, the prophet described how the faithful who had died then rose again and entered a New Jerusalem, a heavenly city, where they enjoyed peace, prosperity, and abundance for a thousand years.[10]

During the Middle Ages, the Sibylline oracles, a collection of prognostications ascribed to the Sibyls, or ancient female seers, remained as popular as the Book of Revelation and emphasized a warrior-king differentiated from Christ himself, a figure who would become a central component of eschatological writings in the Middle Ages. Salvaged in an edition from the sixth or seventh century, Sibylline prophecies contained classical Roman, Gnostic, and early Christian influences and "persisted alongside the eschatologies derived from the Book of Revelation, modifying them and being modified by them."[11] Sibylline prophecy, moreover, incorporated and complemented Jewish and Christian prophetic currents, and then, around 350 AD, as the Byzantine Church fractured between the two sons of Constantine, the Sibylline prophecy known as the Tiburtina declared Constantine's handsome son Constans, who ruled in the west, the savior. After Constans's murder, the prophecy foretold that he would rise again as a Greek Emperor who would reunite both sides of the Church, a common goal for Christian eschatological heroes.[12]

Other prophecies regarding a messianic warrior-king continued to circulate in the Middle Ages. In the Sibylline prophecy Pseudo-Methodius, the savior is referred to as the Emperor of the Last Days. It describes how the Ishmaelites, once defeated by Gideon, return to attack and seduce Christians from the one true faith. The emperor then appears to save the loyal and punish those who waffled. After a long period of peace and prosperity, he travels to Jerusalem to lay down his crown at the Golgotha, after which the Antichrist appears, but the hero, with a sword in his mouth (like in the Book of Revelation), destroys the Antichrist and initiates the Last Judgement. He then dies to eventually be reborn, like the Emperor Constans.[13]

At the end of the twelfth and beginning of the thirteenth centuries, Byzantine and Saracen prophecies attributed to an Arab philosopher named Acham Turuley also circulated in Spain. These announced the imminent arrival in Constantinople, Egypt, and finally, the Holy Land of a blond king from the west with a "handsome face," a characteristic also noted in the Tiburtina. Although they were written originally as an expression of the terror felt by the Byzantines and the Saracens regarding a possible crusade by the King of France or the Hohenstaufen of the Holy Roman Empire, many believed that the hero would come from Hispania; at this time, it was the westernmost area in the "known world."[14]

While influenced by prophecies originating outside Iberia, writers in medieval Spain also developed their own prophetic traditions. Sometime between 619 and 624, Isidoro de Sevilla wrote *Historia Gothorum*

Wandalorum Sueborum (*History of the Goths, Vandals, and Suebi*), a triumphant history of a fertile and prosperous Visigothic Empire. Copies of the history circulated, and then in the ninth century, the kings of Asturias (the bastion of Christianity after the Muslim conquest of 711) began claiming descent from the Visigoths through the mythic figure of Pelayo, son of Rodrigo, the last Visigothic king. Pelayo reportedly defeated the Muslim invaders at the first battle of the Reconquista in 722: Covadonga. Later, chroniclers of Castile and Leon characterized their monarchs as the "saviors of Spain" who would restore the kingdoms to the millenarian splendor described by Isidoro.[15] By the fifteenth century, a "destruction-renovation" schema had developed within Iberia; prophecies attributed to Isidoro de Sevilla stated that after the defeat of the Muslims, the "final monarchy" would restore the Visigothic Empire.[16]

In both Spain and France, an eclectic borrowing of prophecy reinforced this schema, as erudite scholars applied Sibylline and neo-Gothic prophecies toward promoting their orders, reforming the Church, and legitimizing or undermining specific rulers. In the twelfth century, contemporary readers of new versions of the Tiburtina characterized Louis VII of France (1120–1180) as the emperor destined to liberate Jerusalem, and by the fourteenth century, the Franciscan John of Rupescissa (Jean de Roquetaillade) predicted that, together, the Pope and King of France (who would also be elected Holy Roman Emperor) would convert the entire world's non-Christian population and unite the Eastern and Western Churches. Furthermore, neo-Gothic prophecies continued to characterize French monarchs as "new Charlemagnes" through the fifteenth century.[17]

In the twelfth century, Joachim de Fiore developed a "theology of history" that would eventually play a significant role in shaping monarchical prophecy and would play an outsized role in the religious and, as we will see, political culture of New Spain. While residing in the Abby of Casamiri just north of Rome, Fiore meditated intently on the Holy Trinity and received a revelation on a Sunday during Pentecost, the feast of the Holy Spirit, which led, eventually, to his development of a three-stage schema of history. Through the study of the similarities between the Old and New Testaments (which corresponded to two distinct ages: the Age of the Father and the Age of the Son), he forecast into the future and predicted the dawning of a third stage of history: the Age of the Holy Spirit, a period marked by abundance, love, and enlightenment. But, before the Second Coming of Christ and the realization of this final stage of history, the Church required reform. On the vanguard of this movement would stand a new religious order of spiritual men, as well as a bold and heroic Pope referred to as the New David.[18]

Although the Papacy embraced Fiore during his lifetime, a more ascetic minority within the recently established Franciscan Order began seeing themselves as agents of the spiritual renewal that would hasten the Second Coming of Christ. This led to a flourishing of controversial Joachimite prophecy within the order, much of which was falsely attributed to Fiore himself. Over a century later, Fiore's theology of history reached the Spanish Kingdoms through the Franciscan Spirituals and the Aragonese scholar and court physician, Arnau de Villanova (c. 1240–1311). While predecessors to Villanova had applied this prophecy to Holy Roman Emperor Frederick II (1194–1250) or to (Saint) Louis IX (1214–1270) or Louis X (1289–1316) of France, Villanova redirected it to argue that the Aragonese monarch would reconquer Jerusalem and establish a Universal Catholic Monarchy.[19] While Fiore had prophesized that a Pope as a New David would reform the Church, Villanova believed that Pedro III would take his place as the New David, conquer Jerusalem, and unify Christendom.[20]

During times of conflict, people continued to seek out prophetic writings to help make sense of destructive change. In a prophecy written as early as the late 1300s but published for the first time in 1500, a Juan Unay or Johan Alamany (a likely pseudonym) borrowed from Villanova and predicted that the Moors and Jews would rise up against Christians and that the Hidden King, the Encubierto, would appear to assist the New David (a Pope) to expel the infidel from the Spanish kingdoms; then, in an elaboration of Joachimite prophecy, he predicted that a figure known as the Encubierto would conquer the Moors in North Africa before taking Jerusalem. After defeating the Antichrist, the Encubierto and the New David would rule together from Seville (the New Jerusalem) for the next thousand years. Although the term "Encubierto" had originally been applied to Fernando II of Aragon, in Valencia, a man claiming to be the Encubierto galvanized rebels during the Revolt of the Germanías, or brotherhoods (1519–1523).[21]

The figures of the New David and the Encubierto gained in popularity and entered the consciousness of people throughout the empire. Christopher Columbus (1451–1506) famously consumed prophecies and firmly believed that Fernando of Aragon would conquer Jerusalem. Around 1500, a Valencian prophecy described how the New David – a lion who awakens to recover his lands – would stabilize Spain and destroy all heresy. Significantly, he "would appear like King David in all his

Prophecy and the Bourbon Succession 99

actions."²² Later prophecies, both in support and against the monarchy also continued to refer to the saviors and revitalizers of Spain interchangeably as the Lion of Judah or as the New David. Lucrecia de León (1567–c. 1595), a visionary hostile to Felipe III, predicted that a millenarian kingdom would be founded in Toledo and ruled over by a "second David" or "other David," a leader who she also referred to as an Encubierto.²³

Medieval prophecies continued to shape political life through the long seventeenth century, and these often centered on the conquest of Jerusalem. In 1510, Julius II named Fernando the Catholic of Castile and Aragon King of Naples and Jerusalem, a title that his grandson Carlos I (Holy Roman Emperor Carlos V) would soon inherit. As kings of Jerusalem and grandmasters of the Order of the Golden Fleece, the most prestigious chivalric order in the world, Spanish monarchs theoretically continued to have the obligation to fight for the recuperation of the Holy Land.²⁴ While largely ceremonial, the title led priests and scholars to regard the monarch of Spain as the destined liberator of Jerusalem. Indeed, Franciscans associated with Jerusalem's Holy Sepulcher periodically asked Spanish kings to lead a crusade to liberate the city.²⁵ With the expulsion of the *moriscos*, or Muslim converts to Christianity, from Spain in 1609, a group of Catholic apologists applied the monikers of Lion and Hidden King to Felipe III, and exalted him as a purifier of Spain and as the eventual ruler of Jerusalem.²⁶

The reign of Felipe II, with the incorporation of Portugal into the *Monarquía Hispánica* (1580–1640), inspired many influential authors to extol the Spanish monarch's providential role.²⁷ In his *Política Española* (1619), Juan de Salazar compared Spaniards to the ancient Israelites and King Pelayo to Moses, who also sought to free his people from captivity. According to Salazar, the current hostilities between the House of Austria and the Ottoman Turks had been predicted in the Book of Daniel and would conclude with the victorious conquest of Jerusalem and the establishment of a Universal Catholic Monarchy with Spain at its head.²⁸

Even on the eve of the War of the Spanish Succession, monarchical messianism lived on. In 1684, Rodrigo Gómez de Aguilera y Saavedra collected prophecies that predicted that Carlos II would conquer Jerusalem and complete Spain's eschatological mission. He echoed the Erythraean Sibyl, a prophetess who presided over the Apollonian Oracle at Erythrae, who supposedly predicted that during the last decades of the seventeenth century, the lion would debilitate the beast and the lamb would be enthroned. In addition, he cited the centuries-old prophecy of

Acham Turuley, as well as the more recent prophecies of the Valencian mystic Nicolás Factor (1520–1583), who foresaw that a Pope known as the "New David" would purify the Church and then unite with the "Encubierto por la Gracia de Dios" (The Hidden King by the Grace of God) to gather an army, cross the Strait of Gibraltar into North Africa, and, eventually, cause the Grand Turk to flee.[29]

Furthermore, by the inception of Bourbon rule, orators working in the viceroyalty proved well-versed in monarchical messianism, possibly inspired by the Franciscan order's pivotal role in shaping New Spain's religious culture. While setting the groundwork for Jesus's return with mass baptisms of the suspected lost tribespeople of Israel, sixteenth-century Franciscan missionaries Christianized New Spain by looking toward the past and seeing the viceroyalty as the site of the original Eden or, looking toward the future, seeing it as the New Jerusalem, the capital of the millennial kingdom of the End of Days. This perspective then spread among the viceroyalty's Augustinians and secular clergy, although it undoubtedly declined in popularity by the end of the sixteenth century. Nevertheless, Joachimite sensibilities left a strong imprint on the viceroyalty. The famous hermit Gregorio López (1542–1596), for example, wrote a commentary on how the Book of Revelation reflected developments in the ancient world from Nero through Constantine and even predicted the rise of Islam.[30] Throughout the seventeenth century, New Spain's chroniclers continued to allude to Joachimite paradigms. As Antonio Rubial García has noted, various chroniclers exalted the viceroyalty's natural abundance and associated it with Paradise or the New Jerusalem: a garden or walled city with twelve doors as described in the Book of Revelation.[31]

During the War of the Spanish Succession, monarchical messianism and Joachimite ruminations, which in the seventeenth century brewed just below the surface, rose and shaped a narrative of Bourbon revitalization. As we will see, orators in New Spain mastered the art of prophetical exegesis and applied the framework of monarchical messianism to the battle for the Crown. They encouraged New Spain's Spanish subjects to rest easy in the comfort of a prosperous Bourbon future.

PROPHECY AND PREFIGURATION IN THE RISE OF THE BOURBON HOUSE

In both Spain and New Spain, supporters of Felipe V and the Archduke Charles applied portents, revelations, and prophetical exegesis to the succession crisis. In Granada in 1705, pro-Bourbon officials captured a leader of a pro-Austrian conspiracy carrying a notebook of prophecies indicating that the Archduke Charles would take the Spanish Crown. Notably, the notebook contained prophecies attributed to Acham Turuley foretelling that a handsome king from Spain would rise to power and that he would conquer and reform the Holy See.[32] Meanwhile, in Mexico City, officials found a prophecy in the home of Gregorio Gasco that predicted that after several setbacks, the Archduke Charles would become the happiest member of the Habsburg dynasty ever to rule over the Spanish Empire.[33]

Various prelates in Spain made sure to publicize the prophecies of Sister Gabriela de San José (1628–1701), a Carmelite nun in Úbeda who received a message from God regarding a French succession shortly before the death of Carlos II. In a publication titled *Demonstración legal y política para desengaño de la plebe* (*Legal and Political Demonstration for the Disillusionment of the Common People*), a text offering advice for confessors during the War of the Spanish Succession, Inquisitor General and Archbishop of Zaragoza, Antonio Ibáñez de la Riva Herrera, cited the prophecy as evidence for Felipe V's legitimate right to the Spanish Crown.[34] News of the prophecy, moreover, circulated in New Spain. Mexico City cathedral prelate Juan Ignacio de Castorena y Ursúa recalled it in detail in an imprint produced to commemorate the cathedral's efforts in support of Felipe V; he described how while giving thanks for the restoration of the king's health after a recent crisis, God informed the holy woman through a talking effigy that Carlos II would soon die and that "a prince from France will come and will maintain the Faith."[35]

In addition to divine revelations, orators also looked to the skies for indications of an imminent Bourbon victory. In a sermon given in the cathedral of Seville in 1704 but that later arrived in Puebla, the Dominican orator Agustín Jacinto de Mesa reminded his audience that a comet had graced the skies in 1702, portending war for the Spanish people. Basing himself on a reading of the Book of Revelation, he equated the war to the Apocalypse and foretold victory for the Bourbon side.[36] Preaching in the cathedral of Guatemala in 1708, Antonio Xardón gave thanks for the birth of Luis I, noting that it was no coincidence that he was born in August, the month of Leo, the sign of the Eucharist, just as the stars transitioned into Virgo, the sign of the Virgin Mary; the Eucharist and Virgin Mary, of course, stood as pillars of Spanish identity (see Chapter 3). He also noted that Leo is the sign of war and that the prince arrived later than expected. His birth in Virgo, therefore, forecast a period of peace, while his conception in Sagittarius, the sign of New

Spain, foretold a happy future for the viceroyalty. Xardón also regarded it as providential that the prince arrived on the feast day of Saint Louis IX, king of France, who died in Tunis in 1270 during the Eighth Crusade and who had transformed into a symbol of an ideal king.[37]

In Mexico City, Puebla, Sepultec, Antequera, and Celaya, skilled orators sought to forecast events and legitimize Felipe V. Early modern men – and especially the erudite trained in the scholastic tradition – understood the importance of scriptural prefiguration and proved adept at identifying hidden meanings and portents. Etymology, for example, represented one of the most powerful tools in an orator's arsenal, and during the War of the Spanish Succession, at least six imprints of sermons or descriptions of ephemeral art produced in New Spain noted the origin of Felipe's name as *os lampadis*, the mouth of a lamp.[38] Prelates compared Felipe to the light of faith, threatened by the darkness of Austria's heretical alliance with Protestant forces, or in keeping with how orators, poets, and artisans commonly characterized Spanish monarchs during elaborate public rituals, as the sun casting benevolent light throughout the empire; the latter characterization was, of course, prefigured by Christ in the Book of Revelation with his "face shining like the sun." In 1707, in the cathedral of Guatemala, the Jesuit Antonio de Valtierra gave a sermon of thanksgiving for the victory in Almansa; basing himself on "common etymology," he compared Felipe V to the inextinguishable "light of faith."[39]

According to Sibylline tradition, the millennium could not commence until disbelief had been eliminated, and so the Emperor of the Last Days had been imagined as streaming forth light, or, in the words of Martin Cohn, as the "indwelling Spirit, which not only surrounds the risen Christ but was also attributed to the future Emperor Constans," a beautiful king with a glowing face.[40] The eschatological hero, therefore, had been commonly characterized as the "light of faith" and a warrior willing to fight against evil. In 1711, as part of Mexico City's long period of public commemorations for the victories at Brihuega and Villaviciosa, the Duke of Linares ordered that funerary honors be held for fallen soldiers at the Colegio Máximo de San Pedro y San Pablo. One of the primary emblems on the seven-story pyramidal catafalque bore a painting of Felipe V riding atop a lion, a representation of the Lion of Judah but also the symbol for Leo, the astrological sign associated with the sun. Artists painted a fragment of the zodiac extending from Leo to Libra and characterized Felipe V as the Savior of Spain and possibly *the* Savior. Indeed, artists depicted his face as the sun, thereby referencing John's description of

Christ in the Book of Revelation. The epigraph accompanying the image read: *Felipus V. Os Lampadis.*[41]

Sermons commemorating distinct royal milestones or military victories borrowed from a constellation of prophetical traditions to unite Spain's subjects in support of Bourbon rule. Orators, for example, indirectly touched on the neo-Gothicism, which had become popular by the sixteenth and seventeenth centuries, and blended it with the idea that Spain's Bourbon dynasty would create a Universal Catholic Monarchy, with Spain as its New Jerusalem. Artisans and orators often blended themes related to Christian universalism and Spanish proto-nationalism, which depended on the idea, prevalent by the sixteenth century, "that a kingdom, together with the nation that went with it, constituted a human community based on descent from an ancient, generally mythic ruler."[42] Medieval and early modern chroniclers often attributed the origin of Spain to Hercules, the mythical figure who purportedly placed columns at the Strait of Gibraltar to mark the limits of the known world. This foundation myth became embodied in engravings of two columns with the Latin motto "Non Plus Ultra," meaning "Not farther than." In 1516, Carlos V adopted the columns as his insignia, but he changed the motto to read "Plus Ultra," linking his reign to the glories of exploration and empire.[43]

Orators and designers of festive art in New Spain often referenced Hercules, a symbol that worked to unify subjects under the banner of empire. The oath ceremony platforms in both Puebla and Guadalajara featured the iconic columns and later, in a sermon of thanksgiving for the pregnancy of the queen, José de las Heras y Alcocer of the Convent of Nuestra Señora de la Merced Redención de Cautivos in Mexico City predicted the arrival of a prince who would drink from his mother's breast and become like Hercules, who became invincible after nursing from Juno.[44] For the celebrations in honor of the royal birth in Puebla, the *comercio*, or volunteer militia of merchants, paraded a triumphal cart carrying a large two-story fortress with towers, decorated with pennants, emblems, and eight canvases; these depicted episodes from the infancy of Hercules.[45] By referencing the mythical foundation of Spain through Hercules, the merchant militia celebrated the foundation of a new ruling dynasty and reaffirmed an imperial identity based on common descent.

Early modern chroniclers also sought to establish a pure "spiritual genealogy" for subjects of the king of Spain, tracing the origins of the Spanish people to Tubal, the grandson of Noah, or to Santiago (James), the apostle and saint who purportedly evangelized in Iberia and later became the Spanish Empire's primary patron. However, by the sixteenth century, chronicles often included genealogies tracing royal bloodlines back to the legendary restorer of Spain, Pelayo, who reportedly inaugurated Christian resistance to the Moors at the Battle of Covadonga. During the war against the Protestant forces of the Grand Alliance, some orators characterized Felipe V as the defender of Spanish Catholicism by equating him to King Pelayo, the first "monarch of Spain." In the imprint of his sermon for the funerary honors for Carlos II in 1701, Puebla's magistral canon José Gómez de la Parra included two genealogies: one traced Felipe V's ancestry to Adam and Eve, and the other went back to King Pelayo to prove Felipe V's relationship to the restorer of Christian Spain.[46] Years later, in his sermon honoring the birth of Luis Fernando, Gómez de la Parra declared Felipe V to be the thirty-sixth male descendant of Pelayo, the first King of Spain.[47]

Similarly, in a sermon in honor of the Virgen de los Remedios in Mexico City, the Franciscan Blas de Pulgar drew comparisons between the newborn crown prince and the Savior. Indeed, both were "restorers"; Christ restored man to God's grace, and the prince, as Christ's lieutenant, promised to restore "not only the ancient splendors of Spain, but most of Christendom," as well as restoring "faith in Jesus Christ." He noted how Mexico City's Virgen de los Remedios safeguarded what he described as the first Spanish monarchy. Citing the loss of Visigothic Spain by King Rodrigo, Pulgar argued that the future of Christian Spain rested with the trunk of the dynastic tree: Prince Pelayo. Like Moses, Pelayo had been saved by his mother from being murdered by being floated down a river in a basket. Citing chronicler of New Spain Agustín de Vetancurt, Pulgar claimed that Pelayo's mother had also placed an effigy of the Virgin Mary in the basket to look after the boy; he argued that this was, of course, the Virgen de los Remedios, the same effigy that centuries later arrived in New Spain.[48]

By making this argument, Pulgar achieved two things: he argued that Luis Fernando would restore Spain to the Edenic days of the Visigothic Empire, but also that New Spain, as the home of the Virgen de los Remedios, would have a direct role in this restoration. He explained that both Isidoro de Sevilla and Zacharias of Rome, the thirteenth-century founder of the Convent of Santa Clara of Alenquer in Portugal, predicted that at the End of Days "a king given by God would reign," and claimed that this was Felipe V. According to the prelate, Isidoro de Sevilla claimed that in the last days, a king would be chosen from a land to the east, which he believed was France.[49] Pulgar specified that he was not a prophet but rather someone who knew a great deal about scripture, and therefore engaged, like many other orators in New Spain, in prophetical exegesis.

THE WARRIOR-KING

Sermons given in New Spain shaped an imperial identity while stressing the messianic implications of Bourbon rule, comparing Felipe V and the first Bourbon crown prince, Luis I, to a host of mythological and historical warriors from Spain's collective history. By the seventeenth century, the warrior-king had become a common archetype for royal portraits, but because Spanish Habsburg rulers had long stopped fighting in battle, Bourbon influencers stressed Felipe V's military prowess and compared the monarch to other warrior-kings featured in the Old Testament, as well as in the Book of Revelation and medieval prophecy. Antonio Ubilla y Medina's chronicle of Felipe V's first few years in power focused mainly on the period following April 1702, when Felipe V embarked from Barcelona for Italy to lead the defense of the Duchy of Milan against the Austrian imperial forces. It contained, moreover, fine engravings of the king in battle (Figure 4.1).[50]

In New Spain, subjects understood that the ascension of the Bourbon dynasty would inevitably lead to war, and visual elements incorporated into oath ceremony platforms announced that Felipe V would assume an active role in the conflict. In Puebla, the oath ceremony platform featured various weapons and shields, and in Guadalajara, a painting depicted Felipe V being armed by his paternal grandfather, Louis XIV, as well as by his father and brothers.[51] In pursuing active and enthusiastic participation in the war (which would earn him the nickname "El Animoso" or "The Spirited"), Felipe V followed the example set by his grandfather, Louis XIV, monarch of France and the greatest military commander in Europe. Thus, as with depictions of his grandfather, Felipe V became the *rex, dux et miles*, that is, king, leader, and soldier, an image exploited by official propaganda through texts and images that spread from the peninsula to the Indies.[52] Moreover, public ceremonies continued to communicate that Bourbon Spain owed a great debt to the Most Christian King. For Louis XIV's funerary honors in Valladolid in 1716, cathedral treasurer and panegyrist José de Alcalá described the Most Christian King as Spain's "shield," and asked: "what triumphs did his always victorious arms not achieve, even when divided into forces, to put in horror and fear the entire world [?]!"[53] Felipe V's supporters logically sought to capitalize on his grandfather's reputation.

FIGURE 4.1 Philip V, King of Spain, 1704. Design by Teodoro Ardemans; engraving by Gérard Edelinck. Chalcographic print in *Succession de el rey D. Phelipe V nuestro señor en la Corona de España* by Antonio de Ubilla y Medina. Biblioteca Nacional de España.

Throughout the war, Bourbon loyalists projected an image of unshakeable military strength. When the Grand Alliance tried to pressure Louis XIV to sign a general peace with conditions unacceptable to Felipe V, the king of Spain let his subjects know. In a letter sent to municipal governments and cathedral chapters throughout New Spain, Felipe V characterized himself as a warrior-king, intent on defending his sovereignty. He relayed how the Grand Alliance persisted in demanding the recognition of the Archduke Charles, adding that they had no intention of respecting the integrity of the Spanish Empire, with Holland planning on keeping the Spanish Netherlands and Portugal on absorbing Castile, Galicia, Extremadura, and the Indies. Felipe rejected rumors that his grandfather would abandon him in exchange for such an offer and reaffirmed his willingness to return at any time to the "fire of war."[54] In 1711, officials in New Spain celebrated the victories in Brihuega and Villaviciosa and stressed how despite confronting many challenges, Felipe V fought and sacrificed for his subjects. In San Luis Potosí, for example, the Jesuit Joaquín Antonio Villalobos characterized the king as a "father" who would shed "the last drop of his blood" in Spain's defense.[55]

Subjects increasingly came to associate the monarch with military prowess.[56] For example, Nicolás Rodríguez Juárez's (1667–1734) portrait of Felipe V in the cathedral of Mexico depicts the monarch in armor and field boots, but, as Iván Escamilla González discovered, the outline of the Spanish *golilla*, or collar, remains visible under his attire; he had been repainted, possibly transformed from Carlos II's "Habsburg" heir for the 1701 oath ceremony, to the victor of the decisive battle of Villaviciosa for the thanksgiving celebrations in 1711.[57] The image of Felipe V as the consummate military commander endured long after the war. In the 1720s, Vicente Bacallar y Sanna, the Marquis of San Felipe and cofounder of the Real Academia Española, wrote a history of the king's military exploits, copies of which also arrived in New Spain.[58]

During the war for the Spanish Crown, orators in New Spain stressed Felipe V's heroism and willingness to sacrifice himself for his subjects, members of an "imagined" imperial community. Several orators emphasized the parallels between Gideon, who defeated the Midianites with only 300 soldiers, and Felipe V, while others compared the Spanish soldiers to the Maccabees, who fought the numerically superior forces of Seleucid King Antiochus IV Epiphanes. Preaching in the Convento de N.P.S. San Francisco in Querétaro, Juan de Guevara made a direct comparison between Felipe V and Judas, the hero of the Maccabean cause.[59]

For various orators in New Spain, military prowess proved particularly "Spanish" and served as a source of national pride. In 1711, the Duke of Linares ordered funerary honors for the Spaniards who died in Brihuega and Villaviciosa, and the Jesuit Casa Profesa of Mexico City scheduled the funerary honors for the eve of the feast day for Santiago, the saint who helped Christian forces defeat the Moors during the Reconquista and who many now claimed helped Spanish forces defeat the Grand Alliance in Brihuega and Villaviciosa.[60] Preaching in Durango, the Franciscan Juan de San Miguel stated that "This is the way they defended their *Patrias*, their Kingdoms, and their Laws, the Joshuas, the Gideons and the Davids in Palestine, the Ceasars in Rome, the Hannibals in Carthage, and the Cids, and Gonzalo Fernandezes in Castile, with swords, with lances, with bullets, with bugles, with drums, with armor, with chainmail, with helmets, and finally, with armies."[61] In a sermon given in Valladolid in honor of the 1710 victories, Tomás Montaño condensed the *topos* of the warrior-king and that of the *rex redivivus*, the sleeping or expired king who miraculously reemerges to rule. He called Felipe V the "glorious emulation of the Fifth Carlos!," the last warrior to rule over Spain.[62] Preaching at the University of Mexico in thanksgiving for Brihuega and Villaviciosa, Juan Ignacio de Castorena y Ursúa highlighted how Felipe V rode into battle on a beautiful Andalucian steed and also drew parallels with the hero on the white horse in chapter 6, verse 2 of the Book of Revelation, who "went forth conquering that he might conquer."[63]

With such a brave ruler, writers entertained hope that Spain would achieve its most elusive goal: the conquest of Jerusalem, a city that took on mythical proportions and that served as a powerful symbol in the Bourbon influence campaign. In Madrid's oath ceremony for Felipe V, organizers referred to the monarch's holy ancestor, Saint Louis IX of France, who attempted to conquer Jerusalem and stressed that Felipe V would finally free the city from captivity.[64] For the celebrations in honor of Brihuega and Villaviciosa at the University of Mexico, organizers placed two statues on the main altar: one of Fernando III of Castile and the other of Saint Louis IX of France. Although together the statues referenced the name of the prince, Luis Fernando, on whose birthday (August 25) the university chose to celebrate, they also evoked the most iconic sacred kings of Spain and France and the most noble objective for all Christian monarchs: religious conquest.[65]

Orators tended to collapse Jerusalem and the New Jerusalem of the End of Days, and both became inseparably associated with Heaven, a reward for the final struggle against the forces of darkness. After the defeat of the Antichrist, John saw "the new Jerusalem, coming down out of heaven from God, prepared as a bride adorned for her husband." While decrying rampant disloyalty within the Spanish kingdoms, orators made sure to emphasize that loyal Spaniards were the "chosen people" who would enjoy this heavenly future.[66] In the sermon of thanksgiving given in 1711 in the University of Mexico, Castorena de Ursúa claimed that Felipe V's reign had been prophesized by Isidoro de Sevilla, who wrote that "in the last days" a king from the east (which he interpreted as France) would rule Spain. Among other details, the prelate stated that he would reign in his youth, purify Spain, conquer Jerusalem, fix a crucifix over the Holy Sepulcher, and be the "Maximum Monarch."[67]

A NEW DAVID FOR THE SPANISH EMPIRE

Despite making numerous comparisons between Felipe V and other warrior-kings, orators in New Spain returned again and again to King David, the son of Jesse (or Isai), who defeated Goliath, succeeded Saul, united Israel and Judea, and prefigured Christ. Among both orators and listeners, King David likely triggered a host of associations. Throughout all phases of the war, prelates argued that Felipe V served as an incarnation of King David. To many, the terrorizing war in Spain resembled the Apocalypse and, as a reminder, a Christ-figure known as the "lion of the tribe of Judah, the root of David" loosened the seven seals. Orators seized on references to Christ's descent from the "root of Jesse," as well as to the prophetical mention of the House of David in the Book of Revelation. One widely disseminated imprint produced in Pamplona in 1711 referred to Felipe V as the "second persecuted David," and the influential text also arrived in Puebla.[68] So, perhaps taking their cue from the Davidic narrative emanating from Spain, orators in New Spain also framed David as a prefiguration of Felipe V, a monarch selected by God to lead a "chosen people."

Characterizations of Felipe V as a second David permeated oratory in Mexico City, seemingly from the very beginning of the crisis. In 1712, Mexico City cathedral canon Miguel Núñez de Godoy published the sermon he gave in 1701 to commemorate the city's oath of loyalty to Felipe V. In the authorization for the printing of the sermon, cathedral canon Miguel González de Valdeosera claimed that it represented a "prognostication or prophecy" for a Bourbon victory, not acknowledging that the priest may have later revised it to fit a Davidic narrative.[69] Regardless, in the 1712 version of the sermon, Núñez de Godoy cited evidence for David as a prefiguration of Felipe V, noting that David was the seventh son of Jesse and that Felipe V represented the seventh Spanish monarch of the House of Austria, never mind that he was technically a Bourbon; significantly, in another point in the sermon, he (speaking to Felipe V) remarked, "You are like us, Spanish, even though you were born in France." He acknowledged the youth and attractiveness of both monarchs, with David being only twenty when he replaced Saul, and Felipe V a mere seventeen when he succeeded Carlos II.[70]

Núñez de Godoy continued to point out parallels and, in so doing, made the succession crisis directly relevant to his viceregal audience. After David moved his court to Jerusalem, he placed a wall around the city to protect it from his enemies, people whom he defined as heretics. Likewise, Felipe V tried to build a "wall" around the Americas to protect it from Dutch and English forces; Núñez de Godoy explained how while traveling to Spain from France, Felipe ordered the ports of New Spain and Peru to be fortified, just like "David wanted to fortify his kingdom with the ark (which he had brought to the new capital in Jerusalem)." Felipe V similarly fortified his rule by paying tribute to the Holy Sacrament, which Núñez de Godoy described as the Spanish Empire's Ark of the Covenant.[71]

At the very least, orators agreed that King David prefigured Felipe V, and that as God favored David, he favored Spain's Bourbon king. In a sermon of thanksgiving given in the Augustinian convent in Celaya in honor of the victories of 1710, Francisco de Aguilera Izaguirre recalled how David's struggle resembled Felipe V's; like David, the king called out to God, who in 1706 helped him force the treacherous Marquis de las Minas, an instrumental ally of the Archduke Charles, out of Madrid, and the following year the king achieved victory in Almansa, he conquered Valencia and Aragon, and finally celebrated the birth of crown prince Luis I. But, like David, the king endured a long struggle, and in 1710, before the decisive victories of Franco-Spanish forces, the king had to leave Madrid again, and echoing David's lament from Psalm 18, verse 8, he described the setting in which the Earth trembled with God's anger.[72]

Aguilera Izaguirre reminded the audience how the ark of the Covenant fortified David, and how Spain's ark – the Holy Sacrament – fortified the Spanish Crown. He characterized the monarch as another David and his Spanish supporters as a "chosen people," arguing that if the victory had transpired in 1706 when 15,000 French troops were in Spain, then the credit would have gone to France. However, in 1710, it was mainly Spanish forces who reportedly pleaded with the French General

Vendôme to engage the enemy, and so Aguilera Izaguirre quoted the general as saying: "Well, if you want to fight so much, go and fight." Just as the Ark of the Covenant gave David the wherewithal to unite Israel, the Holy Sacrament gave Felipe V and his "chosen people" the fortitude to defeat the iconoclastic Grand Alliance.[73]

In a sermon of thanksgiving in Sepultepec, Bernardo Unibárbia described how Felipe V proved the very "portrait of David," stating, significantly, that the "press" had made this very clear. Citing a pastoral letter from Archbishop Belluga of Murcia (see Chapter 2), he argued that both David and Felipe V had been chosen to rule by God, adding that just as David had to flee Jerusalem twice because of the threat posed by his enemies Saul and Absalom, Felipe V had to flee Madrid twice because of its occupation by the Grand Alliance. He added that David killed four giants as well as four squadrons of Philistines, while the "Four Philistine Giants" Germany, Portugal, England, and Holland attacked Spain. After Felipe V and General Vendôme defeated them in Brihuega and Villaviciosa, the Bourbon king gave thanks like David.[74]

David giving thanks proved a popular theme for sermons in New Spain, and these tended to have prophetical overtones. As part of the celebrations for Brihuega and Villaviciosa, the rector of Mexico City's Colegio de San Juan Letrán, Lorenzo Antonio González de Sancha, argued that like David, Felipe V gave thanks for his victories, leading God to afflict his oppressors. Indeed, Felipe V and his Spanish soldiers defeated a "goliath" in the form of 30,000 enemy soldiers.[75] Similarly, in his celebration of the 1710 victories in the Franciscan Convento de la Asunción in Toluca, Baltasar de Carrera told his congregants that just like David gave thanks to God for his victories, so should Spanish subjects hold masses of gratitude.[76]

The Bourbon victories at Brihuega and Villaviciosa certainly invited comparisons between Felipe V and David, and orators throughout New Spain highlighted the similarities of the situations faced by both men. Preaching in the Convento de N.S.P. San Francisco in Querétaro, Juan de Guevara summarized the setbacks that befell Bourbon forces in the months preceding the December 1710 victories. He relayed the horrible news that arrived in New Spain on August 20, 1710, regarding the loss of Zaragoza and the defeat of the army of Felipe V, as well as the occupation of Madrid. Standing on the main altar, the orator described how Protestant soldiers dismembered images of the Virgin Mary and hurled Eucharist wafers to the ground. However, he also reminded his audience that just as God assured David's victory against his enemies, he secured Felipe V's succession.[77]

By pointing out the similarities between the experiences of David and Felipe V, orators signaled that God supported the Bourbon king, who was bound to create his own ruling lineage from the root of Jesse and conquer Jerusalem, which, by the seventeenth century, had become a multivalent symbol that conjured images of the New Jerusalem or Heavenly City at the End of Days. Indeed, the New Jerusalem, the Republic that floated down from the heavens, symbolized the future, the millennial age, or, to use Fiore's term, the Age of the Holy Spirit. With Felipe V guiding his subjects, Spaniards would become the chosen people of the last stage of history.

Erudite ecclesiastics in New Spain understood how to utilize prophetical exegesis to bolster the legitimacy of Felipe V and perhaps anticipated that their sermons could sway those teetering on the edge of disloyalty, including fellow clerics and anyone exposed to apocalyptic ideas. In a sermon for the victories in Brihuega and Villaviciosa, Valladolid's cathedral prebend Tomás Montaño characterized the Archduke Charles as the Antichrist, infectiously spreading heresy throughout the Spanish kingdoms.[78] In a sermon To Make Amends to the Holy Sacrament given in Pátzcuaro in this same year, José Brabo mused that nothing scared a monarch of "two worlds" more than the eclipsing of the sun, which, as noted, served as a multivalent symbol representing faith, the Eucharist, and the monarch. He declared that the sacrilegious acts committed against the Eucharist made it seem like the Antichrist had spread his dark influence.[79] He recalled how, in John's vision, when the sixth seal opened, the sun darkened as if dressed for mourning, and the moon began weeping blood, foreshadowing the sacrilege committed against both the Eucharist and the Immaculate Conception during the War of the Spanish Succession. Yet, Brabo urged his listeners to fear not because Felipe V, the "David of our times," would defeat the Antichrist.[80]

In 1711 in Sepultepec, Unibárbia framed his entire sermon of thanksgiving around chapter 5, verse 5 of the Book of Revelation, when one of the ancients exclaimed, "Behold the Lion of Judah, the root of David." Unibárbia argued that the lion and the lamb slain on the throne nearby were one and the same, and maintained that the one who fights on the battlefield is a lamb on the throne. However, in a somewhat confusing, although clearly nationalist addition, he asked if the passage revealed that Jesus Christ defeated the enemy like a lion or whether it predicted that Felipe V would achieve victory fighting alongside the "Spanish lions."

Regardless, he saw the present state of war reflected in the Book of Revelation; the horrendous sacrilege committed against churches, effigies, and holy wafers testified to the unfolding of the final conflict between good and evil. In the Book of Revelation, four creatures surrounded the lamb's throne, and these, according to Unibárbia, represented the "orders" within the Christian Republic, namely the lion (princes and military), the eagle (ecclesiastics), the human (the administrative bureaucracy), and the donkey (the common people). All bowed down and gave thanks before the Holy Sacrament for the victories in Brihuega and Villaviciosa. Then, after illustrating that the war and the sacrilege had been prophesized in the Book of Revelation, he added that Felipe V proved willing to lay down his life for Spain, just like David had sacrificed himself repeatedly for Israel.[81]

THE IMMACULATE CONCEPTION AND COMPOSITE IDENTITY

Although orators in New Spain evoked Jerusalem and King David in their treatment of Felipe V's providential role, perhaps no symbol helped refer New Spain more to war and millenarian prophecy than the Virgin Mary, and particularly the Immaculate Conception. As discussed in Chapter 2, various forms of propaganda that arrived in New Spain testified to the royal family's devotion to miraculous Marian images, and particularly the Virgen de Atocha. But, while different kingdoms and regions within Spain's composite monarchy had their own miraculous advocations of the Virgin Mary, the Immaculate Conception, an advocation highly associated with the mysterious evolution of God's plan, helped to exalt both Spain and New Spain and their interrelated, but distinct, sets of "chosen people."

Like other areas within the empire, the kingdom of New Spain housed several miraculous images of the Virgin Mary. Furthermore, viceregal leaders mirrored the king's piety by appealing to local devotions on his behalf, devotions generally aimed toward addressing material concerns like hunger, pestilence, and natural disaster.[82] In 1707, Antequera held a mass in honor of its most celebrated image of the Virgin Mary, the Virgen de la Soledad, two days before the feast day of San Felipe, a day that also marked the anniversary of a destructive earthquake. Famed bishop and orator Ángel de Maldonado invited the audience to contemplate their fears of earthquakes along with the fear of the disloyal in Spain, who, through their actions, unleashed a "tempest." While he appealed to the Virgen de la Soledad's protection, he compared the disaffected Spaniards to the Israelites who turned on King David but who still failed in their attempts to overthrow him.[83]

While Antequera appealed primarily to the Virgen de la Soledad, the court of Mexico called on several miraculous Marian images. In requesting divine aid, the viceroy, the Duke of Alburquerque and municipal council of Mexico, first appealed to the Virgen de los Remedios, and possibly chose to do this because of her special relationship with the Crown, a relationship that grew stronger following the Mexico City riot of 1692 when plebeians, in a demonstration of despair over rising grain prices, burned down half the viceregal palace. One week after the riot, officials brought her to the capital, where she stayed until 1695.[84] In 1702, Archbishop of Mexico and interim viceroy, Juan de Ortega Montañes, ordered that the Virgen de los Remedios be brought from her shrine to the cathedral for a mass and sermon of thanksgiving in honor of the safe arrival of the fleet in Havana, and to request her continued protection. Then, toward the end of 1706, the most difficult year for Bourbon forces thus far, the Duke of Alburquerque sent a decree to Mexico City's municipal council stating that his "love and fidelity" for the king obligated him to ask for the intercession of the Virgen de los Remedios. The viceroy ordered that she be brought to the Parish of the Vera Cruz on December 14, where she would remain until January 7. On this day, she would be taken in a solemn procession to the cathedral.[85]

Yet, of all Marian images, miraculous effigies of the Immaculate Conception proved most effective at uniting subjects throughout the empire. Beginning in the thirteenth century, Spanish monarchs became the main supporters of the mystery of the Immaculate Conception, and in 1612, Felipe II named her patroness of the Spanish Empire. All of Spain's future monarchs would lobby the papacy for recognition of the immaculate conception of Mary's mother. Then, amid war in 1708, Clement XI declared the Immaculate Conception obligatory belief, albeit not dogma.[86] Because the Bourbon victories at Brihuega and Villaviciosa in December 1710 occurred during the octave of the feast day of the Immaculate Conception, the Bourbon Crown ordered that thanksgiving masses be held in her honor, as well as in honor of the Holy Sacrament, as both served as "twin pillars" of Spanish identity and the primary targets for sacrilegious acts.

Officials in New Spain appealed to the Virgin Mary throughout the course of the war, and especially to the Immaculate Conception, who contemporaries believed appeared in John's Revelation as the travailing woman clothed in the sun. By appealing to the Immaculate Conception, contemporaries recognized her special patronage over Spain, but by appealing to local images of the Immaculate Conception, orators centered New Spain in the succession crisis and expressed a composite identity. Since the late Middle Ages, the Virgin Mary had been commonly depicted as a militant warrior or bulwark, serving to protect Spanish forces from the infidel during key battles during the Reconquest. By the fifteenth century, the Immaculate Conception had become firmly associated with the travailing woman in the Book of Revelation, and European artists began depicting her as standing atop a crescent moon with twelve stars surrounding her head.[87] New Spain became a kingdom peppered with Marian shrines, and in the second half of the seventeenth century, Mexico City enjoyed the protection of four "bulwarks": Nuestra Señora de la Piedad to the south, Nuestra Señora de la Bala to the east, Nuestra Señora de los Remedios to the west, and Nuestra Señora de Guadalupe to the north, an image representing the Immaculate Conception; she stands atop a crescent moon but is also surrounded by sunbeams, or "clothed in the sun," like the Marian figure in the Book of Revelation.[88]

In the seventeenth and eighteenth centuries, people throughout Spain's vast empire recognized the Immaculate Conception as a prophetical figure. For example, Gregorio Tenorio (1602–1682), a Creole Franciscan in Lima, proclaimed that a Joachimite-style "third age" would begin when the Papacy recognized the Immaculate Conception as dogma.[89] Furthermore, Spanish American clergy came to regard the Immaculate Conception as a symbol for the Heavenly Jerusalem, the center of the messianic age. In *La mística ciudad de Dios* (*The Mystical City of God*), the Conceptionist mystic María de Ágreda (1602–1664) equated the Immaculate Conception with the Woman of the Apocalypse and the Heavenly Jerusalem. Although censored by the papacy in 1690, the revelations made to Ágreda were well known in New Spain.[90] Citing Ágreda, in 1711 Castorena y Ursúa argued that the presence of the Immaculate Conception in John's vision foretold Felipe V's victory.[91]

Later, after Franco-Spanish forces defeated the Grand Alliance in Brihuega and Villaviciosa, cathedrals, convents, and parishes throughout the empire gave thanks to the patroness of the Spanish Empire, awarding her and the Holy Sacrament credit for the victories. Bishop of Oaxaca Ángel de Maldonado later gave a sermon of thanksgiving for the victories in Mexico City's cathedral but dedicated it to the Virgen de los Remedios, Mexico City's other key Marian devotion enlisted for the Bourbon cause.[92] Indeed, as will be discussed in the following chapter, in

1707 she served as the focus of a novena in honor of the first pregnancy of the queen.

By holding pro-Bourbon commemorations in honor of devotions particular to New Spain, viceregal officials centered the viceroyalty in the succession crisis and, in a sense, *creolized* the war. As is well known, by the late seventeenth century, the Virgen de Guadalupe had become a symbol of a burgeoning Creole consciousness, and she also played a large role in the court of Mexico's commemorations. Although supposedly discovered in 1531, people began associating the Virgen de Guadalupe with the Woman of the Apocalypse with Miguel Sánchez's 1648 publication, in which he described her as New Spain's "first *criolla*" threatened by a dragon representing Tenochtitlan.[93] Because of her increasing popularity, the viceregal administration and the city's ecclesiastics recognized the utility of channeling devotion from the Virgen de Guadalupe toward Felipe V. It is no coincidence that the viceroy chose to hold a novena coinciding with May 4, the feast day of the namesake of the monarch, San Felipe, for the inauguration of the sanctuary of the Virgen de Guadalupe in 1709. During the festivities, the Bourbon standard graced the dome of the basilica, while indigenous dancers and musicians performed in front, expressing composite identities rooted in empire, religion, locality, and ethnic group.[94]

In this same year, an expedition led by the English corsair Woodes Rogers attacked the galleon Nuestra Señora de Begoña as it returned from Manila and approached Cabo San Lucas. Its captain prayed to the Virgen de Guadalupe and vowed to hold a novena of gratitude if she saved the vessel. Upon his safe return to Mexico City, he did just that, and the Jesuit Juan de Goikoetxea, one of the orators who participated in the novena for the inauguration of the basilica, also participated in the novena of gratitude for the miracle. In addition to thanking the virgin for saving the ship, he took the opportunity to ask for the safe arrival of the recent *flota* to Spain. Finally, Goikoetxea asked for confirmation upon its return that the king and queen "live, and triumph because of our intercession."[95]

By holding masses of appeasement and gratitude in honor of the Immaculate Conception, orators acknowledged the special relationship between Spain and the mystery, a bond reinforced by the sermons that the Crown ordered after Brihuega and Villaviciosa. However, the Virgen de Guadalupe also allowed Spanish subjects in New Spain to express Spanish identity and regional pride simultaneously through the same miraculous image. In a sermon in honor of the royal birth dedicated to the Virgen de Guadalupe, Castorena y Ursúa acknowledged that she distinguished New Spain through her apparition. Thirty-seven years before she became official patroness of the viceroyalty of New Spain, the ex-rector of the University of Mexico declared that the "Most holy Maria of Guadalupe is a universal patron of these kingdoms." He equated the "twelve" golden rays that emanated from her (and that mimicked the crown atop the Immaculate Conception's head) to Mexico City's twelve patron saints, adding that these were like the twelve doors to the Heavenly Jerusalem. Listeners could conclude that Mexico City would serve as the center of the millenarian age.[96] Indeed, in Mexico City, the Virgen de Guadalupe, an image representing Mary in her Immaculate Conception, had also come to stand for the New Jerusalem: heaven on earth or, by extension, the Republic of the future.

Then, as part of New Spain's celebrations for the victories of 1710, the Duke of Alburquerque hosted a mass and sermon at the shrine of the Virgen de Guadalupe. The Franciscan orator Manuel de Argüello argued that the Virgin of Guadalupe represented both the Woman of the Apocalypse and the Temple of Solomon, stating that as the Virgin, she defeated the dragon, and as the Temple of Solomon, she destroyed snakelike leaders (the Grand Alliance). In his dedication to the imprint of the sermon, the *oidor* Juan Díez de Bracamonte compared the Virgen de Guadalupe to the vision of the Virgin Mary described in the Book of Revelation, stating that the "children of the Mexican Eagle [are] welcomed by the wings of her patronage."[97] While factoring Mexico City into the Spanish Empire's holy war, Argüello suggested that divine support kept the Americas loyal. Indeed, he noted that Lima had her patroness, Saint Rose, and that Mexico City had the Virgin of Guadalupe, and that both are symbolized by the rose – the flower of silence. He credited these devotions with preventing disloyal utterances or conspiracies against Felipe V in the Americas, a highly exaggerated claim.[98]

CONCLUSION

To Felipe V's subjects in the viceroyalty of New Spain, the War of the Spanish Succession likely resembled the final battle between good and evil. Scripture, ancient oracles, and medieval prophecies all directed contemporaries to perceive the conflict as an eschatological struggle. Furthermore, many prophecies that had been reproduced and retooled since the fifteenth century emphasized the King of Spain's messianic role. Confronted with the end of the Spanish Habsburg line, a dynasty closely associated with sovereignty over Jerusalem, orators in New Spain appropriated a vast repertoire of prophetic utterances to reassure New Spain's population regarding Felipe V's ultimate victory and, as we will see, of Spain's prosperous future. Orators in New Spain did not directly cite Joachimite prophecy in their characterizations of the war or of Bourbon rule, but his theology of history undergirded much of their thinking, and especially their imaginings of the future. As we will see, New Spain's orators predicted that Spain's restored and revitalized future would be a fertile one, marked by a limitless supply of heirs to serve on the Spanish throne and the prosperity of the king's loyal subjects.

5

Rebirth

In mid-January 1711, the city of Durango celebrated an oath of loyalty to a three-and-a-half-year-old boy: the Prince of Asturias, Luis I. While people enjoyed music in the main plaza on January 18, they witnessed a curious spectacle: a triumphal cart pulled by elaborately costumed mules. Seated inside, spectators could see a little boy dressed in finery. According to the *alférez real* and author of the official account of the festivities, accountant of the Hacienda Real, or Royal Treasury, Juan Felipe Orozco y Molina, the child "represented our Prince so vividly that if our hearts were not imprisoned there in [Madrid at] his royal feet, we would have surrendered them to the reality of his representation." Behind the cart rode the city's *alférez real* on horseback. Fittingly, he led a group of elites who, in the author's words, "constitute the body of the City."[1]

After Orozco y Molina rose upon a large platform constructed especially for the event, two individuals representing Europe and America took turns reciting a loa, or laudatory poem, taking the form of a friendly discussion regarding which "world" would be the first to acclaim the young prince heir to the "Catholic Monarchy." Presiding from the triumphal cart, the "prince" expressed so much affection for both Europe and America, the two worlds chose to come together as "one body, and one voice for the festivities."[2] Afterward, the *official mayor*, or supervisor, of the Real Hacienda, José Manrique, recited another loa about how recent successes indicated that God's patronage over Spain would continue under the Bourbon dynasty.

The festivities extended over several days, and on January 20, the feast day of the gallic martyr San Sebastián, the *alférez real* led the city in the main event: an oath of loyalty in front of a large portrait of the prince.

After he and the event's *padrino* tossed coins to the joyous crowd, Orozco y Molina claimed to hear divine voices announce "that by the Catholic arm of our acclaimed Prince we are to see the four sects spread throughout the four parts of the world prostrate on the ground and separated from the Faithful."[3] The *alférez real* capped off days of celebration by hosting a theatrical performance centered on the achievements of Alexander the Great, the son of Philip of Macedonia. But, as a prelude, someone read yet another loa, and "A beautiful and graceful child appeared on a throne who represented our tender Infant, with a naked sword in his left hand, and hanging from it the four sects attached to the soles of his feet, encouraging our Spaniards in their loyalty with loving words." Orozco y Molino then expressed hope for the dawn of the "Age of the Holy Spirit."[4]

Orozco y Molina's account of Durango's elaborate festivities for the royal oath ceremony testifies to how ideas regarding sacred monarchy transferred to the Prince of Asturias and nurtured the discourse surrounding the Bourbon succession. In the periphery of New Spain, organizers sought to make the *Monarquía Hispánica's* first Bourbon prince as corporeally present as possible. Not only did they present him via a large portrait, but they also represented him using two young children, whose beauty and age connoted renewal, and whose physical presence inspired American and European subjects to collectively express their belonging to the *cuerpo del rey*. As we have seen, through visual renderings, Felipe V extended his presence throughout the empire, but as this chapter illustrates, the pregnancy of the queen and the eventual birth of Luis Felipe Fernando José (commonly referred to as Luis Fernando) on August 25, 1707, the feast day of Saint Louis IX of France, transformed the crown prince into a central focus of sacred kingship. Given that the prince's birth ended forty-six years of infertility in Spain's ruling house, his mere arrival confirmed the belief for many that God favored the Bourbon cause.

On February 10, 1707, the Crown ordered municipalities and religious corporations to hold public rogations as acts of thanksgiving and to assure a healthy birth. No previous head of the Spanish monarchy had asked subjects to participate in public rogations on behalf of their pregnant wives and unborn children, but the pregnancy of the queen-consort and the arrival of Luis Fernando dominated public life in New Spain intermittently over the course of the next four years. Possibly, as Gloria Angeles Franco Rubio has suggested, the widespread popularity of María Luisa Gabriela de Saboya contributed to the decision to announce her first pregnancy and thereby encourage enthusiasm for the crown prince.[5] María Luisa Gabriela de Saboya, the daughter of Victor Amadeus, Duke of Savoy, and sister of Maria Adelaide, the wife of the French delphine, married Felipe V by proxy in 1701, just five days shy of her thirteenth birthday. Before her departure to meet Felipe V in Barcelona, Pope Clement XI met the queen-consort in Nice and gave her the Golden Rose, a meticulously crafted solid gold rose bestowed by the papacy on influential Catholics. After the king left to fight in Italy in April 1701, María Luisa served as regent and ingratiated herself to her husband's subjects, providing updates on his campaigns from the balcony of the Real Alcázar. When British naval ships attacked Cádiz in 1702, she offered her own jewels to buy the necessary weaponry for its defense and continued to wield political influence after Felipe V's return to Spain from Italy in 1703. Before the Portuguese occupation of Madrid in 1706, she fled and took up residence with the court at Burgos.[6] From there, she and Felipe V took the risk of announcing her pregnancy and asking for public rogations on behalf of a healthy birth; if the queen-consort miscarried, it may have indicated for many that God preferred the Archduke Charles.

The risk, however, paid off, and through a series of public commemorations, orators promised that the birth of a Bourbon successor would lead to imperial renewal. To paraphrase the *cédula real* issued on February 10, the king desired to recognize how God continued to bless both him and his kingdoms. While official word did not arrive in New Spain until November, in early June the Duke of Alburquerque learned the joyous news from Jean de Monségur, the captain of an *aviso* ship recently attacked during its voyage to Veracruz. In a copy of his memoirs dedicated to Felipe V (a kind of *arbitrio*), Monségur stated that the news of both the victory at Almansa and the pregnancy of the queen resulted in indescribable demonstrations of joy, as it "dispelled the sorrowful rumors that the enemy had spread throughout the Indies." While the captain clearly alluded to discouraging, pro-Habsburg rumors, Monségur believed that now no one could continue to doubt that God had "chosen Your Majesty to restore good order and once again make justice, abundance, and happiness reign in the monarchy."[7]

The Duke of Alburquerque immediately ordered Mexico City's municipal council and religious corporations to move ahead with public demonstrations of gratitude and specifically requested that councilmen organize three days of luminaries. The city, in turn, responded by personally congratulating the viceroy as a surrogate for the king. Since the

Virgen de los Remedios currently resided within the cathedral, the *cabildo* also elected to organize a novena in her honor, with distinct religious houses hosting masses and sermons on each of the nine days. As customary for all novenas for the Virgen de los Remedios, the *cabildo* distributed *hachas*, thick candles with several wicks, to be burned in the windows of leading officials throughout the nine evenings and ordered the performance of theatrical comedies. As one of the city's councilmen made clear, as the "head" of "these kingdoms," it was the municipal council of Mexico City's obligation to organize varied commemorations to celebrate the happy news. When the *cabildo* later received official notification through a royal decree on December 2, 1707, councilmen reacted with "*alboroto*" or raucous joy.[8]

Other municipalities like Puebla, San Luis Potosí, and Durango took their cue from Mexico City and proceeded with their own demonstrations before official news arrived. Then, in an enthusiastic repeat of events, before the *cédula* arrived with word of Luis Fernando's birth, the Duke of Alburquerque found out via a communication from the governor of the Canary Islands in December 1707 and notified the *cabildo* formally early February 1708. Again, citing its role as the "head" of the viceroyalty, the municipal council ordered festivities to begin that very month and continue through Ash Wednesday of Holy Week and then resume after Easter Sunday, incorporating a novena, luminaries, comedies, bullfights, and a masquerade procession of the guilds, with each squadron representing a planet and corresponding city within New Spain, and with the silversmith's triumphal cart representing the newborn crown prince and Mexico City.[9] Official word of the royal birth arrived the following month, and other cities proceeded with their own demonstrations. Despite the large sums needed to mount events of this kind, municipalities found creative ways to achieve the expected level of majesty. In the Villa de Córdoba, officials allowed themselves into the home of the deceased *alcalde mayor* to acquire gunpowder, which they claimed was on the verge of spoiling. They then used it for the military salutes in honor of the birth of the crown prince.[10]

In April 1709, Madrid acclaimed Luis Fernando as the Prince of Asturias, and from henceforth he would be known as Luis I. Felipe V informed municipalities, dioceses, and religious orders throughout the empire so that they could hold their own commemorations. Most of these occurred in 1710, and in December, Franco-Spanish forces defeated the Grand Alliance in Brihuega and Villaviciosa, sealing military victory for Bourbon Spain. Despite not necessarily being about the prince directly, many of the commemorations held in 1711 in honor of the victories also referenced the role of the prince in renewing the empire. Between masses and a variety of profane demonstrations, Mexico City celebrated the victories continuously for over six weeks over the course of several months.[11] These were followed the subsequent year with inaugural masses and sermons To Make Amends to the Holy Sacrament, as well as the funerary honors in 1714 for the queen-consort, who died prematurely at just twenty-five years of age.

Throughout this long period of public demonstrations, Bourbon supporters telegraphed the legitimacy of the dynasty, which, from the perspective of many, had obviously earned God's favor. Seen from another, no less mystical, perspective, the prince's birth testified to the fecundity of the Bourbon house, a dynasty famous for the many legitimate and illegitimate sons of Louis XIV. Furthermore, many orators quickly came to see the prince as the Spanish Monarchy's long-prophesized messianic hero "shining like the sun," or the future king who derived from the root of Jesse or who had been foretold by the Sybils and late medieval monarchical prophecy. In expressing his hope for a Joachimite-style Age of the Holy Spirit, Orozco y Molina testified to the endurance of millenarian ideas at the end of the long seventeenth century.

This chapter examines the ideas of sacred kingship surrounding the arrival of crown prince Luis Fernando, as well as the role accorded to his mother, María Luisa, in inaugurating a new dynastic age and possibly even a new millenarian age corresponding with a third stage of history (see Chapter 4). From the beginning of the succession crisis in 1701 through at least 1714, artisans, artists, and orators employed symbols derived from nature, as well as scripture, to promise perpetual fertility in Spain's ruling house. From the perspective of many contemporary observers, the queen played a messianic role in the succession crisis. Through her literal and figurative role of birthing a ruling dynasty, she assured the rebirth of the Spanish Empire.

While sermons given throughout the viceroyalty had characterized the king as a messiah or New David, many identified Luis I, the product of two famed Catholic dynasties, as the promised messiah. New Spain's orators, moreover, elicited emotions of joy, gratitude, and awe from their listeners, and invited their audiences to regard the Spanish Crown's decades of infertility as a collective affliction, remedied miraculously by God through the Bourbon house. By referencing regenerative symbols derived from nature, as well as scripture and prophecy related to the root of Jesse, orators and artists promised that a Davidic dynasty would bring forth a golden age.

FERTILIZING THE BODY POLITIC

Spain's Habsburg monarchy had long struggled with assuring succession through the production of healthy male heirs. Although Felipe IV fathered thirteen legitimate children with two wives, only four survived into adulthood. María Teresa (1638–1683) married Louis XIV in 1660, and Margarita Teresa (1651–1673) married Holy Roman Emperor Leopold I in 1666. Of Felipe IV's sons, his oldest, Baltasar Carlos (1629–1646), died at just seventeen, and Felipe Próspero (1657–1661) died just fifteen days before the birth of Carlos II. In letters written to his friend and spiritual advisor, the famed mystic María de Agreda, Felipe IV expressed belief that through the death of his children and the multiple miscarriages of his wives, God had punished Spain for his many extramarital affairs.[12]

As Emily Kuffner has shown, at the court of the young Carlos II, concerns over fertility deepened. Likely hoping to avoid dynastic uncertainty in the future, in 1673, Tomás de Murillo y Velarde, a personal physician to the Spanish royal family, published a treatise on rare and migrating herbs with extensive annotations regarding mandrake and its positive effect on fertility. The doctrine of signatures sustained that the secret to a plant's medicinal purpose derived from its appearance and served as the basis of Murillo y Velarde's defense of mandrake as a fertility aid. Indeed, in the mandrake's roots, he saw the thighs of a virile man and cultivated the plant in the court garden for the use of the noble ladies who suffered from bareness, which he perceived as prevalent throughout Spain. By using the drug to tend to women, Murillo y Velarde betrayed the popular belief holding women primarily responsible for infertility. Using Old Testament matriarchs as examples, Spanish subjects tended to regard barren women as cursed by God. Nearly a decade following the marriage of Carlos II and María Louisa de Orleans, pasquinades began circulating throughout Madrid, blaming the queen for failing to produce an heir.[13]

Throughout the Spanish Empire, the metaphor of the human body shaped political relations and understandings regarding imperial belonging, as we have seen. However, the metaphor of the patriarchal family also shaped understandings of empire, and a biblical passage from Ephesians blended the two metaphors of body and family together. It reads, "Wives, be subject to your husbands as you are to the

Lord. For the husband is the head of the wife just as Christ is the head of the church, the body of which he is the Savior."[14] Contemporaries understood the relationship between king and subject as corporeal, mystical, and patriarchal. Even before the death of Spain's last Habsburg monarch, many viewed infertility in the royal family as a shared experience, and as anxiety regarding an impending succession crisis heightened, it extended to the Americas. In 1686, the diarist Antonio de Robles recorded popular rejoicing in Mexico City over a false rumor from Cartagena that María Luisa de Orleans was finally pregnant. Then, in 1694, subjects in the viceregal capital celebrated yet again over another false rumor that Carlos II's second wife, Mariana de Neuburgo, expected a child.[15]

Beginning with María Luisa Gabriela de Saboya's pregnancy in 1707, New Spain's prelates began recalling their audiences' shared experience with infertility. In San Luis Potosí, in a sermon aptly titled *La importancia de la fecundidad* (*The Importance of Fertility*), the Franciscan Antonio de Salazar compared the miracle bestowed on Spain through the queen's pregnancy to the miracles bestowed upon barren women in scripture. He began his sermon with an exclamation of gratitude for the pregnancy of Spain's "Most Beautiful Rachel, its discreet Abigail, and its prudent Esther, DOÑA MARÍA LUISA GABRIELA DE SABOYA (emphasis his)." According to the prelate, the queen – like all women – deeply desired children, since her entire purpose in life lay in becoming a mother. He speculated that this is what Rachel meant when she said to Jacob, "Give me children or I shall die."[16]

Several orators referred to the matriarch Rachel, comparing her not only to María Luisa Gabriela de Saboya but also to the Spanish Empire. Clearly, in its current configuration, the empire would have "died" without a successor, and coming out of prolonged infertility, orators encouraged contemporaries to empathize by referencing scripture. In a sermon given during the novena in Mexico City, the Mercedarian José de las Heras y Alcocer described a fertile woman as a happy woman and extended the comparison to empires, made happier with the pregnancy of queens. He began the sermon with Rachel's declaration to Jacob and then explained that among the Hebrews, barrenness produced "ignominious infamy."[17] Throughout the empire, people were encouraged in a myriad of ways to identify with the fertility struggles of the royal family. Indeed, the *cédula real* announced the birth as the "greatest consolation and new verification of the pieties and benign protection with which he [God] looks at us."[18]

To provoke empathy and frame the pregnancy of the queen-consort as, in a sense, predestined and/or miraculous, sermons referenced the plight of the infertile in the Old and New Testaments, as well as the happy and fortuitous outcomes of their prolonged sterility. In a sermon sponsored by the Bishop of Valladolid in Guanajuato, José de Abarsuza compared the *Monarquía Hispánica* to the infertile matriarch Hannah before she had been blessed with Samuel. He stated that "Spain was quite afflicted, like another Hannah, or rather I would say the Church of the Catholic Monarchy, by the sterility, which it had suffered for so many years."[19]

In addition to Hannah, orators compared the Spanish Empire to Elizabeth and Zacharias, the parents of John the Baptist. In Puebla, the Franciscan Jacinto Bernárdez de Rivera compared the infertility of the Spanish to this couple who continued to age without producing the "desired fruit."[20] In a sermon given as part of the novena for the queen's pregnancy in Mexico City, cathedral canon Miguel Gonzalez Valdeosera asked the Virgen de los Remedios to assure a "happy birth, that has been desired for many days," and compared the people of New Spain to Elizabeth seeking the aid of her cousin, the Virgin Mary. During her pregnancy, Mary visited Elizabeth, and when she spoke, the baby reacted, leaping inside her. Mary, he concluded, blessed the child, and assured Elizabeth that it would be born healthy, an assurance that Mexico City now solicited from the Virgen de los Remedios.[21] At some point before the birth of the crown prince, the king endowed the annual feast day of John the Baptist on June 24 in the Colegio de San Juan de Letrán. In 1707, John the Baptist's feast day occurred a month before the viceroy announced the queen's pregnancy, and yet Juan Antonio Santibánez gave a sermon acknowledging the miraculous pregnancies of women throughout scripture but of course emphasized the pregnancy of Elizabeth. In the imprint's dedication to the viceroy, Santibánez celebrated the queen's comparably miraculous pregnancy and the viceroy's loyalty in organizing the celebrations that took place the following month.[22]

Upon learning of the pregnancy in 1707, the Bishop of Durango hosted a mass and sermon as well. The Franciscan Juan de San Miguel gave the sermon and described how the comportment of the monarch's subjects effected the ability of the king and queen to procreate, as if king and kingdom shared one mystical body. At one point, he asked why, in 1707, after "so many" years of marriage, did the queen finally become pregnant? Although with hindsight, the queen's young age and the king's prolonged absences likely explain why it took so long, San Miguel argued that this was part of God's plan, as he commonly rewarded his most loyal servants with miraculous pregnancies of male children after long periods of sterility. However, as is well known, God punished, and continued to punish, nations of people for their sins. So, to the question as to why it took so long for the queen to become pregnant, San Miguel answered that "the Kingdom is to blame; for more than forty years, Spain has been sterile," lacking in both virtue and loyalty. He reminded listeners that neither of the wives of Carlos II conceived a child and neither had María Luisa Gabriela de Saboya conceived a child, until now. He concluded emphatically that "the sterility of Spain" had "rubbed off" on the past three queens. The friar then continued with the story of the slave Hagar's conception of Ishmael, with Abraham following forty years of hardship for the Hebrew people. He correlated this to Spain's recent "forty" years of affliction, which, tellingly, "consumed the heart and dried the blood from the body of that Holy King Carlos II."[23] Collective sin and disloyalty, therefore, caused sterility in the royal house and almost destroyed the body politic; although it killed the literal body of the king, it failed to destroy the figurative *cuerpo del rey*.

Orators, therefore, encouraged subjects to regard their lives and destinies as enmeshed with those of the king, forming one mystical body, or to imagine themselves as part of the monarch's patriarchal family, undergoing a shared struggle with infertility. According to various prelates, the viceroyalty longed for an heir as much as an infertile woman longed for a child. In his sermon given for the novena to the Virgen de los Remedios, González Valdeosera, for example, emphasized the "anxieties," "sadness," and "dismay" of New Spain's subjects, which had been transformed into joyful celebration because of the "infallible" news that had arrived through letters from Spain. He asked audience members to take the birth of a male heir as a given, and declared an end to "fear," as "we now have a Prince born in Spain."[24]

Preaching in Puebla, Bernárdez de Rivera made a correlation between infertile couples in scripture and the Spanish people during the reign of Carlos II. He noted how God helped the infertile Anne and Joachim after hearing their laments and supplications. Similarly, "When the monarchy suffered most from the sterility of the infertile," and when the Spanish nation engaged in the most repeated "pleas, prayers, sacrifices, [and] tears, then the divine providence of the heavens allowed for the birth of the legitimate successor."[25] Preaching on the third day of the novena in honor of the pregnancy in the Mexico City cathedral, Blas del Pulgar, the guardian of the Franciscan convent in Tlaxcala, played on sentiment, reminding his audience that thirty years had passed since Carlos II first married and that people throughout the empire had repeatedly offered sacrifices and tears, as well as public and private orations, for a succession. But, he explained, God never troubled people with sterility without later providing a "singular prodigious succession." He recalled how, with God's aid, Isaac, Samson, Samuel, and John the Baptist emerged after prolonged sterility.[26]

Therefore, by, in a sense, fertilizing the *Monarquía Hispánica*, the Bourbon dynasty promised stability, renewal, and prosperity. Indeed, a future golden age depended on continuous succession, which, by the seventeenth century, meant male heirs. Bourbon influencers, therefore, sought to speak to the collective anxieties of Spaniards regarding dynastic succession. The Latin root of fecund, *fecundus*, means fruitful, and throughout the sixteenth and seventeenth centuries, botanicals and fruit functioned as common symbols in paintings to connote human fertility and abundance.[27] Throughout the 1690s, Louis XIV's agents in Madrid disseminated imprints designed to familiarize Spaniards with the progeny of the Bourbon house and to showcase the strength of his lineage.[28] One imprint from 1699 featured the king surrounded by his numerous children and grandchildren. Furthermore, surrounding the explanatory plaque at the bottom of the engraving, spectators could spy a fleur-de-lys (the French lily), as well as an ouroboro connecting two cornucopias filled with fruit and wheat, clearing connoting perpetual fertility.[29]

Flowers, and especially roses (representing Spain) and lilies (representing France), figured prominently in the decorations for the oath ceremonies in Spain and New Spain. Viewed within the proper context, plants, flowers, and fruit evoked the promise of spring, or of rebirth and hope for the future. Furthermore, they helped to associate the garden of Paradise and the New Jerusalem strongly in people's minds. As described in Genesis, in the beginning "the Lord God planted a garden in Eden, in the east, and there he put the man whom he had formed. And out of the ground the Lord God made to spring up every tree that is pleasant to the sight and good for food. The tree of life was in the middle of the garden, and the tree of the knowledge of good and evil."[30] Ezekiel had a paradisical vision of the restored Temple as a garden promising perpetual life, containing trees whose "leaves will not wither, nor their fruit fail, but they will bear fresh fruit every month, because the water for them flows from the sanctuary. Their fruit will be for food, and their leaves for healing."[31] The Book of Revelation described the New Jerusalem as a gated city that descended from the sky but also described "the river of the water of life, bright as crystal," as well as a tree of life which bore twelve types of fruit each month and whose leaves also served to heal nations of people.[32]

Botanical metaphors and especially those related to mythological trees had a strong impact on Judeo-Christian culture and the development of sacred kingship in the Monarquía Hispánica. By the sixteenth century, trees had become strongly associated with monarchical power, as conferred through lineage, and reaffirmed through the growing popularity of royal genealogical trees and histories. In Tirso de Molina's La prudencia de la mujer (1554) (The Prudence of the Woman), the legitimate heir to the Castilian throne, Fernando IV, grandson of Alfonso X, is hidden safely from the enemy inside the trunk of a tree, and when discovered, his location confers legitimacy and an almost supernatural mystique.[33] Ceremonial emblems, moreover, reinforced the association between trees and monarchy. In Juan de Borja's Empresas morales (1680) (Moral Emblems), the Book of Daniel inspired an emblem of a massive and lush tree covering all the birds, animals, and fruits of the world. The story of Daniel explains how all terrestrial power, including that of kings, derives from God, and the commentary accompanying the emblem makes clear that the tree referenced by Daniel and depicted in the emblem represents a great world empire.[34] Furthermore, a nostalgia for a lost golden age, represented as Paradise, inspired intellectuals throughout the sixteenth and seventeenth centuries in their use of botanical imagery. In both Spanish and Portuguese America, numerous chroniclers suggested that Paradise could be physically located in the New World.[35]

Tangled within an interrelated web of understandings, botanical references invited Spanish subjects to contemplate the future. Fiore famously decorated his manuscripts with drawings of trees to serve, in the words of Marjorie Reeves, as symbols of "continuing human history whose branches must spread out throughout the centuries."[36] The natural world could, therefore, communicate a multiplicity of messages, but in this context, they revolved around fertility and hope for a millenarian-style golden age. Lilies, for example, represented the French monarchy since the thirteenth century, but their long stems also promised virility and fecundity. Roses, of course, had been long associated with Castile, but also with the Virgin Mary, whom Saint Jerome associated with a *hortus conclusus*, or a locked garden, as described in the Song of Songs: "a garden locked is my sister, my bride."[37] Saint Ambrose, in turn, famously explained that in Paradise, the rose grew without thorns, which represented sin, and referred to the Virgin Mary as the "rose without thorns."[38]

Given the multivalent ways symbols derived from nature resonated, it is understandable that in Spain and New Spain, orators and artisans chose to draw heavily from the natural world in framing Felipe V's succession. For the king's inaugural entrance into Madrid, organizers decorated ephemeral structures with Castilian roses and French lilies, and during the sermon given for the funeral honors of Carlos II in the Franciscan convent of Tlaxcala, Maximiliano López de Pro called Carlos II the "Rose of Castile," which withered with death.[39] Similarly, the organizers of the *jura* ceremony celebrated in Texcoco used poetry and ephemeral art to describe the unification of the two ruling dynasties, represented as Castilian roses and French lilies.[40] For the oath ceremony in Guadalajara, the royal standard bearer wore a coat embroidered with roses, while his lackeys all donned verdant green; the *jura* platform bore both roses and lilies, signaling toward a fertile and abundant future.[41] Yet, subjects at court witnessed what may have been the most poignant and dramatic use of botanical imagery during Mexico City's oath ceremony. In a central location on the *jura* platform, silversmiths placed a finely crafted silver lily, and from the stem, it sprouted a golden Castilian rose.[42]

According to the doctrine of signatures, phallic-like stems represented the most fertile part of a flowering plant. The magistral canon of Puebla, José Gómez de la Parra, made this point in a preamble to a sermon given in honor of the birth of Luis Fernando. In it he celebrated the fecundity of the Bourbon house and referenced the funerary sermon he gave for Carlos II in 1701, an imprint of which he lamented had been lost during the naval attack at Vigo in 1702.[43] In the sermon, which he based largely on the Gospel of John, he compared Carlos II to the Savior, who in turn compared himself to the "grain of wheat" that falls alone to the ground but through death bears "fruit." Given a mere seven to eight years after a long period of scarcity and disease, this reference likely activated memories of deprivation and hope for future abundance, at least for some. Gómez de la Parra then linked this narrative of agricultural fertility to the fertility of the monarchy, stating that Carlos II "conceived" Felipe V through his last will and testament, just as God made David the King of Israel through his words: "Ask me, and I will give you your inheritance, that is your own; because you are the First-born Son."[44]

Similarly, in 1707, Santiago de Guatemala celebrated the retaking of Madrid by Felipe V's forces in 1706. In his sermon, the Jesuit Antonio de Valtierra stated that Carlos II chose Felipe V as his "primogeniture," because France is a "land so fecund with princes" that they grow like flowers.[45] When celebrating the royal birth in Santiago de Guatemala, the

Jesuit Antonio Xardón described Luis Fernando as the "fruit" of one of the few Hispanic olive branches remaining on the Habsburg trunk, emphasizing that this line had been able to continue, thanks to the union of Louis XIV and María Teresa.[46]

Orators in New Spain used imagery pulled from the natural world to reconcile the French and Spanish ruling dynasties, and with news of the queen's pregnancy, Bourbon supporters throughout the empire amplified a message of rebirth. Rejoicing at news of the queen's pregnancy in Toledo, one prelate described the queen as the "fertile lily, which in the midst of the thorns of so much bloody war, unleashes the new royal flower of our prince."[47] Preaching in San Luis Potosi in honor of the pregnancy, Antonio de Salazar prayed that the unborn child – the "flower" of the best lily of France, Felipe V – would be born a Castilian rose.[48]

The Dominican convent of Antequera chose to celebrate the birth of the prince on May 7, 1708, the day the order honored the Crown of Thorns of Jesus Christ. In his sermon, Dionisio Levanto claimed that like Christ, Felipe V wore a Crown of Thorns, but that after the birth of the prince on August 25, 1707, lilies began to replace the barbs. He also relayed the story of how in 1205, the barren and desperate Queen Blanche of France turned to the Virgin Mary, symbolized, of course, by the rose. The Virgin Mary blessed the queen with a son who would become Saint Louis IX of France. The speaker made clear that with the help of the first Bourbon crown prince, Spain would open like a flower in spring. He asked his listeners: "Turn your eyes now to our Spain, and even at the risk of drawing a sigh from your loyal breasts, [sic] remember, that at the beginning of that century the flowers of our Crown withered."[49]

In that same year, in the convent of San Bernardo de México, prolific orator Castorena y Ursúa gave a sermon in honor of the prince. In his aptly titled *Fructo de bendicion de la rosa de Castilla, y la flor de lyz francesa* (*Blessed Fruit of the Rose of Castile and the French Fleur-de-lis*), Castorena y Ursúa described the infant as the "rose of Castile," which had been born from the "fruit of France" with the help of San Bernardo, on whose feast day, August 20, the queen experienced the first pangs of childbirth. He credited the saint with "fertilizing" the empire, noting that in the same year that Mexico City elected San Bernardo (1699) as a patron saint, New Spain experienced bountiful harvests and the prince of Bavaria died, making it necessary for Carlos II to select Felipe as his successor.[50] According to the prelate, the etymology of the saint's name reflected his role in this historic moment, as he claimed that it is composed of two distinct words: *ber*, meaning fountain, and *nardus*, a beautiful and fragrant grass commonly used to "arouse" and help to assure the "happy propagation." Castorena y Ursúa concluded that "the beautiful young Sapling of Our Prince is the fruit of the King, and of San Bernardo; the King, as Father, and of San Bernardo, as patron."[51]

Botanical imagery helped to emphasize the theme of renewal through at least 1714, when Maria Luisa died. In the funerary honors held in the cathedral of Mexico on October 27, 1714, the catafalque equated the queen-consort to a rose and her husband and surviving sons to lilies. As the Jesuit Lucas del Rincón made clear in his description, the queen represented the rose who died at the height of her beauty and power, leaving behind three "*pimpollos*," or saplings. A specific emblem depicted a rose threatened by fire and embraced by a skeleton, representing death. However, as Rincón made clear, fire served as a tool that horticulturalists used "to irritate, and propagate the fecundity of its root." Given this, he felt that the Bourbon succession remained assured by the "royal plants" produced by the queen.[52]

THE BOURBON MESSIAH

Botanical symbolism embodied the promise of renewal but one that took on millenarian implications thanks to the king's marriage to María Luisa Gabriela de Saboya. Since at least the twelfth century, Popes and other influential prelates have identified the rose as a sacred symbol with messianic significance, and by the twelfth century, high-ranking clergy linked the flower to Davidic prophecy. Innocent III (1161–1216) identified the "rod" described by Isaiah that grows from the stem of Jesse as undeniably a rose.[53] According to Isaiah, then "a Branch shall grow out of his roots: And the spirit of the Lord shall rest upon him." In foretelling the arrival of a messiah derived from the root or stem of Jesse, Isaiah prophesized an age of righteousness and peace, stating that the "wolf also shall dwell with the lamb, and the leopard shall lie down with the kid; and the calf and the young lion and the fatling together; and a little child shall lead them."[54] In New Spain, this passage became a reference used to explain the significance of the birth of Luis Fernando. According to numerous orators, the crown prince descended from the root of Jesse and not in a purely mystical or metaphoric way. Numerous orators claimed that the Savoy family literally descended from the House of David through the Virgin Mary, a rose without thorns.

It is unclear where New Spain's orators got the idea that the Savoy family descended from the Virgin Mary, but the claim served to sacralize the young prince as a descendant of David and Jesus Christ. In 1701, María Luisa Gabriela de Saboya received the honor of the golden rose from Clement XI while traveling to meet her husband for the first time. The Pope tried to remain neutral for most of the war, so the bestowing of the gift is significant. It is this that perhaps led orators in New Spain to claim that the queen descended from the family of the Virgin Mary, and, therefore, the "root of Jesse." It is, of course, even more likely that the Savoy family's possession of the Holy Shroud (a relic with the supposed imprint of Christ's body) nurtured this belief. The Savoy family acquired the controversial relic in 1453, but people may have come to believe that it had been passed down within the Savoy family since Jesus's death. Regardless, orators in various cities throughout New Spain repeated the statement – as if it were fact – that the Savoy family descended from the family of the Virgin Mary. Genealogies in Mathew and Luke linked the Virgin Mary to the House of David, and by the twelfth century, pictorial representations of the Tree of Jesse commonly included the Virgin Mary.[55]

In his sermon of supplication for a healthy birth in the Church of San Francisco in San Luis Potosi, Salazar informed his audience that the prince descended from the Virgin Mary through his mother. Significantly, he argued that the prince would act as a "Redeemer and Liberator of the Spains."[56] During his sermon in honor of San Luis Potosí's oath ceremony for Luis I years later, Salazar explained how Isaiah prophesized that a prince would be born who was desired by all and "like a fragrant Flower, he would spring from the fertile root of Jesse." He concluded that given his mother's ancestry, Luis I was clearly that fragrant flower.[57]

Orators throughout New Spain did not tire of remarking on the Savoy family's lineage. While giving thanks for the birth of the prince in Puebla's Franciscan Convento de las Llagas, Bernárdez de Ribera argued that the birth of the prince had been prophesized by Ezekiel when he saw four cherubs with distinct faces: human, representing the prince; lion representing majesty; ox (which he claimed was a mule) representing Spain; and eagle, representing Mexico City, clearly centering the viceroyalty in this transformative event. Ezekiel, moreover, prophesized that the line of David would be restored, and so Bernárdez de Ribera declared that the prince was the "heir of David," descendant of the Virgin Mary.[58]

Orators in New Spain exalted the Bourbon monarch and crown prince as sacred rulers, like David, Solomon, and Christ. However, they went further and claimed that the crown prince descended from Jesse, and would act as a messiah like the one prophesized by Isaiah, "who judges and seeks justice and is swift to do righteousness."[59] Preaching in honor of the oath ceremony in Durango, Antonio Garcia Valdés cited Psalm 132: "The Lord swore to David a sure oath from which he will not turn back: 'One of the sons of your body I will set on your throne.'" Since she descended from the House of David, the prelate argued that by providing a "womb," Mary acted as an extension of David's body. Furthermore, he contended that because the House of Savoy descended from the Virgin Mary, Luis I fulfilled the promise that God had made to David to keep his heirs on the throne forever.[60] According to Garcia de Valdéz, "when the prince of Spain is born from a branch of the Imperial tree of the Most Holy Mary," that ruling dynasty will endure.[61]

Orators utilized prophetical exegesis related to the House of David and a coming millenarian age to understand the war and legitimize Bourbon rule. In the Book of Revelation, John had a complex vision of the Eleventh Hour, which included the root of David loosening the seven seals and a pregnant woman "clothed in the sun" struggling to give birth as a dragon waited to devour the newborn. In these events, Bourbon influencers encouraged audiences to recognize the current war and to identify the prince as the child carried by the woman clothed in the sun. Various prelates assured their audiences that Luis I would grow into a messiah like Christ, a prince of peace.

According to John's vision, at the end of a great struggle between the forces of Heaven and Hell, Christ binds the Beast for a thousand years, and then a New Jerusalem comes down from the heavens, and Christ announces himself as the "root and the offspring of David, and the bright and morning star."[62] As Rubial García has illustrated, in the seventeenth century, New Spain's intellectuals often imagined the New Jerusalem as an Edenic garden or as a walled city made of gold and crystal, with twelve doors covered in gems. By the eighteenth century, orators and artists in New Spain commonly mixed representations, representing the New Jerusalem as an enclosed garden, similar to Paradise, but retaining the twelve doors.[63] Some orators, as noted in Chapter 3, equated the New Jerusalem with Mexico City. But, regardless of divergent interpretations, botanical imagery like trees, flowers, and vines represented the dawn of a new age of abundance. Preaching in San Luis Potosí in praise of the queen's fertility and in supplication for a healthy birth, Salazar compared the queen to the Woman of the Apocalypse. He relayed how John saw a vision of a beautiful woman, or better stated, a "queen," with twelve stars surrounding her head like a Crown. Heavily pregnant, she was "desirous to give birth to the fruit of her womb, because [he] was to govern an entire world." He cited Isaiah as stating that "a rod will be born from the root of Jesse, and from this rod the beautiful flower of a tender child [will emerge]."⁶⁴ For the novena held in Mexico City in 1707, Heras y Alcocer described John's vision of a "beautiful queen" struggling to give birth while surrounded by enemies.⁶⁵

For many Bourbon influencers, the infant born amid war would be a "Prince of Peace," who would inaugurate an Edenic golden age. Preaching in the cathedral of Mexico for the novena in 1707, the Franciscan Blas del Pulgar emphasized Christ's Davidic descent through the Virgin Mary, adding that it was widely known that the noble House of Savoy descended from the Tree of Jesse. Luis Fernando's parentage, therefore, assured Bourbon rule, and as arguably forecast in the Book of Revelation, a warrior-savior (a Lion) from the line of David would save Spain from apocalyptic war and forecast a peaceful future. Paraphrasing Mark 11, verse 10 – "blessed is the kingdom of our father David which is coming to us" – Pulgar stressed that it was no coincidence that the "root of Jesse" existed through the Savoy family line and that a member of that family became queen of Spain. The prince's birth on the feast day of Saint Louis IX of France also indicated that a united Christendom lay ahead, through the "Restorer of the Holy Land and the ultimate ruin of the Ottoman Empire, and the Mohammedan sect."⁶⁶ Furthermore, he emphasized the prince's sacred power, stating, "He is not an average Prince of the earth, he who has been born in Spain; he has much of Heaven [in him]."⁶⁷

Various prelates promised that this sacred prince would inaugurate a final stage of history. Described in both Isaiah and the Book of Revelation as a New Jerusalem or as a walled city and garden, the millenarian age would be one of peace and abundance, and, according to Pulgar, Spaniards "*daran saltos*" or would jump for joy, as the immediate future following the war would take the shape of the age following the return of Christ. At this time, peace and unity would reign. The Roman Empire/ Grand Alliance symbolized by a great beast would no longer make war against the "Lamb." Instead, "he would lay down with him," and the "insolent Philistines" would flee this land "because the newborn Infant would threaten them with his happy Birth." He declared that the king, represented by the lion; the queen, represented by the lamb; and the prince, as the calf, would live in "peace, union, and quietude."⁶⁸

Pulgar referenced centuries-old monarchical prophecy to explain the arrival of Luis Fernando, the first in what he hoped would be a long line of Spanish Bourbon princes. Other prelates directly identified the prince as a Last World Emperor-type figure who would inaugurate a new stage of history. In the license for the publication of the sermon given in Durango in honor of the birth of the first Bourbon crown prince, the rector of the University of Mexico, Manuel Butrón y Moxíca, made declarations that directly reflected Sibylline and Joachimite prophecy. He stated that like Christ, Luis Fernando was born from the root of Jesse, and for this reason, he had the right to inaugurate a third stage of history that would correspond with a new or third testament. He cited the Apollonian oracle at Erythrae, which supposedly claimed that a prince with a handsome face would be born in Spain and that he would "conquer the whole world." Butrón y Moxíca cited the prophecy as also reading that "the Lion will violently break all of Asia into pieces, until it starves it and until [he] smashes the beast and places above the beast's scepter the lamb."[69] He interpreted this as meaning that Luis Fernando, son of Felipe V, would destroy the Ottoman Empire and that he would take the lamb from the collar of the Golden Fleece and place it on the Ottoman throne. Significantly, he added that while many oracles predicted that the Emperor of the Last Days would be a Catholic King from Spain, others applied it to Most Christian Kings of France. He made known his belief that the Emperor of the Last Days would descend from *both* ruling dynasties. In the actual sermon, Juan de San Miguel, the Franciscan guardian of the Convent of San Antonio, claimed that Luis Fernando would rule over the entire world, including England, Portugal, and the Holy Roman Empire, and that the faith will take root again everywhere it was lost, including Africa and Asia, and especially Palestine.[70]

San Miguel also compared the infant prince to the biblical Samson, whose name derives from the Hebrew for "sun." However, San Miguel argued that the Book of Revelation predicted the current succession crisis, with María Luisa Gabriela de Saboya prefigured by the travailing woman and the Grand Alliance represented by the dragon ready to devour the newborn infant. In John's vision, an eagle whisked the woman away, and San Miguel saw Spain's Catholic King and France's Most Christian King represented in the animal's wings. According to San Miguel, both monarchies "finally united" in their common pursuit against the forces of evil. He concluded by noting that the prince had brought about this union. The defeat of the Antichrist would lead to worldwide conquests for the Catholic Church, the unification of Christendom, the conquest of Jerusalem, and a long period of peace, prosperity, and abundance.[71] Franciscans and wealthy officials in Durango, therefore, characterized the prince as a Universal Catholic Monarch and eschatological hero in several distinct commemorations. As a reminder, in 1711 officials presented the crown prince as conqueror of the sects spread throughout the four parts of the world and the inaugurator of an "Age of the Holy Spirit."

Yet, priests in municipalities throughout the viceroyalty commonly characterized the crown prince as a messianic hero. Preaching during the novena for the Virgen de los Remedios in 1707 in honor of the pregnancy of the queen, the Augustinian Fernando de Toro Altamirano stated that a prince who would "rule the world" had been prophesized by John in the Book of Revelation.[72] Various orators attributed miraculous powers to the infant. Preaching in Puebla in honor of the birth, cathedral canon Gómez de la Parra characterized the infant prince as capable of defeating the enemy and described him as an infant-warrior and even as a *rex redivivus*. In the sermon, the cathedral canon stressed the crown prince's glorious lineage and even cited a printed genealogy of Felipe V created by Ubilla y Medina. He traced the king's ancestry back to San Fernando, King of Castile and conqueror of Seville and Cordoba, as well as to Santa Isabel, Queen of Portugal, San Luis IX, and even Charlemagne. According to Gómez de la Parra, in Luis Fernando, these great heroes would be reborn.[73] And, perhaps not coincidentally, the triumphal cart sponsored by Puebla's merchant militia compared the child to the infant Hercules, the quintessential archetype for a Spanish hero.[74] In Mexico City, in 1713 the Third Order of Saint Francis sponsored the printing of a sermon dedicated to its patron, San Louis IX de Francia, revered as an ideal Christian monarch, and as a defender of the faith and would-be conqueror of Jerusalem. According to Alfonso Mariano del Río, his virtues transferred miraculously to his namesake, Luis I.[75]

Throughout the many commemorations in honor of the crown prince, officials made sure to present Luis I through visual devices. In the case of Durango, officials presented him through stand-ins and portraiture. For the cathedral of Mexico's celebration of the oath of loyalty to Luis I, the painter Juan Correa (1646–1716) created a full-body portrait of the prince (Figure 5.1). It rested on a stage under the dome of the cathedral, decorated with tapestries embroidered with a variety of flowers, and under a canopy embroidered with gold tulips.[76] It reconciled both ruling dynasties by presenting the prince in French attire within a setting reminiscent of the Real Alcázar de Madrid's Salón de Espejos, with a lion resting at his feet; these recalled the so-called Spanish lions associated with the Habsburgs, the lions of Solomon, and the "lion of Judah."[77] For the cathedral of Valladolid's mass and sermon in honor of the 1710

FIGURE 5.1 The Prince Our Lord Don Luis Fernando, 1710. Oil on canvas by Juan Correa. Metropolitan Cathedral, Mexico City. Secretaría de Cultura–INAH. Photograph by Pedro Ángeles Jiménez, Manuel Toussaint Photographic Archive, Instituto de Investigaciones Estéticas, UNAM.

victories, organizers placed paintings of the king, queen, and prince on the altar.[78] Similarly, when the University of Mexico held its celebration in honor of the victory, it showcased paintings of the entire royal family, including the prince. The university also chose to hold its commemoration on the crown prince's birthday, August 25, the feast day of San Luis IX de Francia, and placed statues of his namesakes, the archetypical sacred kings San Luis and San Fernando.[79]

In the end, how people internalized messages regarding the crown prince and new Bourbon dynasty cannot be understood with complete precision, but through close readings of sermons and ceremonies pitched to audiences throughout the viceroyalty, we can glean shared understandings of divine kingship and the sacrality of the Spanish body politic. Furthermore, for many, the crown prince had "much of Heaven in him," just like Blas de Pulgar claimed in 1707. For the celebrations in honor of the royal birth in Guichiapa, the "*cabeza*" of the province of Xilotepec, a priest named Antonio de Escoto gave a sermon on the feast day of the Purification of Mary, an occasion that commemorated how Mary, in accordance with Jewish law, entered the Temple in Jerusalem forty days after the birth of Christ to be purified and to present her child in the ceremony known as the redemption of the first-born. Escoto acknowledged the brutal war over the succession currently taking place in Spain and implored the Virgin Mary's aid on behalf of Franco-Spanish forces. Significantly, the town's Spanish *alcalde mayor*, Don Diego de Solis Cachero, commissioned a painting of the infant for the community to pray before for the defeat of the "heretics."[80]

CONCLUSION

In the summer of 1711, municipalities and religious corporations throughout New Spain began celebrating the decisive victories in Brihuega and Villaviciosa, and the following year, churches followed with the inaugural *Fiesta de Desagravios al Santísimo Sacramento*. This almost closed out the extensive series of ceremonies resulting from the succession crisis. The cathedral of Mexico celebrated the "final punishment" of Felipe V's enemies with spectacular celebrations featuring, among other elements, an enormous *gigante* or paper mâché doll, sitting near its dome and shooting out fireworks from its arms.[81] During the capital's summer of revelry, Felipe V's subjects released pent-up tension and breathed a collective sigh of relief and not only for the military victories but also for securing what many predicted would be a seamless succession of progeny.

FIGURE 5.2 Engraving from *Llanto de Flora: desatado en sepulchrales rosas sobre el magestuoso túmulo que la Imperial corte mexicana erigió al obsequio, y votó a la memoria de su florida reyna Doña María Luisa Gabriela de Saboya* ... (Mexico: Herederos de la Viuda de Miguel de Ribera, 1715), 192. John Carter Brown Library at Brown University.

And whether the king did secure a "seamless" succession depends on one's perspective. Felipe V willingly gave up the throne of Spain to his son, Luis I, in January 1724, but in August 1724, smallpox took the young king's life, forcing Felipe V's return to the throne. However, at the time of her death in 1714, the queen-consort still had three surviving sons. Although Luis I died less than eight months into his reign, one of the three, Fernando (1713–1759), would live to succeed his father after his death in 1746. However, after the death of the childless Fernando VI, the Crown passed from María Luisa Gabriela de Saboya's last surviving son to Fernando VI's half-brother, Carlos III, in 1759. Technically speaking, with the death of María Luisa Gabriela de Saboya's heirs, the line of David died in Spain. Whether anyone publicly acknowledged this is another matter.

Through his second marriage, Felipe V produced more children who would secure the dynasty's hold on the Spanish throne. But, at the time of the queen-consort's death in 1714, people had little reason to fear dynastic uncertainty or doubt a prosperous future for the empire. With three surviving sons at the time of her death, the empire seemed secured by her "saplings." Mexico City residents could find strength in the catafalque erected in the cathedral for the queen. Decorated with one thousand candles, the ephemeral structure covered almost the entire floor below the cupola and featured twenty-two statues representing virtues, each clutching a bouquet of flowers, as well as emblems featuring roses intended to represent the queen. At the very top of the pyramidal structure, onlookers could admire a lily growing upwards until just grazing the side of the dome (Figure 5.2).[82] If mourners in Mexico City harbored doubts regarding the future of the Spanish Empire, they could cast their eyes upwards toward that lily which, like the Tree of Life in the New Jerusalem, ascended boldly toward the future.

Conclusion

The War of the Spanish Succession touched, and even upended, the lives of people throughout New Spain's social and spatial hierarchy, as rumors of a possible Dutch or English invasion circulated amongst the viceroyalty throughout its duration. Fearing both external and internal threats, the Bourbon Crown sought to retain the *Monarquía Hispánica*'s lucrative and strategically important viceroyalty in a myriad of ways that included sending French naval ships to guard its coastlines, reinforcing its vulnerable presidios, and selling appointments within the imperial administration to members of the Creole elite. However, the Bourbon Crown also retained its hold on New Spain by controlling the nature and circulation of information, and by overwhelming the public sphere with writings, sermons, rumors, and visual imagery that strengthened the position of the Bourbon house.

The *Monarquía Hispánica*'s succession crisis triggered financial hardship and feelings of insecurity and vulnerability among large segments of New Spain's population, while also providing financial, political, and economic opportunities to others, spiking interest in succession-related news. While some subjects in New Spain read printed reports from Europe, others listened to rumors and gossip. Furthermore, priests relayed information about the war and the virtues of the new Bourbon king in an extraordinary number of commemorative sermons. In New Spain's early eighteenth-century public sphere, information regarding the Habsburg challenger also circulated, but to a limited degree that demanded subterfuge, with individuals issuing subtle cues as to their monarchical leanings. For people with dissenting opinions to remain safe, they needed to refrain from expressing them, even as Bourbon supporters inundated the viceroyalty with propaganda. Visual imagery – whether ceremonies, costumes, ephemeral art pieces, or portraiture – also contributed to the creation of a public sphere that magnified the virtues of the Bourbon dynasty. However, the image of the king and crown prince also became refracted by the legacy of sacred kingship, revealing a clear idea of how contemporaries understood the Spanish Empire, and their place within it.

An analysis of the discourse surrounding the Bourbon succession in New Spain reveals that contemporaries saw themselves as belonging to an empire but one imagined as the sacred body of the king. The degree to which the corporeal metaphor shaped the political culture of the Spanish Empire may not have been made so strikingly apparent if not for the way the War of the Spanish Succession forced supporters of Bourbon rule to articulate shared ideas regarding political legitimacy and, perhaps more importantly, imperial belonging. During times of crisis, members of communities often articulate and reaffirm that which collectively defines them, and in the early modern Spanish world, bureaucrats, artists, and intellectuals encouraged adhesion to the empire, kingdom, and locality when confronted by the real or perceived threat of war, instability, and ethnic and religious plurality. This was certainly true during the War of the Spanish Succession, which represented a serious physical, material, and existential threat. In reaffirming and calling for unity, contemporaries treated the body of the king and the body of Christ as a conflated entity capable of unifying all Spanish subjects and absorbing composite identities. Writers and orators recalled medieval prophecy and symbols associated with Habsburg rule and drew on corporeal and messianic notions of kingship to promise that the Bourbon succession would bring about imperial resurrection and renewal.

In recalling deeply ingrained and widely shared understandings, supporters of dynastic change did not promise that a Bourbon victory would merely preserve the status quo. Instead, they promised that a Bourbon victory would permit the imperial body to rise again or to be reborn, a promise embodied in the birth of crown prince Luis I, the root of Jesse. As botanical motifs and scriptural references made clear, the future would be one of prosperity, with the certainty that Spain's Bourbon Crown would bring about messianic change. Many orators promised a utopian age, and with the birth of Luis I, a New David as Spain's sacred king.

These discourses reflected – and helped to shape – an imagined community that predated the rise of the modern nation-state. Rooted in notions of common descent and, to a large extent, imagined ethnicity, this community embraced legendary "ancestors" such as Hercules and Pelayo, along with saints and devotions tied to Spain's sacred history, including Fernando of Castile, Santiago, and the Immaculate Conception. At the same time, the corporeal conception of empire made space for expressions of local pride and allowed for a degree of cultural and political pluralism. Royal ceremonies required the formal participation of key *cuerpos* – such as the Republic of the Indians and other governing or social institutions – whose presence affirmed the composite nature of imperial rule.

The corporeal metaphor (and its association with life, death, and messianic kingship) channeled and shaped both religious and political understandings throughout the early modern Spanish world. Before and during the war, people in New Spain performed their belonging to the empire, with each jurisdiction and corporation demonstrating its loyalty to the monarch under the guidance of its own "head," whether a viceroy, governor, *alcalde mayor*, or head town. Throughout the entirety of the war, corporeal metaphors worked in an intense and magnified way, drawing on a semiotic tangle of repetitive references to Old Testament kings, Jesus Christ, medieval rulers, the sun, and the Eucharist in both sermons and images. Orators and artisans, moreover, deployed botanical symbolism to recall life and death, and to promise fertility and abundance. With the birth of the first Bourbon crown prince of Spain, many clerics recognized the "resurrection" of the *cuerpo del rey* and encouraged their parishioners to see the ascension of the Bourbon dynasty as a rebirth. Ceremony and oratory, moreover, encouraged subjects in New Spain to see themselves as Spanish subjects, devoted to the Eucharist. Ceremonies like the funerary honors for fallen soldiers, moreover, served to honor all of those "national" heroes who died for Spain.

By the end of the war, the Bourbon Crown had already taken steps toward replacing the *Monarquía Hispánica*, the Spanish Empire's composite body politic, with a more centralized Crown, and this would be followed by commercial and fiscal reforms. Nevertheless, the promise of reform would prove slow to realize, and supporters of Bourbon rule continued to draw on corporeal metaphors even while they took tenuous steps to supplant the *Monarquía Hispánica* with an absolutist structure. When Felipe V stepped down and turned the monarchy over to Luis I in 1724, some orators continued to make strong allusions to sacred kingship. For Luis I's *jura* in Tula in what is now the state of Hidalgo, Francisco de la Concepción Barbosa gave a sermon that compared the sovereignty of Felipe V to the sovereignty of God the Father, who sent his son to serve as king while he still "lived" in Heaven. Likewise, although Felipe V chose to step down, he "transubstantiated" into Luis I. To underscore this interpretation, Barbosa cited from the *Pange lingua gloriosi corporis mysterium* (*Sing, My Tongue, the Glorious Mystery of the Body*) by Saint Thomas Aquinas (1225–1274), the Latin hymn sung during the consecration of the Eucharist. He then noted how the "woman clothed in the sun" in John's vision was to give birth to a king, and how this prophecy came true with the birth and ascension of Luis I. Yet, while exalting the sacrality of the Spanish Empire's Bourbon monarch, Barbosa celebrated the viceroyalty's importance to the empire. He referenced the prophecy of Ezekiel, who saw a triumphal cart pulled through the sky by an eagle, a common symbol for Mexico City. According to the priest, the triumphal cart represented the Spanish Monarchy, with both Luis I and the viceroyalty of New Spain symbolized by the eagle pulling it along.[1]

Then, with the tragic death of Luis I seven months later, orators continued to rely on traditional symbols and metaphors. In the Convento Real de Jesús María in Mexico City, Luis de la Peña bemoaned the passing of the king at just seventeen years of age, and described him as a "flower" and a "sapling."[2] For the funerary honors hosted by Viceroy Juan de Acuña y Bejarano, the first Marquis of Casafuerte, in the cathedral of Mexico City, José Antonio de Villerías y Roelas compared the death of the prince to the setting of the sun.[3]

THE SACRED KING LIVES ON

Over time, the Bourbon monarchy took concerted steps toward transforming the *Monarquína Hispánica* into a more centralized and uniform formulation. But, in bringing absolutism to the empire, administrators did not necessarily consider the dense web of symbols and understandings that nurtured ideas regarding Spanish kingship. What is more, Spain's Bourbon dynasty continued to associate its rule with symbols of sacred monarchy through ceremonies like the *Fiesta de Desagravios al Santísimo Sacramento*. Supporters framed Felipe V's defense of the faith as part of the origin story of the Spanish Bourbons, one that permitted the dynasty to appropriate the cult of the Eucharist from their Habsburg predecessors. The Hieronymites, the order responsible for the administration of the Real Monasterio de San Lorenzo de El Escorial, commissioned *Felipe V, vencedor de la herejía* (*Felipe V, Conqueror of Heresy*) by Felipe de Silva to commemorate the king's victory at Villaviciosa. Completed around 1712, it depicts Felipe V to the left of the monastery-palace of El Escorial, a symbol

FIGURE C.1 Felipe V, Conqueror of Heresy, c. 1712. Felipe de Silva, oil on canvas. Commissioned by the Hieronymite order, this painting commemorates Philip V's victory at the Battle of Villaviciosa (1710). Monasterio del Escorial.

of the New Jerusalem, with the queen and the crown prince to the right. Behind the monarch is an allegorical representation of Faith holding the Blessed Sacrament, with the Immaculate Conception crowning the entire image. At the foreground of the image writhes a dragon, representing the heretical enemy being stabbed by both Felipe V and the crown prince, Luis (Figure C.1).[4] As noted, Felipe V installed the feast day in honor of the Blessed Sacrament in 1711, instructing that it be honored throughout the empire perpetually on the Sunday preceding the feast day of the Immaculate Conception. In municipalities throughout New Spain, councilmen attended the annual mass and sermon "*en cuerpo*," or as the "body" of their municipality through Independence. By ordering this annual commemoration, the Crown helped to inscribe Felipe V's defense of the faith and the cult of the Eucharist on the historical memory of the empire.

Yet, over time, the idea of sacred kingship would become increasingly unstable, as new policies and representations of monarchy challenged its

Conclusion 147

very foundation. On the one hand, the Bourbon Crown continued to recall the legacy of archetypal sacred kings. In 1753, for example, New Spain's viceroy instituted public celebrations on the annual feast day in honor of San Fernando, the "titular saint of our king."[5] On the other hand, the image of the king as an infallible ruler began to suffer. As Gabriel Torres Puga examined, by the 1760s, the public sphere had become more robust, with print and manuscript material critiquing the Jesuit Order escaping the control of censors and awakening a diversity of public opinion. Part of the debate regarding the Jesuits centered on the possible beatification of Bishop Juan de Palafox y Mendoza (1600–1659), who, while serving in Puebla, came into conflict with the order. By rejecting his episcopal authority, the bishop argued that the Jesuits rejected the authority of the king as awarded to him through the *Patronato Real*, the Spanish Crown's patronage over the Church, and its control over ecclesiastical appointments and portions of Church revenue. After Carlos III became monarch of Spain in 1759, it became clear that the Inquisition and the Bourbon Crown no longer shared the same opinion regarding Jesuit autonomy. Whereas the Inquisition banned the publication of Palafox y Mendoza's letters regarding the Jesuits, Carlos III asked the Pope to repeal the ban, and then had the letters published in luxurious binding under royal license.[6] To complicate matters, rumors spread regarding the Jesuit Order's recent expulsions from both the Portuguese and French empires, as well as supposed plans by specific residents within New Spain to create an independent republic with support from England. Significantly, literature regarding this plan first began circulating during the Seven Years' War (1756–1763).[7]

Acting on secret orders from the Crown, on June 25, 1767, the Marquis de Croix expelled the Jesuit Order from the viceroyalty. Four weeks later, the *audiencia* of Mexico published Carlos III's decree pertaining to the expulsion, stating that "silence must be imposed on this matter to all his subjects."[8] Nevertheless, sermons, poems, satires, and other writings for and against the order already circulated widely and helped to divide public opinion. In a counterpoint to the traditional understanding of the Spanish monarch as a "defender of the faith" or even a messiah, some texts referred to Carlos III as a "heretic." In the years immediately following the expulsion, prophecies circulated, but not about a Last World Emperor, a New David, or the birth of Spain's messiah. Instead, prophecies circulated about the return of the Jesuit Order.[9]

Viceregal administrators tried to stabilize New Spain in the usual way: by utilizing public ceremony and oratory to "speak" to subjects. Since at least 1765, New Spain had been undergoing a broad reform of its military, a project that placed intense pressure on the finances of municipal councils. In 1767, while keeping the secret that the expulsion of the Jesuits would take place in one short week, the viceroy ordered that 5,000 soldiers in Mexico City participate in the procession on the Thursday of Corpus Christi, a display of military power that had not happened previously.[10] Then, the following November, the viceroy hosted a commemoration intimately associated with Bourbon rule: the annual funerary honors for fallen soldiers. In an extraordinary move not seen since the War of the Spanish Succession, he also had the sermon printed.

To rescue the ceremony from its painful association with the Jesuit Order, the viceroy had it moved from its traditional home in the Jesuit Casa Profesa to the Franciscan convent on the same street, the Calle de los Plateros (Street of the Silversmiths). The printed sermon included a dedication to the viceroy that lauded his military achievements.[11] Then, in 1768, the viceroy chose to move the funerary honors to the cathedral, where it would continue to be celebrated through Independence. Cathedral canon Gregorio de Omaña gave the sermon and played on historical memory to legitimize current events. He began by celebrating the military for doing what was needed to defend the empire, regardless of the difficulty. He evoked key military figures from Spain's past, including conquistadors like Cortés, the Pizarros, the Almagros, and the Alvarados, and praised them for dying like men, and stated that they were worthy of immortality. As Omaña explained, their heroism naturally led to stains on their honor and, for this reason, the pious Carlos II established the annual masses throughout the empire. He praised Spain's military for repeatedly saving empire and Church from destruction, and tellingly, acknowledged Carlos III's father, Felipe V, in his struggle against the Grand Alliance during the War of the Spanish Succession. Right after the victory at Villaviciosa, Omaña described how Felipe V ordered 20,000 masses said for the dead in the monastery next door to the battle site.[12]

While refining their understandings of sacred kingship to meet the changing context and actions of the Crown, many struggled to reconcile the image of the sacred king with someone increasingly subject to scrutiny. For the cathedral of Mexico City's funerary honors for Carlos III in 1789, magistral canon José Serruto y Nava praised the monarch for professionalizing the military in both Spain and the Americas. He extolled the establishment of new regiments, squadrons, and military orders, and the generous distribution of grades, positions, prizes, and distinctions. Furthermore, the orator reminded his audience how the monarch modernized his empire in ways that had directly benefitted his subjects, lighting the streets of cities, and founding schools and hospitals in countless locations.[13]

But, in this résumé-like recounting of Carlos III's life, there remained little of the aura of sacred kingship expressed at the beginning of the century. This is not to say that orators stopped presenting the monarch as a "defender of the faith." Serruto y Nava recounted how Felipe V gave Carlos III a sword, stating, "This has been mine, of my Father Felipe and my Grandfather Luis, and I leave it to you, so that not forgetting our ancestors, you may employ it in defending the Religion." The sermon stressed that just like his ancestors, Carlos III respected the twin pillars of Spanish Catholicism: the Blessed Sacrament and the Immaculate Conception. It described how he surrendered his coach so that the Host could be taken with dignity to the bedside of a sick man, and how when the monarch established the Military Order of Carlos III, he placed it under the protection of the Immaculate Conception (1771). However, Serruto y Nava made no mention of the monarch's providential role or how these actions reaffirmed the sacred pact between God and Spain. Instead, he emphasized the king's pious example "And not only to the multitude of his subjects, and to the rest of the faithful who now occupy the Universe, but to all the generations that will succeed until the end." He concluded by stating that because of Carlos III's good works, his memory would always be "edifying."[14] Now, no longer an agent of Providence, the king served as an agent of progress, something achieved by encouraging ingenuity and industry. But, with all the gratitude that orators demanded for the king's specific accomplishments, what of his failures? If his achievements warranted praise, people likely understood that his missteps deserved criticism.

Skepticism regarding the king's infallibility increased with time. A king praised as like God the Father in 1724, transformed into a "heretic" in the eyes of many by 1767, only to be referred to as an edifying example who should be appreciated for all he did, with no mention of his mistakes. Nevertheless, deeply entrenched ideas continued to shape cultural understandings and expressions through Independence, even as some of the Crown's actions and policies could be perceived as anathema to sacred kingship. During New Spain's struggle for independence, as Fernando VII (1784–1833) remained imprisoned by Napoleon Bonaparte (1769–1821), two competing royal images persisted: a messianic redeemer and a fallible autocrat stripped of sacred authority. When the priest Miguel Hidalgo and military captain Ignacio Allende launched a movement for Independence in

1810, they, along with other first-wave insurgents, donned the so-called mask of Fernando, or what royalists perceived as feigned allegiance to Fernando VII. According to traditional interpretations, many insurgents cynically claimed to be fighting on behalf of the monarch for fear of alienating the popular classes, who remained loyal to "El Deseado" ("The Desire One").

Scholars have significantly nuanced this interpretation, illustrating that for many insurgents, adherence to monarchism in some form or another was more than a cynical ruse.[15] Eric Van Young, for example, illuminated the degree to which ideas of sacred kingship continued to influence the rural poor in New Spain during the struggle for Independence (1810–1821), something he regarded as an expression of "naïve monarchism," "indigenous messianism," vestiges of Joachimite prophecy, or a survival from the Habsburg era.[16] But, as *The Rebirth of the Spanish Empire* has illustrated, the Eucharistic and messianic idea of kingship prevalent at Independence did not represent a mere holdover from Habsburg Spain. Rather, early Bourbon supporters appropriated and amplified an idea of sacred kingship to legitimize Spain's new ruling dynasty. Furthermore, the idea of the monarchy as the body of the king – a sacred body composed of other *cuerpos* – persisted despite Bourbon innovations to both the administrative structure of the Spanish Empire, and to the image of the king.

As the empire fragmented, many cleaved to the body of the king, not only to be saved from the material hardship that preceded the Hidalgo Revolt in the *Bajío* region but to hold on to God and empire, something that people throughout New Spain had been cognitively trained to do. In November 1810, a group of male and female insurgents near Celaya claimed that the king physically resided in New Spain and ordered Miguel Hidalgo to take up arms in his name. Tellingly, the insurgents also claimed that the king rode around the countryside in a black coach, reminiscent of that which often carried the Eucharist; significantly, he also wore a reflective silver mask to turn himself invisible, like a "Hidden King" or Encubierto, or to, perhaps, evoke the sun. Witnesses claimed that people knelt before the coach and walked away happy, as if blessed. Furthermore, like the presence of Jesus Christ in the Eucharist, the monarch defied the laws of space and time, appearing in different locations at roughly the same time throughout the wars of Independence. In various expressions of popular millenarianism recounted by Van Young, people claimed that the king would redistribute wealth and remedy injustices.[17]

Although New Spain's rural people clearly projected messianic expectations onto the Crown, for many others, monarchy remained the ideal, and hence, Independence leaders established an "empire" as their first experiment in state-building (1822–1823). Afterward, many conservatives remained closeted monarchists and continued to apologize for, or even outrightly celebrate, monarchy. Also, in what can be interpreted as the ultimate expression of the deep structures undergirding the political culture of nineteenth-century Mexico, conservatives eventually pinned their hopes for a Second Mexican Empire on an Austrian Habsburg, the ill-fated Maximilian I (1832–1867). Finally, in the populism of national leaders like Antonio López de Santa Anna (1794–1876) and Porfirio Díaz (1830–1915), we can see reflections and amplifications of people's messianic expectations, and in the alarming rise of populist authoritarians throughout the world today, we can discern the naïve, and often betrayed, hope for salvation.

The ways in which thought patterns tied to sacred kingship both shaped and conflicted with evolving representations of Bourbon absolutism – and the extent to which these patterns endure – merit further investigation. This study has offered an interpretation of how people sustained and shaped a concept of empire during a transformative period of dynastic change, arguing that Bourbon supporters in New Spain established the dynasty's legitimacy on a complex conception of monarchy nurtured over centuries. In a moment of deep insecurity and uncertainty, orators, bureaucrats, satirists, and artists relied on the semiotics of sacred kingship to invest people in a reinvigorated Spanish Empire. Their efforts remind us that even in times of rupture, political imagination draws power from inherited symbols – and that power, like sovereignty, persists not merely through institutional authority but through shared cultural understandings.

Notes

Introduction

1 Agustín de Mora, *El sol eclipsado antes de llegar al zenit: Real pira que incendió à la apagada luz del rey N.S.D. Carlos II en la Santa Iglesia Catedral Metropolitana de la ciudad de México* (Mexico City: n.p., 1701).
2 Víctor Mínguez Cornelles, *Los reyes solares: Iconografía astral de la monarquía hispánica* (Castelló de la Plana: Publicacions de la Universitat Jaume I, 2001), 35–68; Jonathan Brown and John Huxtable Elliott, *A Palace for a King: The Buen Retiro and the Court of Philip IV* (New Haven: Yale University Press, 2003); Peter Burke, *The Fabrication of Louis XIV* (New Haven: Yale University Press, 1994).
3 Mora, *El sol eclipsado*.
4 For a discussion of events leading up to the war, see Henry Kamen, *Philip V of Spain: The King Who Reigned Twice* (New Haven: Yale University Press, 2001), 1–33.
5 Revelation 12:1.
6 Mínguez Cornelles, *Los reyes solares*, 263.
7 Mínguez Cornelles, *Los reyes solares*, 260.
8 Mora, *El sol eclipsado*, not numerated.
9 James George Frazer, *The Golden Bough: A Study in Magic and Religion* (New York: Simon and Schuster, 1995; orig. pub. 1890). David Graeber and Marshall Sahlins discuss the endurance of Frazier's argument that deep structures shape ideas of sacred kingship. They recognize the importance of Frazier's emphasis on ideas of sacrifice, fertility, and regeneration undergirding premodern and, to a large degree, early modern notions of sacred kingship. See *On Kings* (New York: Hau Books, 2017).
10 See Marc Bloch's classic study *The Royal Touch: Sacred Monarchy and Scrofula in England and France*, trans. J. E. Anderson (New York: Routledge, 2015; orig. pub. 1973). For a specific analysis of the presentation of the king's sacred body during funerary rituals in France, see Ralph E. Giesey, *The Royal Funeral Ceremony in Renaissance France* (Geneva: Droz, 1960).

11 Teofilo F. Ruíz, *Spain's Centuries of Crisis: 1300–1474* (Oxford: Wiley, 2008), especially chapter 6.
12 Víctor Mínguez Cornelles, "Los emperadores taumaturgos: curaciones prodigiosas desde Trajano a Napoleón," *Potestas*, no. 5 (2015): 43–81.
13 Víctor Mínguez Cornelles, "Reyes enfermos e imperio renovado. Las muertes de Felipe IV, Carlos II, Luis XIV, Luis I y Felipe V en la Nueva España (1665–1746)," *Romance Notes* 56, no. 3 (2016): 415.
14 Mínguez Cornelles, *Los reyes solares*, 157–166.
15 Antonio de Posada, *Sermon funeral de las sumptuosas honras, que en el Convento de San Francisco de la ciudad de la Vera-Cruz, celebró el dia 23 de abril de 1701 a n. gran rey, y catholico monarca Dn. Carlos II de inmortal memoria* (Mexico City: Imprenta de Juan Joseph Guillena Carrascoso, 1701), 2, 13. During Mexico City's funerary honors for Philip III in 1666, Isidro Sariñana also referenced this etymology. See *Llanto del occidente en el ocaso del mas claro sol de las Españas* (Mexico City: Viuda de Bernardo Calderón, 1666).
16 Blas del Pulgar, *Oracion panegyrica, y declamacion funebre, en las solemnes exequias, que celebrò el Real Convento de N.P.S. Francisco de Mexico, dia 13. de mayo de 1701 por muerte del Rey Nuestro Señor, el Señor D. Carlos II. Rey de las Españas, y las Indias, el Catholico, el Pio, el Religioso* (Mexico City: Herederos de la Viuda de Francisco Rodriguez Lupercio, 1701), 7.
17 Maximiliano López de Pro, *Caminos de verdad, mansedumbre, y justicia. Señales que dexo estampadas en ellos la S.A.C. y R. Magestad de el Señor D. Carlos Segundo, Rey de las Españas (…) en las honras que le hizo el Imperial Convento de N. P. S. Francisco de la ciudad de Tlaxcala el dia 11 del mes de agosto, del año de 1701* (Puebla: Imprenta del Capitán Sebastián de Guevara, 1701), 5v–6.
18 Helen Rawlings, *The Debate on the Decline of Spain* (Manchester: Manchester University Press, 2012), 31–49.
19 J. H. Elliott, "Self-Perception and Decline in Early Seventeenth-Century Spain," *Past & Present*, no. 74 (1977): 41–61.
20 Christopher Storrs, *The Resilience of the Spanish Monarchy, 1665–1700* (Oxford: Oxford University Press, 2006).
21 Luis Ribot, "El rey ante el espejo: historia y memoria de Carlos II," in *Carlos II: el rey y su entorno cortesano*, ed. Luis Ribot (Madrid: Centro de Estudios Europa Hispánica, 2009), 13–52.
22 Silvia Z. Mitchell, "The Spanish Habsburg Court during the Reign of Carlos II (1665–1700)," *The Court Historian* 23, no. 2 (December 2018), 107–112; Silvia Z. Mitchell, "Women and Children First: Court Ceremonial during Carlos II's Minority, 1665–1675," *The Court Historian* 23, no. 2 (December 2018), 135–151.
23 Ribot, "El rey ante el espejo," 23–30.
24 Henry Kamen, *Spain in the Later Seventeenth Century, 1665–1700* (London: Longman, 1980), 390–391.
25 Antonio de Robles, *Diario de sucesos notables (1665–1703)*, vol. 2 (Mexico City: Editorial Porrúa, 1972), 18.

26 For a discussion of the rumors surrounding Carlos II's health, see Tom Töle, *Heirs of Flesh and Paper: A European History of Dynastic Knowledge around 1700* (Berlin: De Gruyter Oldenbourg, 2022), 20–59.
27 Richard L. Kagan and Fernando Marías Franco, *Urban Images of the Hispanic World, 1493–1793* (New Haven: Yale University Press, 2000), 28.
28 Cristina Borreguero Beltrán, "Imagen y propaganda de guerra en el conflicto sucesorio (1700–1713)," *Manuscrits: revista d'història moderna*, no. 21 (2003): 96.
29 Antonio Feros, *Speaking of Spain: The Evolution of Race and Nation in the Hispanic World* (Cambridge, MA: Harvard University Press, 2017); Anthony P. Cohen observed long ago that communities tend to define themselves when attacked from without. See *The Symbolic Construction of Community* (London: Routledge & Kegan Paul, 1985).
30 Karen Melvin looks at the process of attaching *novohispanos* to the broader empire in "Charity without Borders: Alms-Giving in New Spain for Captives in North Africa," *Colonial Latin American Review* 18, no. 1 (2009): 75–97. Also see Alejandro Cañeque García, *Un imperio de mártires: Religión y poder en las fronteras de la Monarquía Hispánica* (Madrid: Marcial Pons Ediciones de Historia, S.A., 2020).
31 In this book, I use both "Spanish Empire" and *Monarquía Hispánica* interchangeably, while remaining attentive to their distinct historiographical and conceptual meanings. I retain both because I am often referring to the imagined whole – the vast and heterogeneous expanse of territory under the sovereignty of the Habsburg and Bourbon Crowns. "Spanish Empire" highlights the global scope and imperial strategies of monarchical rule, especially in relation to Bourbon centralization and New World propaganda. *Monarquía Hispánica*, a term more common in contemporary sources, reflects the composite structure of the early modern monarchy: a union of kingdoms and jurisdictions governed by shared sovereignty but distinct laws and institutions. My choice to use both also mirrors the flexible and often fluid vocabulary of early eighteenth-century actors, who invoked different idioms of rule depending on context and audience.
32 See J. H. Elliott, "A Europe of Composite Monarchies," *Past & Present* 137 (November 1992): 48–71.
33 For an analysis of Felipe V's early policies toward the Crown of Aragon, see Joaquim Albareda i Salvadó, *Felipe V y el triunfo del absolutismo: Cataluña en un conflicto europeo, 1700–1714* (Barcelona: Generalitat de Catalunya, Entitat Autònoma del Diari Oficial i de Publicacions, 2002).
34 Allan J. Kuethe and Kenneth J. Andrien, *The Spanish Atlantic World in the Eighteenth Century: War and the Bourbon Reforms, 1713–1796* (New York: Cambridge University Press, 2014).
35 Linda Curcio-Nagy, *The Great Festivals of Colonial Mexico City: Performing Power and Identity* (Albuquerque: University of New Mexico Press, 2004); Frances L. Ramos, *Identity, Ritual, and Power in Colonial Puebla* (Tucson: University of Arizona Press, 2012), especially chapter 2. Ángel López Cantos illustrates this for Puerto Rico and Guatemala in *Juegos, fiestas y diversiones en la América Española* (Madrid: Editorial MAPFRE, 1992).

36 Analola Borges, "Los aliados del Archiduque Carlos en la América virreinal," *Anuario de estudios americanos* 27 (1970): 321–370; Luis Navarro García, "Cambio de dinastía en Nueva España," *Anuario de estudios americanos* 36 (1979): 111–168; Luis Navarro García, *Conspiración en México durante el gobierno del Virrey Alburquerque* (Valladolid: Casa-Museo de Colón; Seminario Americanista de la Universidad de Valladolid, 1982); Pedro E. Pérez-Mallaina Bueno, *Política naval española en el Atlántico (1700–1715)* (Sevilla: Escuela de Estudios Hispano-Americanos de Sevilla, 1982).

37 Luis Navarro García, "Los oficios vendibles en Nueva España durante la Guerra de Sucesión," *Anuario de estudios americanos* 32 (1975): 133–154; Alfredo Moreno Cebrián and Núria Sala i Vila, *El "premio" de ser virrey: Los intereses públicos y privados del gobierno virreinal en el Perú de Felipe V* (Madrid: Consejo Superior de Investigaciones Científicas, 2004); Francisco Andújar Castillo, *Necesidad y venalidad: España e Indias 1704–1711* (Madrid: Centro de Estudios Políticos y Constitucionales, 2008); Christoph Rosenmüller, *Corruption and Justice in Colonial Mexico, 1650–1755* (Cambridge: Cambridge University Press, 2019).

38 Aaron Alejandro Olivas, "Loyalty and Disloyalty to the Bourbon Dynasty in Spanish America and the Philippines during the War of the Spanish Succession (1700–1715)" (PhD, University of California, Los Angeles, 2013); Christoph Rosenmüller, *Patrons, Partisans, and Palace Intrigues: The Court Society of Colonial Mexico, 1702–1710* (Calgary: University of Calgary Press, 2008).

39 Iván Escamilla González, *Los intereses malentendidos: El consulado de comerciantes de México y la Monarquía Española, 1700–1739* (Mexico City: Universidad Nacional Autónoma de México, Instituto de Investigaciones Históricas, 2011).

40 María Teresa Pérez Picazo, *La publicitista española en la Guerra de Sucesión*, vols. 1–2 (Madrid: Consejo Superior de Investigaciones Científicas, 1966).

41 See *Guerra de religión entre príncipes católicos: el discurso del cambio dinástico en España y América (1700–1714)* (Madrid: Ministerio de Defensa, 2002). For his analysis of the types of propaganda disseminated throughout the war, see *Propaganda e información en tiempos de Guerra: España y América (1700–1714)* (Madrid: Silex, 2009).

42 For an excellent study that takes this approach, see Jodi Campbell, *Monarchy, Political Culture, and Drama in Seventeenth-Century Madrid: Theater of Negotiation* (New York: Routledge, 2016).

43 Iván Escamilla González, "Razones de la lealtad, cláusulas de la fineza: poderes, conflictos y consensos en la oratoria sagrada novohispana ante la sucesión de Felipe V," in *Religión, poder y autoridad en la Nueva España*, ed. Iván Escamilla González, Alicia Mayer, and Ernesto de la Torre Villar (Mexico City: Universidad Nacional Autónoma de Mexico, 2004), 179–204; Frances L. Ramos, "Succession and Death: Royal Ceremonies in Colonial Puebla," *The Americas* 60, no. 2 (2003): 185–215; Frances L. Ramos, "Arte efímero, espectáculo, y la reafirmación de la autoridad real en Puebla durante el siglo XVIII: La celebración en honor del Hércules borbónico," *Relaciones* 25, no. 97 (Winter 2004): 179–218.

44 Frances L. Ramos and Iván Escamilla González, "Sucesión y renovación del cuerpo de la monarquía: Las representaciones de Felipe V y la familia real en Nueva España durante la Guerra de Sucesión," *Colonial Latin American Review* 31, no. 3 (2022): 381–410.
45 See David González Cruz, "Celebraciones de victorias militares de la monarquía hispánica en sus dominios de Europa y América (siglos XVII y XVIII)," in *Ocio y vida cotidiana en el mundo hispánico en la edad moderna*, ed. Francisco Núñez Roldán (Sevilla: Editorial Universidad de Sevilla-Secretariado de Publicaciones, 2007), 231–244; Frances L. Ramos, "Un puñal, un tóxico, que quita la vida de toda una monarquía: ceremonias públicas, sermones panegíricos, y el discurso anti-inglés en la víspera de Utrecht," in *Resonancias imperiales: América y el Tratado de Utrecht*, ed. Iván Escamilla González, Matilde Suoto Mantecón, and Guadalupe Pinzón Ríos (Mexico City: Instituto de Investigaciones Dr. José María Luis Mora, 2015), 121–148; Frances L. Ramos, "War, Legitimacy, and Ceremony in 18th-Century Mexico City: The Annual Funerary Honors for Fallen Soldiers," in *A Companion to Viceregal Mexico City, 1521–1821*, ed. John F. López (Leiden: Brill, 2021), 114–133.
46 Ramos, "Arte efímero," 179–218.
47 Ramos, "Un puñal," 121–148. This can also be translated as the Feast of Reparation to the Most Blessed Sacrament.
48 See Yu. M. Lotman and B. A. Uspensky, "On the Semiotic Mechanism of Culture," *New Literary History* 9, no. 2 (1978): 211–232.
49 See Benedict Anderson, *Imagined Communities: Reflections on the Origin and Spread of Nationalism* (London: Verso, 2006; orig. pub. 1983).
50 Alejandra B. Osorio, "The Copy as Original: The Presence of the Absent Spanish Habsburg King and Colonial Hybridity," *Renaissance Studies* 34, no. 4 (2020): 704–721.
51 David I. Kertzer, *Ritual, Politics, and Power* (New Haven: Yale University Press, 1988), 11.
52 Osorio, "The Copy as Original," 704–721.
53 Salvador Alejandro Lira Saucedo analyzes the visual tropes employed in dynastic rituals conducted during the war. See "El discurso visual en la transición dinástica de Austrias a Borbones," in *Semiótica e historia*, ed. Carmen Fernández Galán Montemayor, Alfredo Tenoch Cid Jurado, and Víctor Manuel Chávez Ríos (Zacatecas: Universidad Autónoma de Zacatecas, 2018), 65–98.
54 Thomas Calvo, "La construcción de una cultura imperial: Zaragoza, Valladolid de Michoacán, Lima y Manila lloran al Príncipe Baltasar Carlos (1647–1648)," in *Convergencias y divergencias: México y Perú, siglos XVI–XIX*, ed. Lilia V. Oliver Sánchez (Guadalajara: University of Guadalajara, 2006), 101–128.
55 Although John Leddy Phelan and Georges Baudot argued that the early friars had a utopian and even millenarian perspective on the evangelization of Mesoamerica, Elsa Frost sustained that the term has been misapplied. For her, millenarianism can only be understood as a popular phenomenon aimed at challenging the status quo. However, as I make clear later, millenarian

propaganda related to a paradisical age following the defeat of the anti-Christ has been historically applied to the reigns of numerous European kings. See John Leddy Phelan, *The Millennial Kingdom of the Franciscans in the New World*, 2nd ed. (Berkeley: University of California Press, 1970); Georges Baudot, *Utopia and History in Mexico: The First Chroniclers of Mexican Civilization (1520–1569)* (Niwot: University Press of Colorado, 1995); Elsa Cecilia Frost, "El milenarismo franciscano en México y el profeta Daniel," *Historia Mexicana* 26, no. 1 (1976): 3–28.

56 Luis Weckman, *The Medieval Heritage of Mexico* (New York: Fordham University Press, 1992); Antonio Rubial García, *El paraíso de los elegidos. Una lectura de la historia cultural de Nueva España* (Mexico City: Fondo de Cultura Económica, 2011). Also see D. A. Brading, "Tridentine Catholicism and Enlightened Despotism in Bourbon Mexico," *Journal of Latin American Studies* 15, no. 1 (1983): 1–22.

Chapter 1

1 Diego Jiménez to the King, Veracruz, November 28, 1712, AGI, México, leg. 562.
2 Andújar Castillo, *Necesidad y venalidad*, 6–7.
3 The general narrative of the war in the Spanish kingdoms is well known. For a recent and comprehensive analysis, see Joaquim Albareda Salvadó, *La Guerra de Sucesión de España (1700 – 1714)* (Barcelona: Crítica, 2012).
4 Albareda Salvadó, *La Guerra de Sucesión*, 122–159.
5 Albareda Salvadó, *La Guerra de Sucesión*, 122–159.
6 Diversas letras patentes del Comisario General de Nueva España y del Ministro Provincial del Santo Evangelio de México, 1703. Archivo Franciscano, BNM-FR, leg. 141, Exp. 1731.1.
7 Albareda Salvadó, *La Guerra de Sucesión*, 122–159.
8 Albareda i Salvadó, *Felipe V y el triunfo del absolutismo*, especially chapter 1.
9 Albareda i Salvadó, *Felipe V y el triunfo del absolutismo*, 60–75.
10 Kamen, *Spain in the Later Seventeenth Century*, 183–189.
11 Albareda Salvadó, *La Guerra de Sucesión*, 122–159.
12 Albareda Salvadó, *La Guerra de Sucesión*, 122–159.
13 For an analysis of the long-term financial and political impact of the War of the Spanish Succession on France, see Guy Rowlands, *The Financial Decline of a Great Power: War, Influence, and Money in Louis XIV's France* (Oxford: Oxford University Press, 2012).
14 For the Pope's position during the War of the Spanish Succession, see David Martín Marcos, *El papado y la Guerra de Sucesión Española* (Madrid: Marcial Pons Historia, 2011).
15 Henry Kamen, *The War of Succession in Spain, 1700–1715* (Bloomington: Indiana University Press, 1969), 20–24.
16 See Ramos, "War, Legitimacy, and Ceremony," 114–133.
17 Kamen, *The War of the Spanish Succession*, 23–24.

18 Jean de Monségur, *Las nuevas memorias del capitán Jean de Monségur*, ed. and trans. Jean-Pierre Berthe (México: Universidad Nacional Autónoma de México, Instituto de Investigaciones Históricas, 1994), 16; Sylvia Sellers-García, *Distance and Documents at the Spanish Empire's Periphery* (Stanford: Stanford University Press, 2014).
19 Based on silver content, 750,000 pesos in the early eighteenth century would be equivalent to approximately US$19.8 million today. Adjusted for purchasing power or economic impact, the value could range between US$45 and US$75 million, depending on the methodology used. See John J. McCusker, *How Much Is That in Real Money? A Historical Price Index for Use as a Deflator of Money Values in the Economy of the United States*, 3rd ed. (Worcester, MA: American Antiquarian Society, 2001), 4–9.
20 Joseph M. H. Clark, *Veracruz and the Caribbean in the Seventeenth Century* (Cambridge: Cambridge University Press, 2022), 226–229; Ben Vinson, *Bearing Arms for His Majesty: The Free-Colored Militia in Colonial Mexico* (Stanford: Stanford University Press, 2001), 29–30; Pablo Miguel Sierra Silva, "Afro-Mexican Women in Saint-Domingue: Piracy, Captivity, and Community in the 1680s and 1690s," *Hispanic American Historical Review* 100, no.1 (2020): 3–34.
21 Viceroy of New Spain to the king, Mexico City, October 5, 1700, AGI, México, leg. 472.
22 King to the viceroy of New Spain, Madrid, March 2, 1700, AGN, RC, vol. 29, exp. 41, fols. 107–109. Also see Christopher Storrs, "Disaster at Darien (1698–1700)? The Persistence of Spanish Imperial Power on the Eve of the Demise of the Spanish Habsburgs," *European History Quarterly* 29, no.1 (January 1999), 5–38. *Escudos* were typically valued at 16 silver *reales* or 2 silver *pesos*. In the seventeenth and eighteenth centuries, an *escudo* represented a high-denomination currency used in large transactions or state finances.
23 See José Ignacio Rubio Mañé, *El virreinato: expansión y defensa*, part 2, vol. 3 (Mexico City: Fondo de Cultura Económica, 1961), 265–321. Documentation included in this collection also shows that some Frenchmen cut dyewood in the lagoon. For an excellent discussion of the dyewood communities, see Jesse Cromwell, "Life on the Margins: (Ex) Buccaneers and Spanish Subjects on the Campeche Logwood Periphery, 1660–1716," *Itinerario* 33, no. 3 (2009), 43–71.
24 Viceroy of New Spain to the king, Mexico City, May 5, 1701. AGI, México, leg. 472.
25 Queen and governors to the Viceroy, the Duke of Alburquerque, Madrid, July 24, 1702, AGN, RC, vol. 31, exp. 36.
26 Borges, "Los aliados del Archiduque," 321–370.
27 Robles, *Diario de sucesos*, 3: 202–203, 209.
28 Robles, *Diario de sucesos*, 3: 269.
29 King to the viceroy of New Spain, Corella, July 26, 1711, AGN, RC, vol. 35, exp. 49.
30 The Viceroy, the Count of Moctezuma, to the King, Mexico City, May 20, 1701, AGI, México, leg. 472.

31 Rubio Mañé, *El virreinato*, 270–272.
32 María Ángeles Eugenio Martínez, *La defensa de Tabasco, 1600–1717* (Seville: Escuela de Estudios Hispanoamericanos de Sevilla, 1971), 101.
33 King to the viceroy of New Spain, Madrid, January 9, 1703, AGN, RC, vol. 31, exp. 138.
34 Eugenio Martínez, *La defensa de Tabasco*, 104.
35 Eugenio Martínez, *La defensa de Tabasco*, 108–109.
36 Cromwell, "Life on the Margins," 55–57.
37 Pérez-Mallaina Bueno, *Política naval*, 46–47.
38 Eugenio Martínez, *La defensa de Tabasco*, 118–123.
39 Eugenio Martínez, *La defensa de Tabasco*, 136.
40 David Marley, *Wars of the Americas: A Chronology of Armed Conflict in the New World* (Santa Barbara: ABC-CLIO, 1998), 223–224; Informe de Cristóbal Villareal, oidor de la real audiencia de México, sobre la recuperación de la Provincia de Apalache, n.d., AGI, México, leg. 477.
41 Cardinal Portocarrero to the Archbishop-Viceroy of New Spain, Madrid, May 8, 1702, in *Cédulario americano del siglo XVIII: Colección de disposiciones legales indianas desde 1680 a 1800, contenidas en los cedularios del Archivo General de Indias*, vol. 2, ed. Antonio Muro Orejón (Seville: Escuela de Estudios Hispano-Americanos de Sevilla, 1969), 51; Robles, *Diario de sucesos notables*, 3: 248; *Índice general de las cartas del arzobispo virrey de Nueva España y de los ministros y comunidades eclesiásticas y seculares de su distrito y jurisdicción*, n.d., AGI, México, leg. 460.
42 Rubio Mañé, *El virreinato*, 2:3, 270–272.
43 Francisco de Seijas y Lobera, *Gobierno militar y político del reino imperial de la Nueva España, (1702)* (Mexico City: Universidad Nacional Autónoma de México, 1986), 28.
44 King to the viceroy, the Duke of Alburquerque, Trujillo, July 7, 1704, AGN, vol. 32, exp. 39, fols. 81–82v.
45 Robles, *Diario de sucesos notables*, 3: 210–211, 301–302.
46 Copia de la carta original que queda en esta señoría de Indias parte de Nueva España de donde se sacó para emitir al excelentísimo Señor Duque de Alburquerque Virrey Gobernador y Capitán General de las provincias de Nueva España y Presidente de la Audiencia, Mexico City, December 12, 1705, AGN, RC, vol. 31, exp. s/n.
47 Eugenio Martínez, *La defensa de Tabasco*.
48 Memorial de Manuel de Landaeta, 1712, AGI, México, leg. 562.
49 Memorial de Manuel de Landaeta, 1712, AGI, México, leg. 562.
50 Viceroy of New Spain to the king, Mexico City, September 20, 1707, AGI, México, leg. 480.
51 Testimonio de los autos hechos sobre las providencias dadas por el excelentísimo virrey, 1707, AGI, México, leg. 480, exp. 1, fols. 1–25.
52 Testimonio de los autos hechos sobre las providencias dadas por el excelentísimo virrey, 1707, AGI, México leg. 480, exp. 1, fols. 1–8.
53 Testimonio de los autos hechos sobre las providencias dadas por el excelentísimo virrey, 1707, AGI, México leg. 480, exp. 3, fols. 13–25. For a discussion of the role of the *casta* population in the "Corn Riot," see Douglas

R. Cope, *The Limits of Racial Domination: Plebeian Society in Colonial Mexico City, 1660–1720* (Madison: University of Wisconsin Press, 1994).
54 Testimonio de los autos hechos sobre las providencias dadas por el excelentísimo virrey, 1707, AGI, México leg. 480, exp. 3, fols. 13–25.
55 Testimonio de los autos hechos sobre las providencias dadas por el excelentísimo virrey, 1707, AGI, México leg. 480, exp. 4–8, fols. 32–192.
56 Pérez-Mallaina Bueno, *Política naval*, 49; King to the viceroy, the Duke of Linares, Corella, July 26, 1711, AGN, RC, vol. 35, exp. 49.
57 Henry Kamen, "The Destruction of the Spanish Silver Fleet at Vigo," *Bulletin of the Institute of Historical Research* 39, no. 100 (November 1966): 165–175.
58 Pérez-Mallaina Bueno, *Política naval*, 9–10, 56.
59 Stein and Stein, *Silver, Trade, and War*, 181.
60 Queen and governors to the viceroy of New Spain, Barcelona, March 31, 1702, AGN, RC, vol. 31, exp. 10.
61 King to the viceroy of New Spain, Madrid, July 31, 1704, AGN, RC, vol. 32, exp. 45; Juan Joseph de Veytia y Linaje to the king, Puebla, September 18, 1706, AGI, México 478; King to viceroy of New Spain, n.p., January 20, 1711, AGN, RC, vol. 35, exp. 8; For the zealousness of Veytia y Linaje and the political disruption caused by the collection in Puebla, see Frances L. Ramos, "Custom, Corruption, and Reform in Early Eighteenth-Century Mexico: Puebla's Merchant Priests versus the Reformist Bureaucrat," in *Corruption in the Iberian Empires: Greed, Custom, and Colonial Networks*, ed. Christoph Rosenmüller (Alburquerque: University of New Mexico Press, 2017), 151–169.
62 See, for example, King to the viceroy of New Spain, Madrid, November 6, 1707, AGN, RC, vol. 33, exp. 82.
63 King to the viceroy of New Spain, Corella, July 24, 1711, AGN, RC, vol. 35, exp. 47.
64 Al virrey de la Nueva España ordenándole cometa a ministros de su satisfacción la averiguación de los que fueron cómplices en la perdida de la Almirante de Barlovento, Madrid, May 20, 1712, AGN, RC, vol. 35, exp. 75; King to the viceroy of New Spain, Madrid, July 9, 1712, AGN, RC, vol. 35, exp. 82.
65 King to the viceroy of New Spain, Madrid, December 20, 1707, in *Cédulario americano*, ed. Muro Orejón, 72–74; the original cédula is referred to in this particular decree.
66 King to the viceroy of New Spain, Zaragoza, January 11, 1711, AGN, RC, vol. 35, exp. 2, fols. 5–7v. The cédula indicates that it was raised to 10 percent in 1709.
67 King to the viceroy of New Spain, Madrid, August 28, 1703, AGN, RC, vol. 31, exp. 91.
68 Andújar Castillo, *Necesidad y venalidad*, 26.
69 Viceroy of New Spain to the king, Madrid, March 1, 1704, in *Cédulario americano*, ed. Muro Orejón, 118–120.
70 Queen and governors to the viceroy of New Spain, January 11, 1701, in *Cédulario americano*, ed. Muro Orejón, 9–10.

71 While collecting donations for the Crown in 1744, local magistrates in Puebla threatened to put locks on the spinning wheels of local weavers. See Frances L. Ramos, "Memoria colectiva y disensión política en la Puebla del siglo XIII, México: el motín en honor del obispo Juan de Palafox y Mendoza," *Historia Mexicana* 62, no. 3 (2013), 1019–1074.
72 Escamilla González, *Los intereses malentendidos*, 81–82; Robles, *Diario de sucesos*, 3: 248.
73 Elienahí Nieves, "Donativo de los hacendados de Nueva España para financiar la Guerra de Sucesión Española, 1709–1716," *América Latina en la historia económica* 28, num. 3 (2021), 1–19.
74 Robles, *Diario de sucesos*, 3: 290, 299.
75 Viceroy, the Duke of Alburquerque, to the king, Mexico City, April 16, 1708. AGI, México, leg. 480.
76 José Ángel del Barrio Muñoz, *Filipinas y la Guerra de Sucesión Española: Avatares y sucesos en un frente secundario (1701–1715)* (Valladolid: Castilla Ediciones, 2015), 39–51.
77 Diego de Gorospe Irala, *Sermon que en la solemnissima declaracion de la jura del serenissimo Señor D. Luys Fernando de Borbon Principe de Asturias N. Señor aclamada en la coronada Villa de Madrid el dia del mes del año passado [Sic] de 1707 y proclamada en la Muy Noble, y Leal ciudad de Manila el dia XIV de enero de este presente año de MDCCXII* (Manila: Convento de N.P.S Francisco, por Francisco de los Santos, 1712).
78 See Ramos, "Custom, Corruption, and Reform," 151–169.
79 Escamilla González, *Los intereses malentendidos*, 86.
80 Rosenmüller, *Patrons, Partisans, and Palace Intrigues*, 79–87.
81 Escamilla González, "Razones de la lealtad," 181.
82 Rosenmüller, *Patrons, Partisans, and Palace Intrigues*, 79–96.
83 Rosenmüller, *Patrons, Partisans, and Palace Intrigues*, 79–96.
84 Guillermina del Valle Pavón, "Servicios financieros del consulado de México para la Guerra de Sucesión dinástica," *Mélanges de la Casa de Velázquez* 46, no. 1 (2016), 77–88.
85 Viceroy, the Duke of Alburquerque, to the king, Mexico City, December 20, 1707, AGI, México, leg. 479.
86 Crown to the viceroy of New Spain, Madrid, December 31, 1701, and the Crown to the viceroy of New Spain, Madrid, January 11, 1701, in *Cédulario americano*, ed. Muro Orejón, 7–8, 8–9.
87 Pablo E. Pérez-Mallaína Bueno, "La Guerra de Sucesión y la reforma del sistema de comunicaciones con América," in *La Guerra de Sucesión en España y América, Actas X Jornadas Nacionales de Historia Militar, Sevilla, 13–17 de Noviembre de 2000* (Madrid: Deímos, 2001), 347–360.
88 Pérez-Mallaína Bueno, *Política naval*, 9–11.
89 Pérez-Mallaína Bueno, "La Guerra de Sucesión," 356.
90 Escamilla González, *Los intereses malentendidos*, 102–103.
91 Rosenmüller, *Corruption and Justice in Colonial Mexico*, 123–152.
92 Andújar Castillo, *Necesidad y venalidad*. The Cámara de Indias, or Chamber of the Indies, functioned as a specialized branch within the Council of the Indies, overseeing the financial aspects of viceregal administration.
93 Andújar Castillo, *Necesidad y venalidad*, 1–15, 25.

94 Navarro García, "Los oficios vendibles en Nueva España, 141.
95 Andújar Castillo, *Necesidad y venalidad*, 265.
96 "Juan de Díez de Bracamonte, Real Academia de La Historia," accessed December 13, 2023. https://dbe.rah.es/biografias/63375/juan-de-diez-de-bracamonte.
97 See Manuel de Argüello, *Accion de gracias, a la soberana reyna del cielo Maria SS. de Guadalupe en su magnifico templo, con que solemnizò el real acuerdo de esta corte, en virtùd de real orden, las victorias, que consiguiò personalmente la magestad del Rey nuestro Señor Don Philippo V. (que Dios guarde) en Viruega, y Villaviciosa los dias 8. y 11. de diziembre del año de 1710* (Mexico City: Viuda de Miguel de Ribera, 1711).
98 Navarro García, "Los oficios vendibles," 146–147.
99 Nieves, "El donativo de los hacendados," 1–19.
100 Navarro García, "Los oficios vendibles," 147–148.
101 Andújar Castillo, *Necesidad y venalidad*, 274–275.
102 Andújar Castillo, *Necesidad y venalidad*, 262–263.
103 Andújar Castillo, *Necesidad y venalidad*, 276.
104 Andújar Castillo, *Necesidad y venalidad*, 278–279.

Chapter 2

1 Robles, *Diario de sucesos notables*, 3: 132–135.
2 See Jürgen Habermas, *The Structural Transformation of the Public Sphere: An Inquiry into a Category of Bourgeois Society*, trans. Thomas Burger (Cambridge, MA: The MIT Press, 1989; orig. pub. 1962).
3 On the early modern public sphere in the Spanish kingdoms, see Fernando Bouza Álvarez, *Papeles y opinión: Políticas de publicación en el Siglo de Oro* (Madrid: Consejo Superior de Investigaciones Cientificas, 2008), Michele Olivari, *Avisos, pasquines y rumores: Los comienzos de la opinión pública en la España del siglo XVII* (Madrid: Ediciones Cátedra, 2014), and Egido, Teófanes, *Opinión pública y oposición al poder en la España del siglo XVIII: (1713–1759)* (Valladolid Universidad de Valladolid, 2002).
4 William Childers, "The Baroque Public Sphere," in *Reason and Its Others: Italy, Spain, and the New World*, ed. David R. Castillo and Massimo Lollin (Nashville: Vanderbilt University Press, 2006), 165–181. Gabriel Torres Puga has also studied the eighteenth-century "public sphere," but roughly sixty years in the future. He understands the "public sphere" as related to the reading cultures of the Enlightenment. *Opinión pública y censura en Nueva España: indicios de un silencio imposible (1767–1794)* (Mexico City: Colegio de México, 2010).
5 Fernando J. Bouza Álvarez stresses that these are key attributes of the early modern public sphere. See *Communication, Knowledge, and Memory in Early Modern Spain* (Philadelphia: University of Pennsylvania Press, 2004).
6 This, according to José Antonio Maravall, was a defining characteristic of seventeenth-century Spanish culture. See *The Culture of the Baroque: Analysis of a Historical Structure*, trans. Terry Cochran (Minneapolis: University of Minnesota Press, 1986; orig. pub. 1975).

7 María Rosa Cal Martínez, "'La Gazeta' de Madrid y la Guerra de Sucesión," *Cuadernos dieciochistas*, no. 3 (2002), 35–56.
8 González Cruz, *Guerra de religión*, 33.
9 Edicto de Inquisición, Mexico City, June 6, 1707, AGN, IV-Edictos de Inquisición, caja 6222, exp. 2.
10 Specifically, the Inquisitors sought couplets that began with *Llegò el día si no me engaño* and ended with *Nos reynarà el Archi-duque* and another that began *Qué importa que lo mande el mismo Rey* and ended with *Mientras se muere el Asno y quien lo arrea*. Edicto de Inquisición, Mexico City, 1707, AGN, IV-Edicto de Inquisición, caja 6604, exp. 50.
11 Francisco Solanes, *El emperador politico, y politica de emperadores: Vida del emperador Ulpio Trajano sacada del panegyrico de Plinio Menor, y otros autores, ilustrada con varias maximas politicas y morales*, 3 vols. (Barcelona: Imprenta de Joseph Llopis, 1700–1706); J. M. Iñurritegui, "Las virtudes y el jurista: El emperador político de Francisco Solanes y el amor a la patria," *Pedralbes: Revista d'Història Moderna*, January 11, 2004: 285–310.
12 Breve de Clemente XI, Mexico City, June 6, 1707, AGN, IV-Edictos de Inquisición, caja 4964, exp. 49.
13 Carlos F. Nunn, *Foreign Immigrants in Early Bourbon Mexico* (Cambridge: Cambridge University Press, 1979), 33; King to the viceroy of New Spain, Campo Real de Algoa, May 30, 1704, in *Cedulario americano*, ed. Muro Morejón, 127–129.
14 King to the viceroy of New Spain, Madrid, April 17, 1703, in *Cedulario americano*, ed. Muro Morejón, 82–84.
15 King to the Duke of Alburquerque, April 20, 1703, AGN, RC 31, exp. 87, fols. 244–247.
16 Apuntamiento de los papeles y respuestas del señor fiscal que incluye el expediente adjunto tocante a Caracas, AGI, México 478. Albareda i Salvadó, *Felipe V y el triunfo del absolutismo*, 45.
17 The Duke of Alburquerque to the king, January 3, 1708, Mexico City, AGI, México, leg. 478.
18 Duke of Alburquerque to Puebla's cabildo, with a note by Juan Joseph de Veytia y Linaje, Mexico City, January 28, 1707, AGMP, RC 10, fol. 191r–191v.
19 King to the viceroy of New Spain, Corella, July 20, 1711, AGN, RC 35, exp. 146, fols. 135–136v.
20 Olivas, "Loyalty and Disloyalty," 78.
21 King to the viceroys, audiencias, and governors of Peru and New Spain, Madrid, October 19, 1706, AGN, RC 33, exp. 15, fols. 85–86v.
22 Olivas, "Loyalty and Disloyalty," 100.
23 Olivas, "Loyalty and Disloyalty," 105–106.
24 Rosenmüller, *Patrons, Partisans, and Palace Intrigues*, 106.
25 See Testimonio de la causa criminal hecha, de Oficio de la Real Justicia contra Juan López Camaño, 1707. AGN, Escribanía, leg. 262A, fols. 30v–54v.
26 El fiscal con Alberto de Rada y Oreña, alcalde mayor de Tepeaca y Tecali, sobre ser desafecto al Rey Felipe V, 1707, AGI, Escribanía, leg. 190A, fol. 2.

27 El fiscal con Alberto de Rada y Oreña, alcalde mayor de Tepeaca y Tecali, sobre ser desafecto al Rey Felipe V, 1707, AGI. Escribanía, leg. 190A, fol. 15.
28 El fiscal con Alberto de Rada y Oreña, alcalde mayor de Tepeaca y Tecali, sobre ser desafecto al Rey Felipe V, 1707, AGI. Escribanía, leg. 190A, fols. 22v–23v.
29 Navarro García, *Conspiración en México*, 68.
30 Olivas, "Loyalty and Disloyalty," 83–85.
31 El fiscal con Alberto de Rada y Oreña, alcalde mayor de Tepeaca y Tecali, sobre ser desafecto al Rey Felipe V, 1707, AGI, Escribanía, leg. 190A, fols. 6, 27v.
32 Olivas, "Loyalty and Disloyalty," 80.
33 See *Romance, en que una viega de noventa años, vezina de los humeros, barrio extramuros de Sevilla, sentada la fogata de su cozina, le riñe, y reprehende á un nieto suyo, porque es servilletero, y lo persuade á que no lo sea.* Seville: Herederos de Tomás Lopez de Haro, n.d. and *Una vieja, vezina de los humeros, barrio extramuros de Sevilla, sentada junto à la fogata de su cozina, le escribe à la Reyna Ana, desengañandola de lo que se han mentido, y diziendole en metafora de un juego de bolas, lo que se ha passado en la entrada del Señor Archiduque en Madrid, y definiendo en verdad a los Servilleteros* (Sevilla: Herederos de Thomás Lopez de Haro, n.d.). BP.
34 Navarro García, *Conspiración en México*, 52.
35 Navarro García, *Conspiración en México*, 48.
36 Navarro García, *Conspiración en México*, 50.
37 Rosenmüller *Patrons, Partisans, and Palace Intrigues*, 109.
38 Olivas, "Loyalty and Disloyalty," 100.
39 González Cruz, *Guerra de religión*, 17–18, note 2; Rosenmüller, *Patrons, Partisans, and Palace Intrigues*, 113–114.
40 Antonio Ubilla y Medina, *Succession de el rey D. Phelipe V, Nuestro Señor en la corona de España: Diario de sus viages desde Versalles a Madrid, el que executó para su feliz casamiento, jornada a Napoles, a Milan, y a su exercito, successos de la campaña, y su buelta a Madrid* (Madrid: Juan Garcia Infanzón, 1704).
41 González Cruz, *Propaganda e información*, 20. For a history of the ministers that surrounded Felipe V, see Monsalve Concepción de Castro, *A la sombra de Felipe V: José de Grimaldo, ministro responsable* (Madrid: Marcial Pons Ediciones de Historia, S.A., 2004).
42 González Cruz, *Guerra de religión*, 37, 42, note 2.
43 Obispo Luis Belluga y Moncada, *Carta pastoral, que el Illustrissimo señor Don Luis Velluga, Obispo de Cartagena, del Conseio de su Magestad, escrive a los fieles de su Opispado [sic] principalmente a la gente sencilla* (n.p., 1706). CVL.
44 González Cruz, *Guerra de religión*, especially chapter 1.
45 See José María Vallejo García Hevia, "Los navíos de aviso y los correos marítimos a Indias (1492–1898)," *Ius fugit: Revista interdisciplinaria de estudio* 7 (1998), 197–268.
46 Duke of Alburquerque to the king, Mexico City, December 14, 1707. AGI, México, leg. 480, n.p.

47 *Copia del testamento cerrado, que en dos de octubre de mil y setecientos, y del codicilio, que en cinco del mismo mes y año hizo la magestad del señor rey D. Carlos II (que esta en gloria)* (Mexico City: Juan Joseph Guillena Carrascoso, 1701). BP.
48 *Memoria del embaxador de Francia Monsiur Briord* (Madrid: Antonio Bizarrón, 1700). BP.
49 See, for example, *Noticias de los felizes sucesos, que vàn consiguiendo las armas del rey N. Sr. D. Felipe Quinto, en el pais de Portugal, por la parte de Ciudad Rodrigo* (Seville: n.p., 1704). BP.
50 *Copia de la carta, que refiere la sublevacion intentada en la ciudad de Granada contra la Catolica Magestad del monarca de las españas Don Phelipe V (que Dios guarde)* (Sevilla: Francisco de Leefdael, 1705). BP.
51 *Gazeta general, y especial noticia de los cinco reynos de las dos Andaluzias, y lo que cada ciudad va executando en servicio de nuestro rey, y señor D. Felipe Quinto, que Dios guarde, y la confirmacion de la muerte del señor Archiduque, y lo demàs que verà el curioso lector* (Seville: Imprenta de Francisco Garay, 1706). BP.
52 *Copia de carta del rey nuestro señor, manifestando à sus amantes vasallos el desseo de mantenerles en la publica quietud, exponiendo hasta la ultima gota de sangre, para la seguridad de sus dominios*, Campo Real de Xadraque, July 7, 1706. BP.
53 *Relacion diaria de lo sucedido en Madrid des(de) que el Rey N. Señor llegò de la jornada de Cataluña, dia 6. de Junio, hasta el dia 7. de agosto de 1706* (Sevilla: N.p, 1706). BP.
54 King to the viceroy of New Spain, Madrid, October 18, 1706, AGN, RC, vol. 33, exp. 15.
55 Gaspar de Piñeda to the viceroy of New Spain, Madrid, July 1707, AGN, RC, vol. 33, exp. s.n.
56 Olivas, "Loyalty and Disloyalty," 93–95.
57 *Copia de la carta, escrita por los grandes de España a Su Mag. Christianissima* (Mexico City: Francisco de Rivera Calderón, 1711). BP.
58 *Relacion de la señalada victoria conseguida por el Rey N. Señor, contra el exercito de los enemigos, el dia 11 de diziembre de 1710. Junto a Villaviciosa, en el distrito de Toledo* (Mexico City: Francisco de Rivera Calderón, 1711). BP.
59 Alicia Mayer, *Lutero en el paraíso: La Nueva España en el espejo del reformador alemán* (Mexico City: Fondo de Cultura Economica, 2008).
60 Juan Ignacio de Castorena y Ursúa, *Parabien de las letras a las armas. Oracion gratulatoria panegyrica. evangelica; que en accion de gracias, en la Real Universidad, por el glorioso triumpho de el invicto monarcha Felipeo V. El Animoso, Rey de las Españas, Emperador de las Indias su Catholico dueño, en el campo de Brihuega, y Villaviciosa* (Mexico City: Herederos de Juan Joseph Guillena Carrasco, 1712), 14.
61 Castorena y Ursúa, *Parabien de las letras*, 16–17.
62 Navarro García, *Conspiración en México*, 47.
63 Pablo Yáñez de Áviles. *España-Francia, union, y amistad antigua de las dos naciones. Utilidad sagrada, y humana de su comunicación. Compendio*

historial, y aparato a los annales corelativos de las dos Coronas. Divido en dos partes. I. Union, y utilidad catholica-moral religiosa, y mystica. II. Union, y utlidad militar civil, eclesiastica, y literaria (Madrid: n.p, 1711).

64 *Carta de un personage de la corte, escrita à un amigo Andaluz* (Seville: Herederos de Thomas López de Haro, n.d). BP.

65 *Copia de carta escrita por el doctor D. Jacinto de Havena, Inquisidor de Murcia, à D. Alonso Castellanos, su tio, abodago de los reales consejos en la corte, su fecha de 29 de diziembre Proximo de 1705* (n.d: n.p.). BP.

66 González Cruz, *Guerra de religión*, 111.

67 First printed in Murcia in 1707, it would be reprinted in Seville in 1708. Luis Antonio Belluga y Moncada, *Sermón que el Obispo de Cartagena ... predicò en su Santa Iglesia, el dia ultimo de la octava que se celebrò a Maria SSma. de los Dolores en su SS, Imagen de las Lagrimas, en acción de gracias por el nacimiento de Nuestro Serenissimo Principe el Sr. don Luis Fernando* (Murcia: Vicente Llofriu, 1707).

68 Luis Antonio Belluga y Moncada, *A nuestros muy amados en Christo, los fieles de esta nuestra diocesi; salud en el Señor* (Seville: Juan de la Puerta, en la Imprenta de las Siete Rebueltas, 1706). BP.

69 See, for example, *Carta que escrive un amigo afecto, leal vasallo de su Rey, y Señor Phelipe V (que Dios guarde) á un intimo suyo desafecto, noticiandole lo sucedido, desde el dia que salió Su Magestad de la corte, hasta que bolbieron a ella sus Catholicissimas armas* (Seville: Thomàs Lopez de Haro, n.d.). BP.

70 *El què es? de la corte. Escrito por un gabacho nuevo, que se precia de serlo, por estàr graduado de doctor en las leyes del amor, respecto, y lealtad, que se debe á su amado rey, y señor natural Don Phelipe Quinto* (Sevilla: Francisco Garay, 1711). BP.

71 *Nueva relacion, y curioso romance en la qual se da cuenta, y declaran las atrocidades que hizieron con un niño, de edad de quatro, à cinco años, en la ciudad de Cadiz, el mes de Agosto deste año de 1708. y del solemnissimo entierro que le hizieron los cabildos, y demas nobleza de dicha ciudad* (Sevilla: Juan de la Puerta, n.d.). BP.

72 *Testimonio de la causa criminal hecha, de Oficio de la Real Justicia contra Juan López Camaño Herrador vecino de esta ciudad por decir ser desafectos a la Catholica Magd. de Nro Rey y Señor Dn Phelipe V*, 1707, AGI, Escribanía, leg. 262A, f. 8.

73 *Crisol de la verdad, y aviso para algunos politicos, que quieren hazer materia de estado los puntos mas principales de nuestra religion Catholica, tolerando como con una permision legal, los ultrages de la religion cometidos en Castilla por los hereges este año de 1710* (Seville: Herederos de Thomás Lopez de Haro, 1710). BP.

74 *Copia de carta circular, que el rey Nuestro Señor se sirvió de escrivir a las ciudades, villas, prelados, iglesias, religiones, y demás personas a quienes en ocasiones de cartas generales, escribe su magestad*, Madrid, July 4, 1709. BP.

75 Argüello, *Accion de gracias, a la soberana reyna*, 4v–5v.

76 José Brabo, *Sermon a los desagravios del Ssmo. Sacramento, por el real cedula de Su Magestad, por el ultraje, que le hizieron los hereges, poniendole en*

precio, y almoneda (Mexico City: Viuda de Miguel de Ribera Calderon, 1712).

77 Bernardo Unibárbia, *Intereses predicados en la festiva accion de gracias, por las victorias conseguidas de nuestro Catholico Rey Felipeo Quinto: celebrò, por mandado de Su Mag. el Real de Minas de Sultepec, en su yglesia parroquial, patente el SSmo. Sacramento, dia del Santo Nombre de Maria à 13 de septiembre. año de 1711* (Mexico City: Herederos de Juan Joseph Guillena Carrascoso, 1711), 22.

78 Pedro Dañón, *Claridad de ojos, apercion de oidos, y verdad de palabras, que manifiestan a vista de el desengaño, las glorias del mayor triumpho, que a influxo de la concepcion de Maria Ssma., consiguió en su octava nuestro Catholico Monarcha D. Filippo Quinto (que Dios guarde) y con zeloso pecho, festivo culto, y devida accion de gracias, mandó celebrar en este Convento de N.P.S. Francisco de Mexico, el dia 15 de julio de 1711* (Mexico City: Viuda de Miguel de Ribera, 1711), 7v–8.

79 Anna Coreth, *Pietas austriaca*, trans. William D. Bowman and Anna Maria Leitgeb (West Lafayette, Ind.: Purdue University Press, 2004), 45–50; Jeffrey Albert Schrader, "The Virgin of Atocha and Spanish Habsburg Devotion to Miraculous Images" (PhD diss, New York University, 2003), 103–104.

80 Schrader, "The Virgin of Atocha," 210, 247.

81 Madrid, *Gaceta de Madrid*, December 28, 1700. JCB.

82 Madrid, *Gaceta de Madrid*, February 22, 1701. JCB.

83 Nueva relacion, y curioso romance, en que se dà cuenta de la feliz empressa, y victorioso reenquentro, que han tenido las armas de nuestro Catolico Monarca Felipe Quinto (que Dios guarde) contra las armas imperiales, juntamente con la salida que hizo la reyna nuestra señora à dar gracias à la Reyna de los Angeles Nuestra Señora de Atocha el dia diez de agosto deste presente año de 1702. Con todo lo demas que verá el curioso, n.p., 1702. BP.

84 Schraeder, "The Virgin of Atocha," 100–101, 77–88.

85 Olivas, "Loyalty and Disloyalty," 81–82.

86 See Cristina Bravo Lozano, "Madrid as Vienna, Besieged and Saved: The ceremonial and political dimensions of the royal cavalcade to Atocha (1683)," *The Hungarian Historical Review* 4, no. 2 (2015), 471–501.

87 Schrader, "The Virgin of Atocha," 315–316.

88 Diario de lo sucedido desde que Su Magestad salió de la corte, hasta primero de diziembre de 1710 (n.p., 1711). BP.

89 *Respuesta, que da el Señor Guido Estaremberg, desde Daroca, al papel de su proèza* (Sevilla: Herederos de Thomás Lopez de Haro, n.d.). BP.

90 Manuel de Ayala y Salcedo, *Parabien a la Iglesia Catholica, en los glorisiosos triunfos de nuestro invicto monarca D. Phelipe Quinto* (n.p, n.d.). BJML.

91 Francisco de Aguilera Izaguirre, *Accion de gracias del convento de N.P.S. Augustin de la ciudad de Nra. Señora de la Concepcion de Zelaya, a Dios Nro Señor Sacramentado por la victoria que en Villaviciosa consiguio nuestro ynclito monarca, y señor D. Felipepo V. Rey de España, y Emperador de las Indias* (Mexico City: Francisco de Rivera Calderon, 1712), 7–8v.

92 Unibárbia, *Intereses predicados en la festiva accion de gracias*, 16–17.

Chapter 3

1 Gabriel de Mendieta Rebollo, *Sumptuoso, festivo real aparato en que explica su lealdad [sic] la siempre Noble, Illustre, Imperial, y Regia ciudad de Mexico, metrópoli de la America, y corte de su Nueva-España. En la aclamacion del muy alto, muy poderoso, muy soberano principe D. Phelipe V su catholico dueño Rey de las Españas executada lunes quatro de abril del año de 1701* (Mexico City: Imprenta de Juan Joseph Guillena Carrascoso, 1701), 7–18.
2 See Ramos and Escamilla González, "Sucesión y renovación," 381.
3 Lucas Antonio de Bedmar, *Real aclamacion, que de orden de la Reyna nuestra señora, y la Junta de Govierno, se executò en esta corte el miercoles 24 de noviembre de este presente año de 1700, levantando el estandarte teal por el Rey Catolico Nuestro Señor Don Felipe Quinto (...) en que se refieren todas las circunstancias que concurrieron à tan real, y magnifico acto* (Madrid: Lucas Antonio de Bedmar, 1700), 2–7; Ramos and Escamilla González, "Sucesión y renovación," 381–382.
4 Romans 12: 4–5.
5 Alfonso IX, King of Castile, *Las siete partidas del sabio rey don Alonso el Nono glosadas por el licenciado Gregorio López*, ed. Gregorio López de Tovar, vol. 1 (Madrid: Oficina de Benito Cano, 1789).
6 D. A. Brading, *The First America: The Spanish Monarchy, Creole Patriots, and the Liberal State, 1492–1867* (New York: Cambridge University Press, 1991), 226.
7 Edward Muir, *Ritual in Early Modern Europe* (Cambridge: Cambridge University Press, 1997), 231–232.
8 Elliot, "A Europe of Composite Monarchies," 48–71.
9 On how New Spain's viceroy served as a simulacrum of the king, see Alejandro Cañeque, *The King's Living Image: The Culture and Politics of Viceregal Power in Colonial Mexico* (New York: Routledge, 2004).
10 Muir, *Ritual in Early Modern Europe*, 230.
11 Actas de cabildo de la ciudad de México, March 8, 1701; March 14, 1701; and March 29, 1701, in *Actas antiguas de cabildo*, vol. 2, *Libros 38–42, 1689–1705* (Mexico City: Imprenta Particular G. Oropeza Velasco, 1911), 1–60.
12 Curcio-Nagy, *The Great Festivals of Colonial Mexico City*, 170, note 55.
13 Castorena y Ursúa, *Raçones de la lealtad*, 27.
14 Jacques Gelis, *History of Childbirth: Fertility, Pregnancy, and Birth in Early Modern Europe* (Cambridge: Polity, 1996), 8.
15 "Madrid," *Gaceta de Madrid*, November 9, 1700, num. 45, n. pag. JCB.
16 Pulgar, *Oracion panegyrica*, 7.
17 Juan de San Miguel, *Espejo para todos los reyes del mundo. Descifrado en la estatua de Nabuchodonosor. Mejorador para los señores reyes de España en el magnífico corazón de la muerte majestad de nuestro Católico Rey Don Carlos II* (Mexico City: Miguel de Rivera), 8–9.
18 Kamen, *Spain in the Later Seventeenth Century*, 178–179, 380; Cope, *The Limits of Racial Domination*, 125–160.
19 Robles, *Diario de sucesos notables*, 3: 70–71, 77–78; Pierre Ragon, "Los santos patrones de las ciudades de México central (siglos XVI-XVII),"

Historia Mexicana 52:2 (October–December 2002): 374. Ramos and Escamilla González, "Sucesión y renovación," 381–410.

20 "Primera relacion extraordinaria de la salida del Rey Nuestro Señor Don Felipe Quinto, de Versalles para estos sus reynos, y breves noticias de su Real Persona, assi propias, como adquiridas," *Gaceta de Madrid*, December 21, 1700. JCB.

21 Miguel Núñez de Godoy, *Prognostico Philippico hallado en la sagrada historia del real propheta David: discurso panegyrico, que en el sermon de la missa de gracias, que por la acclamacion de nuestro rey, y señor Don Philippo Quinto [que Dios guarde]celebrò la Sancta Iglesia Cathedral de Guadalaxara patente el Sanctissimo Sacramento. En veinte y seis de julio del año de 1701* (Mexico City: Francisco de Ribera Calderon, 1712), 7–8.

22 Miguel de Amescua, *Ramillete compuesto de las mas hermosas fragrantes flores, que en varias, y diversas estaciones de tiempos llevó la antiguedad en sus mas floridos heroes, y en los huertos de las indias se juntaron en las rosas de Castilla, y flores de lis* (Mexico City: Herederos de la Viuda de Francisco Rodriguez Lupercio, 1701), 17v–18v.

23 Antonio López Alonso, *Carlos II el Hechizado* (Madrid: Ediciones Irreverentes, 2003), 17.

24 "Primera relacion extraordinaria de la salida del Rey Nuestro Señor Don Felipe Quinto, de Versalles para estos sus reynos, y breves noticias de su Real Persona, assi propias, como adquiridas," *Gaceta de Madrid*, December 21, 1700. JCB.

25 Mendieta Rebollo, *Sumptuoso, festivo real aparato*, 2.

26 Navarro García, "Cambio de dinastía en Nueva España," 132–135; Joseph Klaits, *Printed Propaganda under Louis XIV: Absolute Monarchy and Public Opinion* (Princeton: Princeton University Press, 1976), 86–112.

27 Martha Sandoval Villegas, "'Traje español' vs. 'traje de francés'. La transición de la casa gobernante, un problema de identidad personificado en la imagen del funcionario. El Caso de Nueva España (finales del siglo XVII, principio del siglo XVIII)", in *El imperio de lo visual. Imágenes, palabra y representación*, ed. Roberto Domínguez Cáceres and Víctor Gayol (Zamora, Michoacán: Colegio de Michoacán, 2018), 322.

28 Escamilla González contributed this analysis to our jointly authored "Sucesión y renovación del cuerpo de la monarquía," 387.

29 Escamilla González contributed this analysis to our jointly authored "Sucesión y renovación del cuerpo de la monarquía." 382.

30 Mínguez, *La invención de Carlos II*, 107–115, 130–133, 143–165.

31 Escamilla González, *Los intereses malentendidos*, 77.

32 Ambrosio Francisco Montoya y Cárdenas Ponce de León, *Diseño festivo del amor obstentiva muestra de la lealtad acclamación alegre con que la Muy Noble, Augusta Imperial ciudad de la Puebla de los Angeles en el diez de abril del año de 1701, juro por su rey y señor natural al invictissimo señor D. Phelipe V de este nombre, monarcha supremo de dos mundos* (Puebla: Herederos del Capitán Juan de Villa Real, 1701), 23r. Ramos, *Identity, Ritual, and Power*, 23–40.

33 Amescua, *Ramillete compuesto de las mas hermosas fragrantes flores*, 14–15; Sandoval Villegas, "'Traje español,'" 338–339.
34 Víctor I. Stoichita, "*Imago regis*: teoría del arte y retrato real in *Las Meninas* de Velázquez," in *Otras Meninas*, ed. Fernando Marías (Madrid: Siruela, 1995), 186–194. Also see Alejandra Osorio, "The King in Lima: Simulacra, Ritual and Rule in Seventeenth-Century Lima," *Hispanic American Historical Review* 84, no. 3 (2004), 447–474, and her excellent "The Copy as Original," 704–721.
35 Louis Marin, *Portrait of the King*, trans. Martha M. Houle (Minneapolis: University of Minnesota Press, 1988), 209. Originally published in 1981.
36 Tomás Montaño, *Vozes de la lealtad, alborozos de la fidelidad: Sòlemnidad plausible, que en accion de gracias por los felices sucessos de las españolas armas, y triumphos de su invensible monarca D. Phillippo V* (Mexico City: Herederos de la Viuda de Francisco Rodriguez Lupercio, 1712), 9v–10.
37 Baltasar de Alcocer y Sariñana, *Festivo triduo, devida aclamacion, á los gloriosos triumphos de las Catholicas armas de nuestro invicto rey de las Españas, del monarcha supremo de las Indias el Señor Don Felipo V (que Dios guarde) devidamente vencedor en los campos de Villaviciosa, contra la opuesta Liga* (Mexico City: Herederos de Juan Joseph Guillena Carrascoso, 1712), 15–55.
38 Marin, *Portrait of the King*, 209.
39 Mora, *El sol eclipsado*; Pulgar, *Oración panegyrica*.
40 See Alejandro González Acosta, *Crespones y campanas Tlaxcaltecas en 1701* (Mexico City: Universidad Nacional Autónoma de México, 2000); J. Picazo, *El segundo Josias, Carlos II, sin segundo como él, y sin primero. Oracion funebre panegyrica, que por la seraphica religion dixo en su Convento Grande de Queretaro, el dia veinte y uno de junio del año passado de mil setecientos y uno* (Mexico City: Herederos de la Viuda de Francisco Rodriguez Lupercio, 1702).
41 Jacinto Bernárdez de Ribera, *Sermon que en accion de gracias ofrecio a Dios, y á su Purissima Madre el Convento de las Llagas de Nuestro Seraphico Padre S. Francisco de la ciudad de la Puebla de los Angeles: por el nacimiento de N. Principe y Señor Don Luiz Phelipe* (Mexico City: Imprenta por la Viuda de Miguel de Ribera Calderon, 1708), A1r.
42 Juan Felipe Orozco y Molina, *Relacion de la plausible real solemnidad con que esta Ilustre, y Leal ciudad de Durango, caveza del Reyno de esta Nueva-Viscaya, celebrò la jura de nuestro principe de las Asturias el Señor D. Luis Fernando, como heredero de los Reynos de España por primogenito de nuestro monarcha, y Señor Felipeo Quinto Emperador de este Nuevo-Mundo, à quienes Dios prospere, y guarde dilata dos años* (Mexico City: Imprenta de Miguel de Ortega, y Bonilla, 1711), 1r–2r.
43 Olivas, "Loyalty and Disloyalty," 68–69.
44 María Cuesta García de Leonardo, "La mano del monarca grande de las Españas: La muerte de los soldados y el poder del Virrey Galve en la Nueva España, 1694," *Anales del Instituto de Investigaciones Estéticas* 38, no. 108 (2016), 51–85.
45 See Ramos, "War, Legitimacy, and Ceremony," 114–133.

46 Anderson, *Imagined Communities*, 9–10.
47 Juan de Goikoetxea, *Philippo Quinto David Segundo, en la piedad primero rey de las Españas; honrando sus fuertes, celebrando exequias á sus militares diffuntos, reyna entre los leones, vençe sus enemigos, restaura los terminos de su imperio, en succession feliz eterniza su solio y se haze un nombre grande, igual con el que oy tiene entre los reyes el renombre de grande. Sermon que predicó el día 5. de noviembre de este año de 1707* (Mexico City: Juan Joseph Guillena Carrascoso, 1707), 9v–10.
48 Amescua, *Ramillete compuesto de las mas hermosas fragrantes flores*, 28v–29.
49 Ramos, *Identity, Ritual, and Power in Colonial Puebla*, 140.
50 Amescua, *Ramillete compuesto de las mas hermosas fragrantes flores*, 29.
51 For an excellent analysis of this relationship, see Thomas Calvo, *Poder, religión y sociedad en la Guadalajara del siglo XVII* (Guadalajara: Universidad de Guadalajara, 1992).
52 Amescua, *Ramillete compuesto de las mas hermosas fragrantes flores*, 26–27.
53 Ramos, "Succession and Death," 199. El argumento del abogado del Coronel José Antonio Ortiz de Casquesta, segundo Marques de Altamira, para comprar el cargo de alférez mayor y regidor de Puebla, March 9, 1715, AGMP, AC 38, fol. 51r–51v.
54 Mora, *El sol eclipsado*, 6–8.
55 Fernando Toro Altamirano, *Sermon panegyrico, en agimento de gracias a el santissimo sacramento, por la feliz noticia de hallarse en cinta la Catholica Magestad de nuestra serenissima reyna de España Doña María Luisa Gabriela de Saboya Nuestra Señora* (Mexico City: Imprenta por la Viudad de Miguel de Ribera, 1707); Bernardez de Ribera, *Sermon que en accion de gracias ofrecio a Dios*.
56 San Miguel, *Sermon que en accion de gracias por el feliz nacimiento*, 2.
57 Chronicler and cleric José Luis de Velasco y Arellano published a poem describing how Mexico City's religious institutions commemorated the victories in Brihuega and Villaviciosa. See *Catholico triumpho, y hacimiento de gracias, que venerando laureles, panegyrisando hazañas, venerando verdades, y admirando valores: consiguieron las reales armas de N.C. Monarcha el Señor D. Phelip V. (que Dios guarde) de las que colligadas con el imperio, solicitaron la ruyna, y dessolacion de nuestra monarchia. Y a los rayos de tantas luces, eclypso sus explendores, la muerte del Sr. Delphin* (Mexico City: Herederos de Juan Joseph Guillena Carrasco, 1712).
58 González Acosta, *Crespones y campanas*, 402.
59 Amescua, *Ramillete compuesto de las mas hermosas fragrantes flores*, 29v.
60 Antonio Carlos de Castañeda, *Reales preceptos executados en accreditados observaciones de affectos con que la ciudad de Tlaxcala manifestó desempeños, assí en los sentimientos por la faltá de Nuestro Rey y Señor Don Carlos Segundo, como en el crecido júbilo a la jura de nuestro rey Don Phelipe Quinto (...)* (Puebla: Herederos del Capitán Juan de Villa – Real, 1701).
61 King to the archbishop and interim viceroy, Barcelona, March 15, 1702, RC, vol. 31, Exp. 7, AGN, 23–24v.
62 Orozco y Molina, *Relacion de la plausible real solemnidad*, 5b.

63 Canon 1, Session 8 in "The General Council of Trent, 1545–63 A.D. – Papal Encyclicals," December 13, 1545, www.papalencyclicals.net/councils/trent.htm.
64 Javier Varela, *La muerte del Rey: El ceremonial funerario de la monarquía española (1500–1885)* (Madrid: Turner Libros, 1990), 75–76; Víctor Mínguez, "La monarquía humillada: un estudio sobre las imágenes del poder y el poder de las imágenes," *Relaciones* 77, no. 20 (1999), 131–134.
65 Frances Calderón de la Barca, *Life in Mexico* (Berkeley: University of California Press, 1982), 66.
66 Posada, *Sermon funeral de las sumptuosas honras*, 6.
67 Auto de cómo se alzaron pendones por el Rey Nuestro Señor D. Felipe V, AMP, AC 34, 648v; José Gómez de la Parra, *Grano de trigo fecundo de virtudes en la vida, fecundissimo por la succession en la muerte, la catholica magestad del rey nuestro senor Don Carlos Segundo* ... (Puebla; Puebla: Herederos del Capitan Juan de Villa-Real, 1701), 11–13. Ramos, "Succession and Death," 197.
68 See, for example, *Diario de lo sucedido desde que Su Magestad salió de la corte, hasta primero de Diziembre de 1710* (n.p. 1711), 569–584. BP.
69 Coreth, *Pietas austriaca*.
70 Juan de Guevara, *Sermon, que los solemnes cultos, que el muy religioso parrochial Convento de N.S.P. San Francisco de la ciudad de Santiago de Queretaro, consagró á Maria SS. N. Señora en el misterio de su concepcion sin culpa, patente el augustissimo señor del cielo, y tierra sacramentado, en accion de gracias por los felices sucessos, que en la Batalla de Brihuega, y Villaviciosa consiguió victorioso de sus enemigos, nuestro amabilissimo, legitimo Rey, y Señor de las Españas. D. Phelippo V* (Mexico City: Viuda de Miguel de Ribera Calderon, 1711), 24–28.
71 Aguilera Izaguirre, *Accion de gracias del Convento de N.P.S. Augustin de la ciudad de Nra. Señora de la Concepcion de Zelaya*, 3v-4.
72 Mora, *El sol eclipsado*.
73 Argüello, *Accion de gracias, a la soberana reyna*, 10.
74 Castorena y Ursúa, *Parabien de las letras*, 12.
75 Posada, *Sermon funeral de las sumptuosas honras*, 6–18.
76 Juan de San Miguel, *Sermón, que en acción de gracias por el feliz nacimiento del príncipe de España nuestro serenísimo señor don Luis Fernando dijo el R. P. F. Juan de San Miguel del orden de N.S.P.S. Francisco ... en el segundo día del novenario con que la Santa Iglesia Catedral celebró dicho nacimiento* (Mexico City: Imprenta Platiniana de los Herederos de Juan Joseph Guillena Carrascoso, 1709), 9–20.
77 Ángel de Maldonado, *Oración evangelica. predicada en el Santuario de N. Señora de la Soledad de Antequera. Domingo de Quasimodo dia de los gloriosissimos aposteles San Phelipe, y Santiago. Dijola el año de 1707 el Ilustrissmo, y Reverendissimo Señor Maestro Don Fray Angel* (Mexico City: Juan Joseph Guillena Carrascoso, 1707), 5.
78 Ángel de Maldonado, "Oracion evangelica, primera. Predicada en la Santa Iglesia Cathedral de Antequera, dia del Apostol Santiago, Año de 1713." in *Oraciones evangelicas predicadas por (...) D. Fr. Angel Maldonado monge del G.P.S. Bernardo* (Mexico City: Herederos de Juan Joseph Carrascoso, 1721), 13.

79 Felipe V to the viceroys of Peru and New Spain, governors, archbishops, bishops, and cities in both kingdoms, Madrid, June 19, 2011, JCB.
80 Brabo, *Sermon a los desagravios del Ssmo. Sacramento*, 2, 12v–13.
81 Miguel Núñez de Godoy, *Desagravios de Christo sacramentado, que en las victorias de nuestro rey, Y señor D. Felipepo V* (Mexico City: Francisco de Ribera Calderón, 1712), 6.

Chapter 4

1 Testimonio de la causa criminal hecha ... contra Juan López Camaño V, 1707, AGI, Escribanía, 262A.
2 Testimonio de la causa criminal ... contra Juan López Camaño, 1707, AGI, Escribanía, 262A, fol. 11v.
3 Alain Milhou, *Colón y su mentalidad mesiánica en el ambiente Franciscanista Español* (Valladolid: Casa-Museo de Colón, 1983), 362.
4 Scholarship on the impact of Sebastianism is abundant, but two studies bear mention as they focus on rumors, and the assumptions and aspirations embedded in Sebastianism. See E. Olsen, *The Calabrian Charlatan, 1598–1603: Messianic Nationalism in Early Modern Europe* (New York: Palgrave Macmillan, 2002) and Ruth MacKay, *The Baker Who Pretended to Be King of Portugal* (Chicago: University of Chicago Press, 2012).
5 Carta de un personaje de la corte, escrita a un amigo Andaluz (Sevilla: Herederos de Thomas López de Haro, n.d.). BP.
6 Carta, y compendio historial de los sucesos más particulares de nuestra España, y sus dominios, del año pasado de 1706. Que escribió en la corte un fiel vasallo de Su Majestad, a instancias de un amigo suyo Sevillano, que la quiere enviar a su correspondiente en Indias. Y otro, con pretexto de copiarla para el mismo efecto (n.p., n.d.). BP.
7 Relación diaria de lo sucedido en Madrid desde que el Rey N. Señor llegó de la jornada de Cataluña, día 6. de junio hasta el día 7 de agosto de 1706 (Sevilla, n.p., 1706). BP.
8 Richard L. Kagan, *Clio & the Crown: The Politics of History in Medieval and Early Modern Spain* (Baltimore: Johns Hopkins University Press, 2009), especially chapter 1.
9 Alain Milhou, "La chauve-souris, le Nouveau David et le roi caché (trois images de l'empereur des derniers temps dans le monde Ibérique: XIIIe–XVIIe s.)," *Mélanges de la Casa de Velázquez* 18, no. 1 (1982), 64.
10 See Elaine Pagels, *Revelations: Visions, Prophecy, and Politics in the Book of Revelation* (New York: Penguin Books, 2012).
11 Norman Cohn, *The Pursuit of the Millennium: Revolutionary Millenarians and Mystical Anarchists of the Middle Ages* (New York: Oxford University Press, 1970), 17.
12 Cohn, *The Pursuit of the Millennium*, 13–16.
13 Cohn, *The Pursuit of the Millennium*, 16–17.
14 Milhou, "La chauve-souris, le Nouveau David et le roi caché," 65.
15 Kagan, *Clio & the Crown*, especially chapter 1.

16 Alain Milhou, "Esquisse d'un panorama de la prophétie messianique en Espagne (1482–1614). Thématique, conjoncture et fonction," in *La prophétie comme arme de guerre. Pouvoirs (XVe–XVIIe) siècles*, ed. Auguste Redondo (Paris: Press de la Sorbonne Nouvelle, 2000), 13.
17 Cohn, *The Pursuit of the Millennium*, 65, 88–89, 102–106.
18 Marjorie Reeves, *The Influence of Prophecy in the Later Middle Ages: A Study in Joachimism* (Notre Dame: University of Notre Dame Press, 1993).
19 Milhou, *Colón y su mentalidad*, 459.
20 Milhou, *Colón y su mentalidad*, 235.
21 For more on how these prophecies likely entered the collective consciousness of Aragonese society, see Amadeo Serra Desfilis, "A Search for the Hidden King: Messianism, Prophecies and Royal Epiphanies of the Kings of Aragon (circa 1250–1520)," *Arts* 8, no. 4 (2019), 1–27. For the Encubierto's role in the revolt, see Sarah T. Nalle, "Revisiting El Encubierto: Navigating between Visions of Heaven and Hell on Earth," in *Werewolves, Witches, and Wandering Spirits: Traditional Belief and Folklore in Early Modern Europe*, ed. Kathryn Edwards (Kirksville, MO: Truman State University Press, 2002), 77–92.
22 Milhou, *Colón y su mentalidad*, 236.
23 Richard L. Kagan, *Lucrecia's Dreams: Politics and Prophecy in Sixteenth-Century Spain* (Berkeley: University of California Press, 1990).
24 Mínguez, *La invención de Carlos II*, 143–144.
25 Chad Leahy and Ken Tully, ed. *Jerusalem Afflicted: Quaresmius, Spain, and the Idea of a 17th-Century Crusade* (London: Routledge, 2020), 11–39.
26 See Grace Magnier, *Pedro de Valencia and the Catholic Apologists for the Expulsion of the Moriscos* (Leiden: Brill, 2010).
27 Manuel Herrero Sánchez, "Spanish Theories of Empire: A Catholic and Polycentric Monarchy," in *A Companion to Early Modern Spanish Imperial Political and Social Thought*, ed. Jörg Alejandro Tellkam (Leiden: Brill, 2020), 32–38.
28 D. A. Brading, *Mexican Phoenix: Our Lady of Guadalupe: Image and Tradition across Five Centuries* (Cambridge: Cambridge University Press, 2001), 33–34.
29 Rodrigo Gómez de Aguilera y Saavedra, *Jerusalem libertada, y restauracion de toda la Palestina. Caida y dessolacion de la secta de Mahoma. Profezia del santo varon Nicolas Factor, anunciandola, y señalando la parte por donde han de entrar los exercitos Christianos à conquistar la morisma. Lamentaciones, y vaticinios dolorosos con que el sabio filosofo Achàm Turuley, natural de Arabia felize, llora la ultima ruina de su agarena gente* (Madrid: Lucas Antonio de Bedmar y Baldivia, 1684). CVL.
30 See Iván Kopylov Sidorovich, ed. *El Tratado del Apocalipsis del beato Gregorio López (1542–1596). Exégesis histórico profética* (Mexico City: Editorial Notas Universitarias, 2021).
31 Rubial García, *El paraíso de los elegidos*, especially chapter 3.
32 González Cruz, *Guerra de religión*, 137, note 189.
33 González Cruz, *Guerra de religión*, 107–108.
34 González Cruz, *Guerra de religión*, 64.

35 Castorena y Ursúa, *Raçones de la lealtad*, 35.
36 Agustín Jacinto de Mesa, *Sermon que en la solemnidad de la Pascua de los Reyes, y epiphania del Señor, predicó en la Santa Metropolitana, y Patriarcal Iglesia de Sevilla, este presente año de 1704* (Seville: Juan de la Puerta, 1704), 14–17.
37 Antonio Xardón, *Nuevo solsticio entre leon, y virgen para exaltacion de España en Sagitario. Horoscopo astrono-mystico al feliz nacimiento del primogenito de las Magestades Catholicas el Señor Don Luis I. Jurado Principe de Asturias ... en la festiva solemnidad que en accion de gracias consagró a Christo Sr. N. Sacramentado el M. Illustre Sr D. Thoribio de Coizio Caballero del Orden de Calatrava, de el Consejo de Su Magestad y su Presidente de la Real Audiencia de Guatemala, Governador y Capitan General de todas sus provincias* (Mexico City: Herederos de Juan Joseph Guillena Carrascoso, 1708), 3–4.
38 Some imprints mention the etymology of the monarch's name in the dedication or in an approbation at the beginning of the text. See sermons by San Miguel (1707), Valtierra (1707), Montaño (1712), and Carrera (1712).
39 Antonio de Valtierra, *Sermon que en solemne accion de gracias por los ultimos successos de la monarchia*, iv.
40 Cohn, *The Pursuit of the Millennium*, 66, 77.
41 Miguel de la Castilla, *Elogio sepulchral a la immortal memoria de los Españoles que murieron en el victoriosa expulsión del ejército enemigo, segunda vez apoderado de la corte de Madrid* (Mexico City: Viuda de Miguel de Rivera, 1711), 10–10v.
42 Kagan, *Clio & the Crown*, 262.
43 Earl Rosenthal, "Plus Ultra, Non Plus Ultra, and the Columnar Device of Emperor Charles V," *Journal of the Warburg and Courtauld Institutes* 34, no. 1 (January 1971), 204–28.
44 José de las Heras y Alcocer, *Sermon que en el solemne novenario, que hizo el Convento Grande de Mexico de el Real Orden de Nuestra Señora de la Merced Redempcion de Captivos, en accion de gracias por la felice noticia de estar en cinta Nuestra Serenissima Señora Dôña Maria Luyza Gabriela Emmanuel de Saboya, Reyna de Espana* (Mexico City: Herederos de la Viuda de Francisco Rodriguez Lupercio, 1707), 11.
45 Ramos, "Arte efímero," 179–218.
46 Escamilla González, "Razones de la lealtad," 186.
47 José Gómez de la Parra, *Famosos triumphos y victoriosos tropheos, que el dia 15 de Julio del año de 1708 el primero de el festivo triduo, que celebró el Ilmo. V. Dean y Cabildo, sede vacante de la Santa Iglesia Cathedral de la ciudad de la Puebla de los Angeles en la Nueva-España en honor de la Immaculada Concepcion de Maria SS. N. S. Su Titular, para dar gracias a Dios N.S. por el feliz nacimiento de Tu Alteza. El Sr. D. Luis I, Principe de las Asturuas* (Puebla: Oficina de D. Joseph Perez, 1709), 20Ir.
48 Blas de Pulgar, *Sermon que en accion de gracias ofrecio a Dios, y a su Santisima Madre, en su devotissima imagen de los Remedios, en su iglesia metropolitana, la Muy Noble, Leal, e Imperial Corte de Mexico. Por el augustissimo parto de la reyna nuestra señora la serenissima Doña Maria*

Luysa Gabriela Emmanuel de Saboya, en que dio a luz, dia de S. Luyz Rey de Francia a 25 de Agosto a Nuestro Principe Luys Phelipe, 3–4.
49 Pulgar, *Sermon que en acción de gracias*, 14–17.
50 Ubilla y Medina, *Succession de el rey*.
51 Ambrosio Francisco Montoya y Cárdenas Ponce de León, *Diseño festivo del amor obstentiva muestra de la lealtad acclamación alegre con que la muy noble, augusta imperial ciudad de la Puebla de Los Angeles en el diez de Abril del año de 1701, juro por su rey y señor natural al Invictissimo Señor D. Phelipe V de este nombre, monarcha supremo de dos mundos* (Puebla: Herederos del Capitán Juan de Villa Real, 1701), 7r–7v. Amescua, *Ramillete compuesto de las mas hermosas fragrantes flores*, 24r–24v.
52 See Burke, *The Fabrication of Louis XIV*.
53 José de Alcalá, *Motivos del dolor, que en las funerales tiernas exequias de el siempre augusto señor, invicto Christianissimo Rey de Francia Luis XIV* (Mexico City: Herederos de la Viuda de Francico Rodriguez Lupercio, 1716).
54 *Copia de carta circular, que el Rey Nuestro Señor se sirvió de escribir a las ciudades, villas, prelados, iglesias, religiones, y demás personas a quienes en ocasiones de cartas generales, escribe Su Majestad* (n.p., n.d.), 143–153. BP.
55 Joachim Antonio Villalobos, *Sermon, que à la fiesta que celebró la ciudad de S. Luis Potosi. A Xpto Nuestro Señor Sacramentado, en accion de gracias por las victorias, que en el campo de Villa-Viciosa alcanzó de sus enemigos, la Catolica Magestad del rey Ntro. Sr. Don Felipeo V. Rey de Españas, y Emperador de las Indias* (Mexico City: Herederos de Juan Joseph Guillena Carrasco, 1712), 27.
56 Miguel Morán, *La imagen del rey. Felipe V y el arte* (Madrid: Editorial Nerea, 1990), 49.
57 Jaime Cuadriello believes that the portrait had been placed in the cathedral between 1718 and 1725 as part of the redesign of the Altar of the Kings. See "The Politicization and Sociability of the Public Image. The King and His Representatives, 1700–1790," in *Painted in Mexico 1700–1790. Pinxit Mexici*, ed. Ilona Katzew (Los Angeles: Los Angeles County Museum of Art, Fomento Cultural Banamex, 2017), 112–139.
58 Vicente Bacallar y Sanna, San Felipe, *Comentarios de la guerra de España e historia de su rey, Felipe V, el Animoso*, Biblioteca de Autores Españoles, vol. 99 (Madrid: Atlas, 1957; orig. pub. 1957).
59 Guevara, *Sermon, que los solemnes cultos*, 3.
60 Miguel de la Castilla, *Elogio sepulchral a la immortal memoria de los Españoles que murieron en el victoriosa expulsión del ejército enemigo, segunda vez apoderado de la corte de Madrid* (Mexico City: Viuda de Miguel de Rivera, 1711).
61 San Miguel, *Sermon, que en accion de gracias*, 11.
62 Montaño, *Vozes de la lealtad*, 8.
63 Castorena y Ursúa, *Parabien de las letras*, 18.
64 "Descripcion del adorno, que se hizo en esta corte a la real entrada de su Magestad Nuestro Catholico Rey Don Felipe Quinto," *Gazeta de Madrid*, 1701. BP.
65 Castorena y Ursúa, *Parabien de las letras*, 3.
66 Aguilera Izaguirre, *Accion de gracias del Convento de N.P.S. Agustin*, 10.

67 Castorena y Ursúa, *Parabien de las letras*, 6–7.
68 María Rosa Cal Martínez, "'La Gazeta' de Madrid y la Guerra de Sucesión," *Cuadernos Dieciochistas*, no. 3 (2002), 48; Jacinto de Aranaz, *El Señor Phelipe es el rey de las Españas verdadero, dado por la mano de Dios torre incontratable, del Segundo David perseguido, y victorioso, guarnecida en tres propugnáculos, justicia, religion, y política; de que penden mil escudos, que defienden su corona* (Pamplona: Francisco Antonio de Neyra, 1711).
69 Núñez de Godoy, *Prognostico Philippico*, n.p.
70 Núñez de Godoy, *Prognostico Philippico*, 6–11.
71 Núñez de Godoy, *Prognostico Philippico*, 11–14.
72 Aguilera Izaguirre, *Accion de gracias del convento de N.P.S. Augustin*, 6–6v.
73 Aguilera Izaguirre, *Accion de gracias del convento de N.P.S. Augustin*, 7v–12v.
74 Unibárbia, *Intereses predicados en la festiva accion de gracias*, 21–21.
75 Lorenzo Antonio González de la Sancha, *Victima Catholica, panegyrico culto, holocausto gratulatorio, demonstracion christiana, que consagro al soberano Jesus Sacramentado en la custodia del sagrado vientre de su Purisima Madre, el Colegio Real de San Juan Letran, de esta Imperial Corte Mexicana, â los felices sucesos de las victoriosas armas de Nuestro Rey y Señor Natural Don Philipo V. que Dios guarde* (Mexico City: Francisco de Ribera Calderon, 1711), 9–10v.
76 Carrera, *Sermon predicado en la solemne funcion*, 1–9.
77 Guevara, *Sermon que los solemnes cultos*, 2–14.
78 Montaño, *Vozes de la lealtad*, 5–5v.
79 Brabo, *Sermon a los desagravios*, 1v–2.
80 Brabo, *Sermon a los desagravios*, 9.
81 Unibárbia, *Intereses predicados en la festiva accion de gracias*, 24–25, 27.
82 William A. Christian, *Local Religion in Sixteenth-Century Spain* (Princeton: Princeton University Press, 1989).
83 Maldonado, *Oración evangelica, predicada en el Santuario*.
84 Linda Curcio-Nagy, "Native Icon to City Protectress to Royal Patroness: Ritual, Political Symbolism and the Virgin of the Remedies," *The Americas* 52, no. 3 (January 1996), 367–91.
85 Actas, December 6, 1706, ACE, Mexico City, ACM, fols. 55–56.
86 Rubial García, *El paraíso de los elegidos*, 232, 238.
87 See Suzanne L. Stratton, *The Immaculate Conception in Spanish Art* (Cambridge: Cambridge University Press, 1994).
88 See Francisco de Florencia, *Zodiaco Mariano* (Mexico City: Consejo Nacional para la Cultura y las Artes, 1995).
89 Phelan, *The Millenial Kingdom*, 122.
90 Rubial García, *El paraíso de los elegidos*, 236.
91 Castorena y Ursúa, *Parabien de las letras*, 10.
92 See Ángel de Maldonado, *Oracion evangelica, que predicò ... en la Sta. Yglesia Metropolitana de Mexico Domingo infra octavo de la Purissima Concepcion de Maria SSma. y segundo de Adviento. Dia en que de orden de S.M. (Dios le guarde) se dieron gracias por los sucessos felizes de el dia nueve, y diez de diziembre en las facciones de Brihuega, y Villaviciosa. Y dia en que se*

solicitaron los desagravios de los arrojos, que cometieron los infieles ... (Mexico City: Herederos de la Viuda de Miguel de Ribera Calderon, 1715).
93 Rubial García, *El paraíso de los elegidos*, 330–332.
94 Juan de Goikoetxea, *La maravilla immarcescible, y milagro continuado de Maria Santissima Señora Nuestra, en su prodigiosa imagen de Guadalupe de Mexico, compite firmezas con su nuevo templo, que la copia: adelanta duraciones al cielo, que á su efigie traslàda: Iguàla permanencias con el augusto sacramento, de quien imita la milagrosa presencia en su pint`ùra. Sermon en el dia octavo del novenario â la dedicacion de su magnifico templo, con el mysterio de la purificacion, y dia de la Aparicion de S,* [sic] *Miguel, celebrô la fiesta, y solemnizô el dia la exc. señora, señora* [sic] *doña Juana de la Cerda, y Aragon, duqueza de Alburquerque, vi-reyna de esta Nueva-España, con la religion de la sagrada Compañia de Iesus* (Mexico City: Imprenta de los Herederos de Juan Joseph Guillena Carrascoso, 1709).
95 Iván Escamilla González, "Yolloxóchitl y flor de lis: Nuestra Señora de Guadalupe de México, patrona de la Monarquía Española, 1710–1810," in *Madre de la patria: la imagen Guadalupana en la historia Mexicana* (Mexico City: Museo de la Basílica de Guadalupe, 2010), 19–28.
96 Castorena y Ursúa, *Fructo de bendicion*, 17.
97 Argüello, *Accion de gracias a la soberana reyna*, n.p.
98 Argüello, *Accion de gracias a la soberana reyna*, 14.

Chapter 5

1 Orozco y Molina, *Relacion de la plausible real solemnidad*, 1–4v.
2 Orozco y Molina, *Relacion de la plausible real solemnidad*, 4v.
3 Orozco y Molina, *Relacion de la plausible real solemnidad*, 4v–6v.
4 Orozco y Molina, *Relacion de la plausible real solemnidad*, 7–7v.
5 Gloria Ángeles Franco Rubio, "Rituales y ceremonial en torno a la procreación real en un contexto de crisis: el primer embarazo de María Luisa de Saboya (1707)," in *Gobernar en tiempos de crisis: las quiebras dinásticas en el ámbito hispánico: 1250–1808* (Madrid: Sílex, 2008), 235–266.
6 Franco Rubio, "Rituales y ceremonial," 235–266. Also see José Antonio López Anguita, "María Luisa Gabriela de Saboya: poder y dinastía durante la Guerra de Sucesión española (1701–1714)," in *Reinas, virreinas y aristócratas en las Monarquías Ibéricas. Estudios sobre mujer, cultura y diplomacia en la Edad Moderna* (Madrid: Dykinson, 2022), 215–245; David González Cruz, "Actitudes e imagen de las reinas en tiempos de crisis: La transición de los Austrias a los Borbones," in *Vírgenes, reinas y santas: modelos de mujer en el mundo hispano*, ed. David González Cruz (Huelva: Universidad de Huelva, 2007), 75–104.
7 Monségur, *Las nuevas memorias*, 4.
8 Francisco Montes González, *Mecenazgo virreinal y patrocinio artístico: El ducado de Alburquerque en la Nueva España* (Seville: Real Maestranza de Caballería de Sevilla, 2016), 352–363.

9 Duke of Alburquerque to the king, Mexico City, December 14, 1707, AGI, México, leg. 480, n.p. Montes González, *Mecenzago virreinal*, 352-363.
10 Oficios de felicitación del Contador de Tributos y el Alcalde Mayor de la Villa de Córdoba por el nacimiento del nuevo príncipe, y relación de las celebraciones," December 1707, AGN, Indiferente Virreinal-Alcaldes Mayores, caja 5223, exp. 102.
11 Ramos, "'Un tóxico,'" 121-148.
12 Emily Kuffner, "Mandrake and Monarchy in Early Modern Spain," *Journal of the History of Sexuality* 29, no. 3 (September 2020), 335-363.
13 Kuffner, "Mandrake and Monarchy," 335-363.
14 Ephesians 5: 22-23
15 Robles, *Diario de sucesos*, 2: 113, 301.
16 Antonio de Salazar, *Importancias de la fecundidad, y desseado parto de la reyna N. Sra. Doña Maria Lvisa de Saboya. Sermon, panegyrico, predicado el dia quinze de septiembre del año de 1707. En el solemne octavario, que celebro en la yglesia del Sr. S. Francisco de la ciudad de S. Luyz Potosi* (Mexico City: Herederos de la Viuda de Francico Rodriguez Lupercio, 1707), 2-8; Genesis 30: 1.
17 Heras y Alcocer, *Sermon que en el solemne novenario*, 1.
18 See Actas de cabildo, March 9, 1708, in *Actas antiguas de cabildo. Libros 43 al 47. Comprendiendo desde el 1 de enero de 1706 a 22 de diciembre de 1713* (Mexico City: Imprenta Particular de G. Oropeza Velasco, 1911), 105-108.
19 José de Abarsuza, *Optimo máximo, fructo de la oración. Sermon panegirico, predicado en la fiesta solemne,que, en accion de gracias, por el feliz, augsto, [Sic] y serenissimo nacimiento de el Principe Nuestro Señor Don Luis Philipo, que Dios guarde, celebró el Illustmo. y Rmo. Sr. Dr. D. Manuel de Escalante Colombres, y Mendoza, Obispo de La Santa Iglesia de Valladolid* (Puebla: Imprenta de Diego Fernández de León, 1708), 8-8v.
20 Bernárdez de Ribera, *Sermon que en accion de gracias*, 3.
21 Miguel González Valdeosera, *Genethliaco elogio, prognostico felice, en la expectacion del real augusto parto: que esperamos segun lo denota el benigno aspecto de la mas brillante americana estrella Maria Sa[n]tissima Virgen, y Madre de Dios, que venera esta Nueva-España con la advocacion de los Remedios* (Mexico City: Juan Joseph Guillena Carrascoso en el Empedradillo, 1707, 7-8.
22 Juan Antonio Santibáñez, *Sermon, que predicó en la real fiesta, que la magestad catholica de nuestro Rey, y Señor D. Phelipe V (que Dios guarde) celebrò en su Real Collegio de San Juan de Letrán de esta mexicana corte el dia 24 de Junio de este año de 1707. á la Natividad del Sr. S. Juan Baptista, que dedica al Ex. Sr. D. Francisco Fernandez de La Cueva, Enriquez. Duque de Alburquerque, Marqués de Cuellar, Conde de Ledésma, Huelama, &c.* (Mexico City: Herederos de la Viuda de Francisco Rodriguez Lupercio, 1707).
23 Juan de San Miguel, *Sermon, que en la última missa de el novenario que hizo la Santa Iglesia catedral de Durango, la qual celebró de pontifical el Illustrissimo, y Reverendissimo Señor D. Ignacio Diez de la Barrera obispo*

de dicha Santa Iglesia en acción de gracias por estar en cinta N. Señora, y Reina Doña Maria Luysa pidiendo juntamente la felizidad de su parto (Mexico City: Juan Joseph Guillena Carrascoso, 1707), 6v–7.
24 González Valdeosera, *Genethliaco elogio, prognostico felice*, 2, 6.
25 Bernárdez de Ribera, *Sermon que en accion de gracias*, 1r–2.
26 Pulgar, *Sermon que en accion de gracias*, 1–2.
27 Jan Baptist Bedaux, "Fruit and Fertility: Fruit Symbolism in Netherlandish Portraiture of the Sixteenth and Seventeenth Centuries." *Simiolus: Netherlands Quarterly for the History of Art* 17, no. 2/3 (1987), 150–168.
28 Luis Antonio Ribot García and Luis Miguel Enciso Recio, *Orígenes políticos del testamento de Carlos II la gestación del cambio dinástico en España: discurso leído el día 17 de octubre de 2010 en la recepción pública del Excmo. Sr. D. Luis Antonio Ribot García y contestación por el Excmo. Sr. D. Luis Miguel Enciso Recio* (Madrid: Real Academia de la Historia, 2010), 32–33.
29 Ramos and Escamilla González, "Sucesión y renovación del cuerpo de la monarquía," 391.
30 Genesis 2: 8–9.
31 Ezekiel 47: 12.
32 Book of Revelation 22:1–2.
33 Isabelle Bouchiba-Fochesato, "El árbol como imagen simbólica del poder," in *El universo simbólico del poder en el Siglo de Oro*, ed. Álvaro Baraibar and Mariela Ínsua (New York/Pamplona: Instituto de Estudios Auriseculares, 2012), 25–34.
34 Juan de Borjas, *Empresas morales, Segunda parte* (Bruselas: Francisco Foppens, 1680), 336, 337. Borjas first published his book of emblems in 1581, but the 1680 edition includes a brand new second part with emblems designed by the author and his grandson, Francisco de Borjas.
35 Rubial García, *El paraíso de los elegidos*; Sérgio Buarque de Holanda, *Visão do paraíso: Os motivos edênicos no descobrimento e colonização do Brasil* (São Paulo: Companhia das Letras, 2010; orig. pub. 1959). On the multivalency of botanical motifs in the decorative arts in New Spain, see Patricia Díaz Cayeros. *Ornamentación y Ceremonia: cuerpo, jardín, y misterio en el coro de la catedral de Puebla* (Mexico City: Universidad Nacional Autónoma de México, 2012).
36 Marjorie Reeves, "The 'Arbores' of Joachim of Fiore," *Papers of the British School at Rome* 24 (1956), 124–136.
37 Jean Delumeau, *History of Paradise: The Garden of Eden in Myth and Tradition* (Champaign: University of Illinois Press, 2000), 124. For a discussion of the meanings of specific flowers and fruit in early modern art, see Lucia Impelluso, *Nature and Its Symbols* (Los Angeles: Getty Publications, 2004).
38 James Hall, *Dictionary of Subjects and Symbols in Art* (New York: Routledge, 2018), 277.
39 "Descripcion del adorno, que se hizo en esta corte a la real entrada de Su Magestad Nuestro Catholico Rey Don Felipe Quinto, el dia catorze de Abril, desde el Buen Retiro a Palacio, con el aparato del arco, Monte Parnaso, y distancia del Prado, y carrera hasta el Palacio," *Gazeta de Madrid*, 1701, BP; López de Pro, *Caminos de verdad*, 2–3.
40 José Francisco de Isla, *Buelos de la imperial aguila Tetzcucana, a las radiantes luzes, de el luminar mayor de dos espheras. Nuestro inclito monarca, el*

catholico rey N. Sr. D. Phelippe Quinto [que Dios guarde]. Cuia siempre augusta real magestad, aclamo jubilosa la americana ciudad de Tetzcuco, el dia 26 de junio de este año de 1701 (Mexico City: Herederos de la Viuda de Bernardo Calderón, 1701).

41 Amescua, *Ramillete compuesto de las mas hermosas fragrantes flores*, 9.
42 Mendieta Rebollo, *Sumptuoso, festivo real aparato en que explica su lealdad*, 18.
43 Gómez de la Parra, *Famosos triumphos*, n.p.
44 Gómez de la Parra, *Grano de trigo fecundo*, 5, 34–35; Psalms 2: 7–8.
45 Valtierra, *Sermon que en solemne accion de gracias por los ultimos successos de la monarchia de España, y singulares providencias à favor de su invencible monarcha*, 1707, 4.
46 Xardón, *Nuevo solsticio entre leon, y virgen para exaltacion de España en Sagitario*, 14–15.
47 Franco Rubio, "Rituales y ceremonial en torno a la procreación real," 245.
48 Salazar, *Importancias de la fecundidad*, 2.
49 Dionisio Levanto, *Oracion panegirica en accion de gracias, que por el feliz nacimiento del serenissimo señor D. Luiz I. Principe de las Asturias celebrò el convento del Señor Santo Domingo de la ciudad de Antequera en el dia siete de Mayo, en que la sacratissima religion de predicadores celebra con annuos cultos la gloriosa Corona de Espinas de Nuestro Redemptor* (Mexico City: Herederos de la Viuda de Francisco Rodriguez Lupercio, 1708), 3v.
50 Castorena y Ursúa, *Fructo de bendicion de la rosa de Castilla, y la flor de lyz Francesa*, 11, 20.
51 Castorena y Ursúa, *Fructo de bendicion de la rosa de Castilla, y la flor de lyz Francesa*, 11–14.
52 Lucas del Rincón, *Llanto de flora: desatado en sepulchrales rosas sobre el magestuoso tumulo, que la imperial corte Mexicana erigio al obsequio, y voto a la memoria de su florida reyna Doña María Luisa Gabriela de Saboya, amada esposa del inclyto rey de las Españas, Don Phelipe Quinto, (que Dios guarde)* (Mexico City: Viuda de Miguel de Ribera, 1715), 29.
53 Charles George Herbermann, *The Catholic Encyclopedia: An International Work of Reference on the Constitution, Doctrine, Discipline, and History of the Catholic Church* (New York: Encyclopedia Press, 1913), 629.
54 Isaiah 11: 6.
55 Margot E. Fassler, "The Tree of Jesse," in Nick Hopwood, Rebecca Flemming, and Lauren Kassell, eds., *Reproduction: Antiquity to the Present Day* (Cambridge: Cambridge University Press, 2018), 672.
56 Salazar, *Importancia de la fecundidad*, 9, 15.
57 Antonio Salazar, *Sermon de Accion de gracias por la acclamacion de el serenissimo Señor Don Luis Fernando en Principe de Asturias, predicado a la Purissima Concepcion de Maria Santissima Nuestra Señora, el dia 27 de Diciembre en que la iglesia celebra a el Sagrado Evangelista San Juan* (Mexico City: Viudad de Miguel de Ribera Calderón, 1713), 4v–5v.
58 Bernárdez de Ribera, *Sermon que en accion de gracias*, 4v–8, 10.
59 Isaiah 16: 5.

60 Antonio García de Valdés, *Sermon que en la gozosa jura que hizo a nro. serenissimo señor el Señor D. Luis Fernando Principe de Asturias: la Muy Noble, y leal ciudad de Durango Reyno de la Nueva-Viscaya* (En Mexico: Por Francisco de Ribera Calderon, 1711), 12–13; Psalm 89: 3–4.
61 García de Valdés, *Sermon que en la gozosa jura*, 8–11.
62 Book of Revelation 22: 16.
63 Rubial García, *El paraíso de los elegidos*, 216–218.
64 Salazar, *Importancias de la fecundidad*, 2–3, 14.
65 Heras y Alcocer, *Sermon que en el solemne novenario*, 9.
66 Pulgar, *Sermon que en accion de gracias ofrecio a Dios*, 10–11.
67 Pulgar, *Sermon que en accion de gracias ofrecio a Dios*, 2.
68 Heras y Alcocer, *Sermon que en el solemne novenario*, 9.
69 San Miguel, *Sermon, que en accion de gracias por el feliz nacimiento*, n.p.
70 San Miguel, *Sermon, que en accion de gracias por el feliz nacimiento*, 27–31.
71 San Miguel, *Sermon, que en accion de gracias por el feliz nacimiento*, 29–31.
72 Toro Altamirano, *Sermon panegyrico, en agimento de gracias a el Santissimo Sacramento*, 3.
73 Gómez de la Parra, *Famosos triumphos*, 201v.
74 Ramos, "Arte efímero," 179–218.
75 Alfonso Mariano del Río. *Sermon de nombre de la venerable Tercera Orden de Penitencia de N.P.S. Francisco de la ciudad de Mexico: de su patrono, y titular el Christianissimo Monarcha San Luis Nono, Rey de Francia* (Mexico City: Viuda de Miguel de Ribera, en el Empedradillo, 1713).
76 Castorena y Ursúa, *Raçones de la lealtad*, 6–7.
77 Ramos and González Escamilla, "Sucesión y renovación," 401.
78 Montaño, *Vozes de la lealtad*, 10–10v.
79 Alcozer y Sariñana, *Festivo triduo*, 27.
80 Antonio de Escoto. *Sermón de hazimiento de gracias, que el feliz nacimiento de nuestro principe Luis Felipepo, y dichoso parto de nuestra augustissima reyna Doña María Luisa Gabriela Manuela de Saboya a los 25 de Agosto del año passado de 1707* (Mexico City: Viuda de Miguel de Ribera Calderón, 1709), 1–11.
81 Castorena y Ursúa, *Raçones de la lealtad*, 12.
82 Rincón, *Llanto de flora*, 1–29.

Conclusion

1 Francisco de la Concepción Barbosa, *Accion de gracias, que con asombros del afecto, y con afectos asombrosos, celebrò la jura, y coronacion de nuestro Catholico Rey, y Señor Don Luis Primero: El dia 2 de octubre, año de 1724. Sermon que en la plausible fiesta, que hizo el Muy Noble, y Siempre Leal pueblo de el partido de Tula, en el religiosissimo Convento de N.S.P.S. Francisco, parrochial de dicho pueblo, y sus contornos* (Mexico City: Juan Francisco de Ortega Bonilla, 1725), 1–15.

2 Luis de la Peña, *La muerte temprana, pero madura de N. Serenissimo Rey, y Señor D. Luis Primero, declamada en el sermon fúnebre ... en las honras, y funerales exequias, que celebró el Sagrado Convento Real de Señoras Religiosas de Jesus Maria, de esta ciudad de Mexico, el dia 26. de Junio de este año de 1725. Con asistencia de los Señores de la Real Audiencia, Regios Tribunales, Nobilisima Ciudad, y un Docto, Religioso, Noble, y numeroso concurso* (Mexico City: Joseph Bernardo de Hogal, 1725), 1–5.

3 José Antonio de Villerías y Roelas, *Llanto de las estrellas al ocaso del sol anochecido en el oriente: solemnes exequias, que a la augusta memoria del serenissimo, y potentissimo señor Don Luis I. Rey de las Españas, celebrò el Excmo. Sr. D. Juan de Acuña, Marquès de Casa-Fuerte, cavallero del Orden de Santiago, y Comendador de Adelfa en la de Alcantara, General de los Reales Exercitos, Virrey Governador, y Capitan General de esta Nueva-España, y Presidente de la Real Audiencia, &c. A cuya disposicion assistieron por comission de Su Exc. los Señores DD. D. Geronimo de Soria Velasquez, Marquès de Villaphermosa de Alfaro, y D. Pedro Malo de Villavicencio, Cavallero del Abito de Calatrva, ambos del Consejo de SM. y sus oydores en esta Real Audiencia, &c.* (Mexico City: Joseph Bernardo de Hogal, 1725).

4 Morán, *La imagen del rey*, 45. Morán mentions the image, seeing it as an example of the king becoming a "defender of the faith" but does not connect it with the iconoclasm committed during the war or the establishment of the annual feast day To Make Amends to the Most Holy Sacrament.

5 Ramos, *Identity, Ritual, and Power*, 42.

6 Torres Puga, *Opinión pública*, 43–61.

7 Torres Puga, *Opinión pública*, 61–69.

8 Torres Puga, *Opinión pública*, 69–76.

9 Felipe Castro Gutiérrez, "Profecías y libelos subversivos contra el reinado de Carlos III," *Estudios de historia novohispana*, no. 11 (1991), 85–96.

10 Torres Puga, *Opinión pública*, 73–74.

11 J. M. Rodríguez, *Oración fúnebre, que en las exequias, que de orden del excelentísimo Sr. D. Carlos Francisco de Croix, Virrey de esta Nueva España &c se celebraron por los militares españoles difuntos, en la Iglesia del Convento Grande de N.S.P.S. Francisco de México, el dia 6 de Noviembre de 1767* (Mexico City: Imprenta del Nuevo Rezado, de los Herederos de Doña María de Ribera, 1767).

12 Gregorio de Omaña, *Oracion funebre que en las anniversarias honras de los militares defuntos de España, celebradas en la Santa Iglesia de Mexico, dijo en presencia del Excmo Sr Marques de Croix ... el dia 19 de noviembre de este año de 1768* (Mexico City: Imprenta Real del Superior Govierno, del Br. Don Joseph Antonio Hogal, 1768), 1–17.

13 José Serruto y Nava, *Reales exequias celebradas en la Santa Iglesia Catedral de México por el alma del Señor Don Carlos III. Rey de España y de las Indias, en los dias 26 y 27 de Mayo de 1789* (Mexico City: Imprenta de D. Felipe de Zúñiga y Ontiveros, 1789), 12–19.

14 Serruto y Nava, *Reales exequias celebradas*, 20–27.

15 See, for example, Marco Antonio Landavazo Arias, *La máscara de Fernando VII: Discurso e imaginario monárquicos en una época de crisis: nueva España, 1808–1822* (Morelia: El Colegio de Michoacán A.C., 2001).
16 Eric Van Young, *The Other Rebellion: Popular Violence, Ideology, and the Mexican Struggle for Independence, 1810–1821* (Stanford: Stanford University Press, 2001), 454–457.
17 Van Young, *The Other Rebellion*, 464–466.

Bibliography

Archives

Archivo de la Catedral de México	ACM
Actas del Cabildo Eclesiástico	ACE
Archivo General de Indias	AGI
Escribanía	
México	
Archivo General de la Nación	AGN
Edictos de Inquisición	
Reales Cédulas (RC)	
Archivo General Municipal de Puebla	AGMP
Actas de Cabildo (AC)	
Reales Cédulas (RC)	

Rare Book Libraries

Biblioteca Burgoa	BB
Biblioteca José María Lafragua	BJML
Biblioteca Nacional de Chile	BNC
Biblioteca Nacional de España	BNE
Biblioteca Nacional de México – Fondo Reservado	BNM-FR
Biblioteca Palafoxiana	BP
Centro de Estudios de Historia de México, Carso	CEHM
John Carter Brown Library	JCB
Real Biblioteca	RB

On-line Depositories

Biblioteca Digital del Museo Nacional del Prado MNP
Cervantes Virtual Library CVL
Google Books GBooks

Select Rarebooks[1]

Abarsuza, José de. *Optimo máximo, fructo de la oración. Sermon panegirico, predicado en la fiesta solemne, que, en accion de gracias, por el feliz, augsto [sic], y serenissimo nacimiento de el principe nuestro señor Don Luis Philipo, que Dios guarde, celebró el Illustmo. y Rmo. Sr. Dr. D. Manuel de Escalante Colombres, y Mendoza, Obispo de la Santa Iglesia de Valladolid ... en la Villa de Santa Fé, Real, y Minas de Huanajuato à 20 de Diziembre de 1707 años*. Puebla: Imprenta de Diego Ferna[n]dez de Leon, 1708. BNC.

Aguilera, Izaguirre, Francisco de. *Accion de gracias del convento de N.P.S. Augustin de la ciudad de Nra. Señora de la Concepcion de Zelaya, a Dios Nro Señor Sacramentado por la victoria que en Villaviciosa consiguio nuestro ynclito monarca, y señor D. Philippo V. Rey de España, y Emperador de las Indias*. Mexico City: Francisco de Rivera Calderon, 1712. BP.

Alcalá, José de. *Motivos de dolor que en las funerales tiernas exequias de el siempre augusto señor, invicto Christianissimo rey de Francia Luis XIV predicò ... y celebro la santa Yglesia de Valladolid, cabeça de el obispado de Michoacan, el dia 14. de noviembre de 1716. años*. Mexico City: Herederos de la Viuda de Francisco Rodríguez Lupercio, 1716. BNC.

Alcocer y Sariñana, Baltasar de. *Festivo triduo, devida aclamacion, á los gloriosos triumphos de las catholicas armas de nuestro invicto rey de las Españas, del monarcha supremo de las Indias el Señor Don Philipo V (que Dios guarde). Devidamente vencedor en los campos de Villaviciosa, contra la opuesta liga, que celebró la Mexicana Athenas con su rector, y claustro, y consagra a dicha real magestad como á su patron, y señor*. Mexico City: Herederos de Juan Joseph Guillena Carrascoso, 1712. BNE.

Alfonso IX, King of Castile. *Las siete partidas del sabio rey don Alonso el Nono glosadas por el licenciado Gregorio López: tomo I [-IV]*. Edited by Gregorio López de Tovar. Madrid: Oficina de Benito Cano, 1789. CVL.

Amescua, Miguel de, *Ramillete compuesto de las mas hermosas fragrantes flores, que en varias, y diversas estaciones de tiempos llevó la antiguedad en sus mas floridos heroes, y en los huertos de las Indias se juntaron en las rosas de Castilla, y flores de Lis*. Mexico City: Herederos de la Viuda de Francisco Rodriguez Lupercio, 1701. BP.

Argüello, Manuel de. *Accion de gracias, a la soberana reyna del cielo Maria SS. de Guadalupe en su magnifico templo, con que solemnizò el real acuerdo de esta corte, en virtùd de real orden, las victorias, que consiguiò personalmente la magestad del rey nuestro señor don Philippo V. (que Dios guarde) en Viruega, y Villaviciosa los dias 8. y 11. de diziembre del año de 1710*. Mexico City: Viuda de Miguel de Ribera, 1711. JCB.

Avendaño Suárez de Sousa, Pedro. *Oración funebre panegyrica, que en las honras, que celebró a la magestad del Señor D., Carlos Segundo, rey de las Españas el Real Convento de Religiosas de Jesus Maria de la ciudad de Mexico, hizo, y dijo el dia 18 de Junio de 1701 años.* [Mexico City?: s.n., ca. 1701]. BNM-FR.
Bedmar, Lucas Antonio de. *Real aclamacion, que de orden de la Reyna nuestra señora, y la Junta de Govierno, se executò en esta Corte el miercoles 24 de noviembre de este presente año de 1700, levantando el Estandarte Real por el Rey Catolico nuestro señor Don Felipe Quinto ... en que se refieren todas las circunstancias que concurrieron à tan real, y magnifico acto.* Madrid: Lucas Antonio de Bedmar, 1700. RB.
Belluga y Moncada, Luis Antonio. *Sermón que el Obispo de Cartagena ... predicò en su Santa Iglesia, el dia ultimo de la octava que se celebrò a Maria SSma. de los Dolores en su SS, Imagen de las Lagrimas, en acción de gracias por el nacimiento de nuestro Serenissimo Principe el Sr. don Luis Fernando.* Murcia: Vicente Llofriu, 1707. CVL.
Bernárdez de Ribera, Jacinto. *Sermon que en accion de gracias ofrecio a Dios, y a su Purissima Madre el Convento de las Llagas de Nuestro Seraphico Padre S. Francisco de la ciudad de la Puebla de los Angeles por el nacimiento de N. Principe y Señor Don Luiz Phelipe.* Mexico City: Imprenta por la Viuda de Miguel de Ribera Calderon, 1708. BJML.
Borja, Juan de. *Empresas morales.* Brussels: Francisco Foppens, 1680. MNP.
Brabo, José. *Sermon a los desagravios del Ssmo. Sacramento, por el real cedula de Su Magestad, por el ultraje, que le hizieron los hereges, poniendole en precio, y almoneda.* Mexico City: Viuda de Miguel de Ribera Calderon, 1712. JCB.
Carrera, Baltasar de. *Sermon predicado en la solemne funcion de la accion de gracias, que por los triumphos, que la magestad de Nuestro Catholico Rey, y Sr. de las Españas Phelipe V contra sus enemigos tiene alcançados de orden y mandato de NMRP Fr Juan de la Cruz ... Este su Convento de la Assumpcion en esta ciudad de Toluca, el dia 6 de agosto de 1711.* Mexico City: Viuda de Miguel de Ribera Calderon, 1712. BP.
Castañeda, Antonio Carlos de. *Reales preceptos executados en acreditados observaciones de affectos con que la ciudad de Tlaxcala manifestó desempeños, assí en los sentimientos por la falta de Nuestro Rey y Señor Don Carlos Segundo, como en el crecido júbilo a la jura de Nuestro Rey Don Phelipe Quinto.* Puebla: Herederos del Capitán Juan de Villa-Real, 1701. BNM-FR.
Castilla de la, Miguel. *Elogio sepulchral a la immortal memoria de los españoles que murieron en el victoriosa expulsión del ejército enemigo, segunda vez apoderado de la corte de Madrid.* Mexico City: Viuda de Miguel de Rivera, 1711. CEHM.
Castorena y Ursúa, Juan Ignacio de. *Fructo de bendicion de la rosa de Castilla, y la flor de lyz francesa, el rey, y la reyna, en nuestro amado principe, que Dios prospera, por intercession del gran San Bernardo, santo frances, patron español de los fructos de Mexico, metropoli de estos reynos, coraçon de la America, y cabeça de la Nueva-España. Oracion panegyrica, que el dia de su fiesta, en el convento de sus religiosas en su iglesia dedicada à Nuestra Señora*

de Guadalupe la Mexicana, y al Santo Abbad. Mexico: Juan Joseph Guillena Carrascoso, 1709. BNC.

Raçones de la lealtad, clausulas de la fineza en elogio de las hazañas, que en los diez años del reynado del catholico monarcha Philipo V el Animoso, rey de las Españas, y de las Indias, ha celebrado la Sta Yglesia Cathedral. Mexico City: n.p., 1711. BNM-FR.

Parabien de las letras a las armas. Oracion gratulatoria panegyrica, evangelica; que en accion de gracias, en la Real Universidad, por el glorioso triumpho de el invicto monarcha Philipo V. el Animoso, Rey de las Españas, Emperador de las Indias su catholico dueño, en el campo de Brihuega, y Villaviciosa. Con asistencia del Exmo Señor vi-rey, Duque de Linares, Real Audiencia, tribunales, claustro pleno, cabildo eclesiastico, observantissimas communidades de todas las sagradas religiones. Mexico City: Herederos de Juan Joseph Guillena Carrasco, 1712. JCB.

Concepción Barbosa, Francisco de la, *Accion de gracias, que con asombros del afecto, y con afectos asombrosos, celebrò la jura, y coronacion de nuestro Catholico Rey, y Señor Don Luis Primero: el dia 2 de Octubre, año de 1724. Sermon que en la plausible fiesta, que hizo el Muy Noble, y Siempre Leal pueblo de el partido de Tula, en el religiosissimo Convento de N.S.P.S. Francisco, parrochial de dicho pueblo, y sus contornos*. Mexico City: Juan Francisco de Ortega Bonilla, 1725. CEHM.

Dañón, Pedro. *Claridad de ojos, apercion de oidos, y verdad de palabras, que manifiestan a vista de el desengaño, las glorias del mayor triumpho, que a influxo de la concepcion de Maria Ssma., consiguió en su octava nuestro catholico monarcha D. Philippo Quinto (que Dios guarde) y con zeloso pecho, festivo culto, y devida accion de gracias, mandó celebrar en este Convento de N.P.S. Francisco de Mexico, el Dia 15 de Julio de 1711*. Mexico City: Viuda de Miguel de Ribera, 1711. JCB.

Díaz de Olivares, Francisco. *Oración en la acción de gracias, que celebro la ciudad de la Puebla de los Ángeles en la iglesia catedral de ella, El día del Apóstol Santiago, patente el Santísimo Sacramento, por las victorias que alcanzo Nuestro Rey Felipe V en el campo de Villaviciosa*. Sevilla, n.p., 1712. CEHM.

Escoto, Antonio de. *Sermón de hazimiento de gracias, que el feliz nacimiento de nuestro principe Luis Philippo, y dichoso parto de nuestra augustissima reyna Doña María Luisa Gabriela Manuela de Saboya a los 25 de Agosto del año passado de 1707*. Mexico City: Viuda de Miguel de Ribera Calderón, 1709. BP.

Gil, Alonso. *Oracion panegyrica en la celebridad que en accion de gracias por el felis nacimiento de nuestro señor, y principe, hizo el Convento de N. P. S. Domingo de la Puebla el dia 18 de Julio de este año de 1708*. Puebla: Imprenta de Diego Fernández de León, 1708. BJML.

Goikoetxea, Juan de. *La maravilla immarcescible, y milagro continuado de Maria Santissima Señora Nuestra, en su prodigiosa imagen de Guadalupe de Mexico, compite firmezas con su nuevo templo, que la copía: adelanta duraciones al cielo, que á su efigie traslàda: iguàla permanencias con el augusto sacramento, de quien imita la milagrosa presencia en su pintura. Sermon en el dia octavo del novenario â la dedicacion de su magnifico templo, con el mysterio de la purificacion, y dia de la Aparicion de S. [sic] Miguel, celebrô la fiesta, y solemnizô el dia la exc. señora, señora [sic] doña Juana de la Cerda, y Aragon, duqueza de Alburquerque, vi-reyna de esta Nueva-España, con la religion de la sagrada Compañia de Jesus.* Mexico City: Imprenta de los Herederos de Juan Joseph Guillena Carrascoso, 1709. JCB.

Philippo Quinto David segundo, en la piedad primero rey de las Españas; honrando sus fuertes, celebrando exequias á sus militares diffuntos, reyna entre los leones; vençe sus enemigos; restaura los terminos de su imperio; en succession feliz eterniza su solio; y se haze un nombre grande, igual con el que oy tiene entre los reyes el renombre de grande. Sermon que predicó el día 5. de Noviembre de este año de 1707. Mexico City: Juan Joseph Guillena Carrascoso, 1707. JCB.

Gómez de la Parra, José. *Grano de trigo fecundo de virtudes de la vida, fecundissimo por la succession en la muerte, la catholica magestad del rey nuestro señor Don Carlos Segundo, que Dio aya: assumpto paneryrico funeral, que predicò a las funebres exequias, que en su magnifica iglesia cathedral celebro el Ilustrissimo Señor Venerable Ecclesiastico Cavildo Sede-Vacante, á expensas de la Nobilissima Imperial ciudad de la Puebla de Los Angeles de la Nueva-España, el dia nuebe de Mayo de 1701. Años.* Puebla: Herederos del Capitán Juan de Villa Real, 1701. BJML.

Famosos triumphos y victoriosos tropheos, que el dia 15 de Julio del año de 1708 el primero de el festivo triduo, que celebró el Illmo. V. Dean y Cabildo, Sede Vacante, de la Santa Iglesia Cathedral de la ciudad de La Puebla de Los Angeles en la Nueva-España en honor de la Immaculada Concepcion de Maria SS. N. S. Su Titular, para dar gracias a Dios N.S. por el feliz nacimiento de Tu Alteza. El Sr. D. Luis I, Principe de Las Asturias. Puebla: Oficina de D. Joseph Pérez, 1709. BNM-FR.

González de la Sancha, Lorenzo Antonio. *Victima catholica, panegyrico culto, holocausto gratulatorio, demonstracion christiana, que consagro al soberano Jesus sacramentado en la custodia del sagrado vientre de su purisima madre, el Collegio Real de San Juan Letran, de esta Imperial Corte Mexicana, â los felices sucesos de las victoriosas armas de nuestro rey y señor natural Don Philipo V. que Dios guarde.* Mexico City: Francisco de Ribera Calderón, 1711. JCB.

González Valdeosera, Miguel. *Genethliaco elogio, prognostico felice, en la expectacion del real augusto parto: que esperamos segun lo denota el benigno aspecto de la mas brillante Americana estrella Maria Sa[n]tissima virgen, y madre de Dios, que venera esta Nueva-España con la advocacion de los Remedios.* Mexico City: Juan Joseph Guillena Carrascoso, 1707. JCB.

Gorospe Irala, Diego de. *Sermon que en la solemnissima declaracion de la jura del serenissimo Señor D. Luys Fernando de Borbon Principe de Asturias N. Señor aclamada en la coronada Villa de Madrid el dia del mes del año passado [Sic] de 1707 y proclamada en la Muy Noble, y Leal ciudad de Manila el dia XIV de enero de este presente año de MDCCXII.* Manila: Convento de N.P.S Francisco, 1712. BP.

Guevara, Juan de. *Sermon, que los solemnes cultos, que el muy religioso parrochial Convento de N.S.P. San Francisco de la ciudad de Santiago de Queretaro, consagró á Maria SS. N. Señora en el misterio de su concepcion sin culpa, patente el augustissimo señor de el cielo, y tierra sacramentado, en accion de gracias por los felices sucessos, que en la batalla de Brihuega, y Villaviciosa consiguió victorioso de sus enemigos, nuestro amabilissimo, legitimo rey, y señor de las Españas, D. Phelippo V. (que Dios guarde).* Mexico City: Viuda de Miguel de Ribera Calderon, 1711. BP.

Heras y Alcocer, José de las. *Sermon que en el solemne novenario, que hizo el Convento Grande de Mexico de el Real Orden de Nuestra Señora de la Merced Redempcion de Captivos, en accion de gracias por la felice noticia de estar en cinta nuestra serenissima señora Dôña Maria Luyza Gabriela Emmanuel de Saboya, Reyna de Espana.* Mexico City: Herederos de la Viuda de Francisco Rodríguez Lupercio, 1707. JCB.

Heredia, Antonio de. *Elogio genethliaco, festivo paean, que en un carro triumphal en la cimientos de nuestro príncipe fiestas, con que esta Muy Noble, y Cesárea ciudad de la Puebla de los Angeles, celebró el feliz nacimiento de nuestro príncipe.* Puebla: Imprenta de D. José Pérez, 1709. CEHM.

Isla, José Francisco de, *Buelos de la imperial aguila Tetzcucana, a las radiantes luzes, de el luminar mayor de dos espheras. Nuestro inclito monarca, el Catholico Rey N. Sr. D. Phelippe Quinto [que Dios guarde]. Cuia siempre augusta real magestad, aclamo jubilosa la americana ciudad de Tetzcuco, el dia 26 de junio de este año de 1701.* Mexico City: Herederos de la Viuda de Bernardo Calderón, 1701. BP.

Levanto, Dionisio. *Oracion panegirica en accion de gracias, que por el feliz nacimiento del serenissimo Señor d. Luiz I. Principe de las Asturias celebrò el Convento del Señor Santo Domingo de la ciudad de Antequera en el dia siete de mayo, en que la sacratissima religion de predicadores celebra con annuos cultos la gloriosa Corona de Espinas de Nuestro Redemptor.* Mexico City: Herederos de la Viuda de Francisco Rodriguez Lupercio, 1708. JCB.

López de Pro, Maximiliano. *Caminos de verdad, mansedumbre, y justicia. Señales que dexo estampadas en ellos la S. A. C. y R. Magestad de el Señor D. Carlos Segundo, Rey de las Españas ... En las honras que le hizo el Imperial Convento de N. P. S. Francisco de la ciudad de Tlaxcala el dia 11 del mes de agosto, del año de 1701.* Puebla: Imprenta del Capitán Sebastián de Guevara, 1701. BJML.

Maldonado, Ángel de. *Afectos a Dios, y al Rey, solicitados por medio de cinco oraciones evangelicas.* Puebla: Imprenta de Diego Fernández de León, 1709. BJML.

Oracion evangelica predicada en la Santa Iglesia Cathedral de Antequera, segundo dia de Pasqua de Resurreccion: y dia primero de el octavario, que celebró dicha Santa Iglesia en hacimiento de gracias de el nacimiento de Nuestro Principe Real de Asturias el Señor Luis Primero. Puebla: Diego Fernández de León, 1709. BP.

Oracion evangelica, que predicò [...]en la Sta. Yglesia Metropolitana de Mexico Domingo infra octavo de la Purissima Concepcion de Maria SSma. y segundo de Adviento. Dia en que de orden de S.M. (Dios le guarde) se dieron gracias por los sucessos felizes de el dia nueve, y diez de diziembre en las facciones de Brihuega, y Villaviciosa. Y dia en que se solicitaron los desagravios de los arrojos, que cometieron los infieles en Christo Bien Nuestro Sacramentado. Mexico City: Herederos de la Viuda de Miguel de Ribera Calderón, 1715. JCB.

Oraciones evangélicas. Mexico City: Herederos de Juan Joseph Guillena Carrascoco, 1721. B.Burgoa.

Mancilla, Antonio. *Piedras tituladas que dejo en España su patron, el gloriosissimo apostol Santiago; para feliz exaltacion, del reyno, del rey, y de su Corona. Sermon con la asistencia del excelentissimo Señor Duque de Alburquerque Virrey de esta Nueva España, y de la noble ciudad de México, predicó el dia 25 de Julio del año de 1708.* Mexico City: Herederos de la Viuda de Francisco Rodríguez Lupercio, 1708. BJML.

Mendieta Rebollo, Gabriel de. *Sumptuoso, festivo real aparato en que explica su lealdad [sic] la siempre Noble, Ilustre, Imperial, y Regia ciudad de Mexico, metropóli de la America, y corte de la Nueva-España. En la aclamacion del muy alto, muy poderoso, muy soberano príncipe. D. Phelipe V so católico dueño.* Mexico City: Imprenta de Juan Joseph Guillena Carrascoso, 1701. GBooks.

Mesa, Augustín Jacinto de. *Sermon que en la solemnidad de la Pascua de los Reyes, y epiphania del Señor, predicó en la Santa Metropolitana, y Patriarcal Iglesia de Sevilla, este presente año de 1704.* Seville: Juan de la Puerta, 1704. BP.

Montaño, Tomás. *Vozes de la lealtad, alborozos de la fidelidad: sòlemnidad plausible, que en accion de gracias por los felices sucessos de las españolas armas, y triumphos de su invensible monarcha D. Phillippo V. que Dios guarde. Consagró la Santa Yglesia de Valladolid de Michoacan, y su meritissimo prelado el Ill. Sr. D. D. Phelipe Ignacio Truxillo, y Guerrero, de el Consejo de Su Magestad, Obispo Electo de Michoacan.* Mexico City: Herederos de la Viuda de Francisco Rodriguez Lupercio, 1712. JCB.

Montoya y Cárdenas Ponce de León, Ambrosio Francisco. *Diseño festivo del amor obstentiva muestra de la lealtad acclamación alegre con que la Muy Noble, Augusta Imperial ciudad de la Puebla de los Angeles en el diez de Abril del año de 1701, juro por su rey y señor natural al invictissimo señor D. Phelipe V de este nombre, monarcha supremo de dos mundos.* Puebla: Herederos del Capitán Juan de Villa Real, 1701. BJML.

Mora, Agustín de. *El sol eclipsado antes de llegar al Zenit: real pira que incendió à la apagada luz del rey N.S.D. Carlos II: El Excelentísimo Señor Don Joseph Sarmiento Valladares, Caballero del Orden de Santiago.* Mexico City: n.p., 1701. BNM-FR.

Núñez de Godoy, Miguel. *Desagravios de Christo Sacramentado, que en las victorias de Nuestro Rey, y Señor D. Philippo V discurrio … en la solemne fiesta que Su Magestad (Dios le guarde) manda celebrar en la Dominica infraoctava de la Concepcion de Maria Señora Nuestra, patente el Sanctisimo Sacrame[n]to.* Mexico City: Francisco de Ribera Calderón, 1712. JCB.

Prognostico Philippico hallado en la sagrada historia del real propheta David. Discurso panegyrico, que en el sermon de la missa de gracias, que por la acclamacion de nuestro rey, y señor Don Philippo Quinto [que Dios guarde] celebrò la Sancta Iglesia Cathedral de Guadalaxara. patente el Sanctissimo Sacramento. En veinte y seis de Julio del año de 1701. Mexico City: Francisco de Ribera Calderón, 1712. JCB.

Omaña, Gregorio de. *Oracion funebre que en las anniversarias honras de los militares defuntos de España, celebradas en la Santa Iglesia de Mexico. Dijo en presencia del Excmo Sr Marques de Croix ... el dia 19 de Noviembre de este año de 1768*. Mexico City: Imprenta Real del Superior Gobierno, del Br. Don Joseph Antonio Hogal, 1768. CEHM.

Orozco y Molina, Juan Felipe. *Relacion de la plausible real solemnidad con que esta ilustre, y leal ciudad de Durango, caveza del reyno de esta Nueva-Viscaya, Celebrò la jura de nuestro principe de las Asturias el Señor D. Luis Fernando, como heredero de los reynos de España por primogenito de nuestro monarcha, y señor Philipo Quinto emperador de este Nuevo-Mundo, à quienes Dios prospere, y guarde dilatados años*. Mexico City: Imprenta de Miguel de Ortega, y Bonilla, 1711. JCB.

Peña, Luis de la, *La muerte temprana, pero madura de N. Serenissimo Rey, y Señor D. Luis Primero, declamada en el sermon fúnebre ... que celebró el Sagrado Convento Real de Señoras Religiosas de Jesus Maria, de esta ciudad de Mexico, el dia 26. de Junio de este año de 1725. Con asistencia de los señores de la Real Audiencia, regios tribunales, Nobilisima Ciudad, y un docto, religioso, noble, y numeroso concurso*. Mexico City: Joseph Bernardo de Hogal, 1725. CEHM.

Picazo, J. *El segundo Josias, Carlos II. Sin segundo como èl, y sin primero. Oracion funebre panegyrica, que por la seraphica religion dixo en su Convento Grande de Queretaro, el dia veinte y uno de Junio del año passado de mil setecientos y uno*. Mexico City: Herederos de la Viuda de Francisco Rodríguez Lupercio, 1702. BNC.

Posada, Antonio de., *Sermon funeral de las sumptuosas honras, que en el Convento de San Francisco de la ciudad de la Vera-Cruz, celebró el dia 23 de Abril de 1701 a n. gran rey, y catholico monarca Dn. Carlos II de immortal memoria, el Sr. D. Manuel de Velazco, y Texada [...]Cavallero de Orden de Santiago*. Mexico City: Imprenta de Juan Joseph Guillena Carrascoso, 1701. BJML.

Pulgar, Blas del. *Oracion panegyrica, y declamacion funebre, en las solemnes exequias, que celebrò el Real Convento de N.P.S. Francisco de Mexico, dia 13. de mayo de 1701. Por muerte del rey nuestro Señor, el Señor D. Carlos II. Rey de las Españas, y las Indias, el Catholico, el pio, el religioso*. Mexico City: Herederos de la Viuda de Francisco Rodriguez Lupercio, 1701. BNM-FR.

Sermon que en accion de gracias ofrecio a Dios, y a su santisima madre, en su devotissima imagen de los Remedios, en su iglesia metropolitana, la Muy Noble, Leal, e Imperial Corte de Mexico. Por el augustissimo parto de la reyna nuestra señora la Serenissima Doña Maria Luysa Gabriela Emmanuel de Saboya, en que dio a luz, dia de S. Luyz Rey de Francia a 25 de Agosto a nuestro principe Luys Phelipe. Mexico City: Viuda de Miguel de Ribera Calderón, 1708. JCB.

Rincón, Lucas del. *Llanto de flora: desatado en sepulchrales rosas sobre el magestuoso tumulo, que la imperial corte Mexicana erigio al obsequio, y voto a la memoria de su florida reyna Doña María Luisa Gabriela de Saboya, amada esposa del inclyto rey de las Españas, Don Phelipe Quinto, (que Dios guarde).* Mexico City: Viuda de Miguel de Ribera, 1715. JCB.

Río, Alfonso Mariano del. *Sermon de nombre de la venerable Tercera Orden de Penitencia de N.P.S. Francisco de la ciudad de Mexico: De su patrono, y titular el Christianissimo Monarcha San Luis Nono, Rey de Francia.* Mexico City: Viuda de Miguel de Ribera, 1713. JCB.

Salazar, Antonio de. *Importancias de la fecundidad, y desseado parto de la reyna N. Sra. Doña Maria Luisa de Saboya. Sermon, panegyrico, predicado el dia quinze de septiembre del año de 1707. En el solemne octavario, que celebro en la yglesia del Sr. S. Francisco de la ciudad de S. Luyz Potosi.* Mexico City: Herederos de la Viuda de Francisco Rodriguez Lupercio, 1707. BNM-FR.

Sermon de accion de gracias por la acclamacion de el serenissimo señor Don Luis Fernando el Principe de Asturias, predicado a la Purissima Concepcion de Maria Santissima Nuestra Señora, el dia 27 de Diciembre en que la Iglesia celebra a el sagrado evangelista San Juan. Mexico City: Viuda de Miguel de Ribera Calderón, 1713. BNM-FR.

San Miguel, Juan de. *Espejo para todos los reyes del mundo. Descifrado en la estatua de Nabuchodonosor. Mejorador para los señores reyes de España en el magnífico corazón de la muerte majestad de nuestro Católico Rey Don Carlos II.* Mexico City: Miguel de Rivera, 1701. BNM-FR.

Sermon, que en la última missa de el novenario que hizo la Santa Iglesia catedral de Durango, la qual celebró de pontifical el Illustrissimo, y Reverendissimo Señor D. Ignacio Diez de la Barrera obispo de dicha Santa Iglesia en acción de gracias por estar en cinta N. Señora, y Reina Doña Maria Luysa pidiendo juntamente la felizidad de su parto. Mexico City: Juan Joseph Guillena Carrascoso, 1707. CEHM.

Sermon que en accion de gracias por el feliz nacimiento de el principe Nuestro Señor D. Luis Fernando dijo el ... guardian del Convento de S. Antonio de Durango, el dia quinto de la infraoactava de la Natividad de la Señora. En la fiesta que celebraron los juezes oficiales reales de la referida ciudad, y reyno de la Vizcaya. Mexico City: Imprenta Nueva Plantiniana de Diego Fernández de León, 1710. CEHM.

Sariñana, Isidro. *Llanto del occidente en el ocaso del mas claro sol de las Españas. Funebres demostraciones, que hizo, pyra real, que erigio en las exequias del Rey N. Señor D. Felipe IIII. El Grande. El Exmo. Señor D. Antonio Sebastian de Toledo, Marques de Manzera, Virrey de la Nueva España, con la Real Audiencia, en la S. Yglesia Metropolitana de Mexico, ciudad imperial del Nuevo Mundo.* Mexico City: Viuda de Bernardo Calderón, 1666. JCB.

Serruto y Nava, José. *Reales exequias celebradas en la Santa Iglesia Catedral de México por el alma del Señor Don Carlos III. Rey de España y de las Indias, en los dias 26 y 27 de Mayo de 1789.* Mexico City: Imprenta de D. Felipe de Zúñiga y Ontiveros, 1789. CEHM.

Solanes, Francisco. *El emperador politico, y politica de emperadores: vida del emperador Ulpio Trajano sacada del panegyrico de Plinio Menor, y otros autores, ilustrada con varias maximas politicas y morales.* Barcelona: Imprenta de Joseph Llopis, 1700. BJML.

Torres Pezellín, José de. *Phelipe Quinto de los santos de este nombre, y quintado por las heridas del martyrio. Sermon que á S. Phelipe de Jesus, Proto-Martyr del Japon, criollo, y natural de la Muy Noble, y Leal ciudad de Mexico, dixo, el dia 5. de Febrero de 1707 años, en la Santa Yglesia Cathedral, con asistencia de los Exmos. Señores Vi-Rey de esta Nueva España, Arçobispo, Real Audiencia, y cabildos eclesiastico, y secular.* Mexico City: Viuda de Miguel de Ribera Calderón, 1707. JCB.

Toro Altamirano, Fernando de, *Sermon panegyrico, en agimento de gracias a el Santissimo Sacramento, por la feliz noticia de hallarse en cinta la catholica magestad de nuestra serenissima reyna de España Doña María Luisa Gabriela de Saboya Nuestra Señora.* Mexico City: Imprenta por la Viuda de Miguel de Ribera, 1707. BNM-FR.

Ubilla y Medina, Antonio. *Succession de el rey D. Phelipe V, Nuestro Señor en la corona de España: diario de sus viages desde Versalles a Madrid, el que executó para su feliz casamiento, jornada a Napoles, a Milan, y a su exercito, successos de la campaña, y su buelta a Madrid.* Madrid: Juan Garcia Infanzón, 1704. BNM-FR.

Unibárbia, Bernardo. *Intereses predicados en la festiva accion de gracias, por las victorias conseguidas de nuestro Catholico Rey Philipo Quinto: celebrò, por mandado de Su Mag. el Real de Minas de Sultepec, en su yglesia parroquial, patente el SSmo. Sacramento, dia del Santo Nombre de Maria à 13 de Septiembre. año de 1711.* Mexico City: Herederos de Juan Joseph Guillena Carrascoso, 1711. JCB.

Valtierra, Antonio de. *Sermon que en solemne accion de gracias por los ultimos successos de la monarchia de España, y singulares providencias à favor de su invencible monarcha. Philippo Quinto,(que Dios guarde). Y lo dedica al S. D. Pedro Colon de Larreatigui del Consejo de Su Magestad en el Real, y Supremo de Castilla.* Mexico City: Viuda de Miguel de Ribera, 1707. JCB.

Velasco y Arellano, José Luis de. *Catholico triumpho, y hacimiento de gracias, que venerando laureles, panegyrisando hazañas, venerando verdades, y admirando valores: consiguieron las reales armas de N.C. monarcha el Señor D. Phelip V (que Dios guarde) de las que colligadas con el imperio, solicitaron la ruyna, y dessolacion de nuestra monarchia. Y a los rayos de tantas luces, eclypso sus explendores, la muerte del Sr. Delphin.* Mexico City: Herederos de Juan Joseph Guillena Carrasco, 1712. JCB.

Verdiguer Isasi, Lucas de. *Acción gratulatoria que la Santa Iglesia Metropolitana de México celebró el Domingo doce del mes de Julio de este presente año de 1711, Estando patente el Santísimo Sacramento, por la feliz victoria que Su Majestad (que Dios guarde) alcanzó de las imperiales armas: el día 9 y 10 de Diciembre del año pasado de 1710.* Mexico City: n.p., 1711. CEHM.

Villalobos, Joachín Antonio, *Sermon, que à la fiesta que celebró la ciudad de S. Luis Potosi. A Xpto Nuestro Señor Sacramentado, en accion de gracias por las victorias, que en el Campo de Villa-Viciosa alcanzó de sus enemigos, la catolica magestad del rey ntro. sr. Don Philipo V. Rey de Españas, y*

Emperador de las Indias. Predicó el dia 20 de Septiembre de este año. Mexico City: Herederos de Juan Joseph Guillena Carrasco, 1712. BP.

Villerías y Roelas, José Antonio de. *Llanto de las estrellas al ocaso del sol anochecido en el oriente: solemnes exequias, que a la augusta memoria del serenissimo, y potentissimo señor Don Luis I. Rey de las Españas, celebrò el Excmo. Sr. D. Juan de Acuña, Marquès de Casa-Fuerte, cavallero del Orden de Santiago, y Comendador de Adelfa en la de Alcantara, General de los Reales Exercitos, Virrey Governador, y Capitan General de esta Nueva-España, y Presidente de la Real Audiencia.* Mexico City: Joseph Bernardo de Hogal, 1725. CEHM.

Xardón, Antonio. *Nuevo solsticio entre leon, y virgen para exaltacion de España en Sagitario. Horoscopo astrono-mystico al feliz nacimiento del primogenito de las Magestades Catholicas el Señor Don Luis I. Jurado principe de Asturias ... En la festiva solemnidad que en accion de gracias consagró a Christo Sr. N. Sacramentado el M. Illustre Sr D. Thoribio de Coizio Caballero del Orden de Calatrava, de el Consejo de Su Magestad y su presidente de la Real Audiencia de Guatemala, governador y capitan general de todas sus provincias.* Mexico City: Herederos de Juan Joseph Guillena Carrascoso, 1708. CEHM.

Yáñez de Avilés, Pablo. *España-Francia, union, y amistad antigua de las dos naciones. Utilidad sagrada, y humana de su comunicación. Compendio historial, y aparato a los annales corelativos de las dos Coronas. Divido en dos partes. I. Union, y utilidad catholica-moral religiosa, y mystica. II. Union, y utlidad militar civil, eclesiastica, y literaria.* Madrid: n.p., 1711. BJML.

Zuazo y Coscojales, Diego de. *Oracion evangelica y panegirica de la Purificacion de Maria Santísima: Que predicó en la Santa Iglesia Metropolitana de Mexico, el dia dos de Febrero, de este ano de 1703.* Mexico City: Imprenta de Juan Joseph Guillena Carrascoso, 1703. JCB.

Modern Editions of Primary Sources

Actas antiguas de cabildo. *Vol. 2: Libros 43–47, años de 1706 a 1713.* Mexico City: Imprenta Particular G. Oropeza Velasco, 1911.

Calderón de la Barca, Frances. *Life in Mexico.* Berkeley: University of California Press, 1982. Originally published in 1843.

Florencia, Francisco de and Juan Antonio Oviedo. *Zodiaco Mariano.* Mexico City: Consejo Nacional para la Cultura y las Artes, 1995.

González Acosta, Alejandro. *Crespones y campanas tlaxcaltecas en 1701.* Mexico City: Universidad Nacional Autónoma de México, 2000.

Kopylov, Iván, ed. *El tratado del Apocalipsis del beato Gregorio López (1542–1596): Exégesis histórico profética.* Mexico City: Editorial Notas Universitarias, 2021.

Monségur, Jean de. *Las nuevas memorias del capitán Jean de Monségur.* Edited and translated by Jean-Pierre Berthe. Serie Historia novohispana, no. 50.

Mexico City: Universidad Nacional Autónoma de México, Instituto de Investigaciones Históricas, 1994.

Muro Orejón, Antonio. *Cedulario americano del siglo XVIII: colección de disposiciones legales indianas desde 1680 a 1800, contenidas en los cedularios del Archivo General de Indias. Vol. 2, Cédulas de Felipe V (1700–1724)*. Seville: Publicaciones de la Escuela de Estudios Hispano-Americanos de la Universidad de Sevilla, 1969.

Robles, Antonio de. *Diario de sucesos notables (1665–1703)*. 3 vols. Mexico City: Editorial Porrúa, 1972.

San Felipe, Vicente Bacallar y Sanna. *Comentarios de la guerra de España e historia de su rey, Felipe V, el Animoso*. Biblioteca de Autores Españoles, vol. 99. Madrid: Atlas, 1957. Originally published in 1725.

Seijas y Lobera, Francisco de. *Gobierno militar y político del reino imperial de la Nueva España (1702)*. Mexico City: Universidad Nacional Autónoma de México, 1986.

Secondary Sources

Albareda i Salvadó, Joaquim. *Felipe V y el triunfo del absolutismo: Cataluña en un conflicto europeo, 1700–1714*. Barcelona: Generalitat de Catalunya, Entitat Autònoma del Diari Oficial i de Publicacions, 2002.

——— *La Guerra de Sucesión de España (1700 – 1714)*. Barcelona: Crítica, 2012.

Anderson, Benedict. *Imagined Communities: Reflections on the Origin and Spread of Nationalism*. Brooklyn: Verso, 1991.

Andújar Castillo, Francisco. *Necesidad y venalidad: España e Indias 1704–1711*. Madrid: Centro de Estudios Políticos y Constitucionales, 2008.

Baraibar, Álvaro, and Mariela Ínsua, eds. *El universo simbólico del poder en el Siglo de Oro*. New York/Pamplona: Instituto de Estudios Auriseculares, 2012.

Baudot, Georges. *Utopia and History in Mexico: The First Chroniclers of Mexican Civilization (1520–1569)*. Niwot, CO: University Press of Colorado, 1995.

Bedaux, Jan Baptist. "Fruit and Fertility: Fruit Symbolism in Netherlandish Portraiture of the Sixteenth and Seventeenth Centuries." *Simiolus: Netherlands Quarterly for the History of Art* 17, no. 2/3 (1987), 150–168.

Bloch, Marc. *The Royal Touch: Sacred Monarchy and Scrofula in England and France*. Translated by J. E. Anderson. New York: Routledge Revivals, 2015. Originally published 1973.

Borges, Analola. "Los aliados del Archiduque Carlos en la América virreinal." *Anuario de estudios americanos* 27 (1970), 321–370.

Borreguero Beltrán, Cristina. "Imagen y propaganda de guerra en el conflicto sucesorio (1700–1713)." *Manuscrits: Revista d'història Moderna* 21 (2003), 95–132.

Bouchiba-Fochesato, Isabelle. "El árbol como imagen simbólica del poder." In *El universo simbólico del poder en el Siglo de Oro*, edited by Álvaro Baraibar and Mariela Ínsua, 25–34. New York/Pamplona: Instituto de Estudios Auriseculares, 2012

Bouza Álvarez, Fernando J. *Communication, Knowledge, and Memory in Early Modern Spain*. Translated by Sonia López and Michael Agnew. Philadelphia: University of Pennsylvania Press, 2004.
Bouza Álvarez, Fernando. *Papeles y opinión: Políticas de publicación en el Siglo de Oro* Madrid: Consejo Superior de Investigaciones Científicas, 2008.
Brading, D. A. "Tridentine Catholicism and Enlightened Despotism in Bourbon Mexico." *Journal of Latin American Studies* 15 (1983), 1–22.
The First America: The Spanish Monarchy, Creole Patriots, and the Liberal State, 1492–1867. New York: Cambridge University Press, 1991.
Mexican Phoenix: Our Lady of Guadalupe: Image and Tradition across Five Centuries. Cambridge: Cambridge University Press, 2001.
Bravo Lozano, Cristina. "Madrid as Vienna, Besieged and Saved: The Ceremonial and Political Dimensions of the Royal Cavalcade to Atocha (1683)." *The Hungarian Historical Review* 4, no. 2 (2015), 471–501.
Brown, Jonathan and J. H. Elliot. *A Palace for a King: The Buen Retiro and the Court of Philip IV*. New Haven: Yale University Press, 1980.
Burke, Peter. *The Fabrication of Louis XIV*. New Haven: Yale University Press, 1994.
Cal Martínez, María Rosa. "'La Gazeta' de Madrid y la Guerra de Sucesión." *Cuadernos dieciochistas*, no. 3 (2002), 35–56.
Calvo, Thomas. "La construcción de una cultura imperial: Zaragoza, Valladolid de Michoacán, Lima y Manila lloran al Príncipe Baltasar Carlos (1647–1648)." In *Convergencias y divergencias: México y Perú, siglos XVI–XIX*, edited by Lilia V. Oliver Sánchez, 101–128. Guadalajara: University of Guadalajara, 2006.
Poder, religión y sociedad en la Guadalajara del siglo XVII. Guadalajara: Universidad de Guadalajara, 1992.
Campbell, Jodi. *Monarchy, Political Culture, and Drama in Seventeenth-Century Madrid: Theater of Negotiation*. New York: Routledge, 2016.
Cañeque, Alejandro. *The King's Living Image: The Culture and Politics of Viceregal Power in Colonial Mexico*. New York: Routledge, 2004.
Cañeque García, Alejandro. *Un imperio de mártires: Religión y poder en las fronteras de la Monarquía Hispánica*. Madrid: Marcial Pons Ediciones de Historia, S.A., 2020.
Castillo, David R., and Massimo Lollini. *Reason and Its Others: Italy, Spain, and the New World*. Nashville: Vanderbilt University Press, 2006.
Castro Gutiérrez, Felipe. "Profecías y libelos subversivos contra el reinado de Carlos III." *Estudios de historia novohispana*, no. 11 (1991), 85–96.
Childers, William. "The Baroque Public Sphere." In *Reason and Its Others: Italy, Spain, and the New World*, edited by David R. Castillo and Massimo Lollini, 165–181. Nashville: Vanderbilt University Press, 2006.
Clark, Joseph M. H. *Veracruz and the Caribbean in the Seventeenth Century*. Cambridge: Cambridge University Press, 2022.
Cohn, Norman. *The Pursuit of the Millennium: Revolutionary Millenarians and Mystical Anarchists of the Middle Ages*. New York: Oxford University Press, 1970.
Cope, Douglas R. *The Limits of Racial Domination: Plebeian Society in Colonial Mexico City, 1660–1720*. Madison: University of Wisconsin Press, 1994.

Cortezo, María Victoria López Cordón, Julio Valdeón Baruque, Bethany Aram, et al. *Gobernar en tiempos de crisis: Las quiebras dinásticas en el ámbito hispánico.* Madrid: SÍLEX EDICIONES, S.L., 2008.

Cromwell, Jesse. "Life on the Margins: (Ex) Buccaneers and Spanish Subjects on the Campeche Logwood Periphery, 1660–1716." *Itinerario* 33, no. 3 (2009), 43–71.

Cuadriello, Jaime. "The Politicization and Sociability of the Public Image: The King and His Representatives, 1700–1790." In *Painted in Mexico, 1700–1790: Pinxit Mexici,* edited by Ilona Katzew, 112–139. Los Angeles: Los Angeles County Museum of Art and Fomento Cultural Banamex, 2017.

Cuesta García de Leonardo, María. "La mano del monarca grande de las Españas: la muerte de los soldados y el poder del Virrey Galve en la Nueva España, 1694." *Anales del Instituto de Investigaciones Estéticas* 38, no. 108 (2016), 51–85.

Curcio-Nagy, Linda. *The Great Festivals of Colonial Mexico City: Performing Power and Identity.* Albuquerque: University of New Mexico Press, 2004.

"Native Icon to City Protectress to Royal Patroness: Ritual, Political Symbolism and the Virgin of the Remedies." *The Americas* 52, no. 3 (1996), 367–391.

Díaz Cayeros, Patricia. *Ornamentación y ceremonia: Cuerpo, jardín, y misterio en el coro de la catedral de Puebla.* Mexico City: Universidad Nacional Autónoma de México, 2012.

Domínguez Cáceres, Roberto and Víctor Gayol, eds. *El imperio de lo visual. Imágenes, palabra, y representación.* Zamora, Michoacán: El Colegio de Michoacán, 2018.

Egido López, Teófanes. *Opinión pública y oposición al poder en la España del siglo XVIII: (1713–1759).* Valladolid: Universidad de Valladolid, 2002.

Eissa-Barroso, Francisco. *The Spanish Monarchy and the Creation of the Viceroyalty of New Granada (1717–1739): The Politics of Early Bourbon Reform in Spain and Spanish America.* Leiden: Brill, 2016.

Eissa-Barroso, Francisco and Ainara Vázquez Varela, eds. *Early Bourbon Spanish America: Politics and Society in a Forgotten Era (1700–1759).* Leiden: Brill Academic Publishers, 2013.

Elliott, J. H. "Self-Perception and Decline in Early Seventeenth-Century Spain." *Past & Present,* no. 74 (1977), 41–61.

The Revolt of the Catalans: A Study in the Decline of Spain (1598–1640). Cambridge: Cambridge University Press, 1980.

"A Europe of Composite Monarchies." *Past & Present,* no. 137 (1992), 48–71.

Escamilla González, Iván. "Razones de la lealtad, cláusulas de la fineza: Poderes, conflictos y consensos en la oratoria sagrada novohispana ante la sucesión de Felipe V." In *Religión, poder y autoridad en la Nueva España,* edited by Alicia Mayer and Ernesto de la Torre Villar, 179–204. Mexico City: Universidad Nacional Autónoma de México, 2004.

Los intereses malentendidos: El consulado de comerciantes de México y la Monarquía Española, 1700–1739. Mexico City: Universidad Nacional Autónoma de México, 2011.

"Yolloxóchitl y flor de lis: Nuestra Señora de Guadalupe de México, patrona de la monarquía española, 1710–1810." In *Madre de la Patria: La imagen guadalupana en la historia mexicana,* 19–50. Mexico City: Museo de la Basílica de Guadalupe, 2010.

Escamilla González, Iván, Guadalupe Pinzón Ríos, and Matilde Souto Mantecón, eds. *Resonancias imperiales: América y el Tratado de Utrecht de 1713*. Mexico City: Instituto Mora, 2015.

Eugenio Martínez, María. *La defensa de Tabasco, 1600–1717*. Seville: Escuela de Estudios Hispanoamericanos de Sevilla, 1971.

Fassler, Margot E. "The Tree of Jesse." In *Reproduction: Antiquity to the Present Day*, ed. Nick Hopwood, Rebecca Flemming, and Lauren Kassell, 672. Cambridge: Cambridge University Press, 2018.

Fernández Galán Montemayor, Carmen, Alfredo Tenoch Cid Jurado, and Víctor Manuel Chávez Ríos, eds. *Semiótica e historia*. Zacatecas: Universidad Autónoma de Zacatecas, 2018.

Franco Rubio, Gloria Ángeles. "Rituales y ceremonial en torno a la procreación real en un contexto de crisis: El primer embarazo de María Luisa de Saboya (1707)." In *Gobernar en tiempos de crisis: las quiebras dinásticas en el ámbito hispánico: 1250–1808*, edited by José Manuel Nieto Soria, María Victoria López-Cordón Coby, 35–66. Madrid: Sílex, 2008.

Frazer, James George. *The Golden Bough: A Study in Magic and Religion*. New York: Simon and Schuster, 1995. Originally published in 1890.

Frost, Elsa Cecilia. "El milenarismo franciscano en México y el profeta Daniel." *Historia Mexicana* 26, no. 1 (1976), 3–28.

Gelis, Jacques. *History of Childbirth: Fertility, Pregnancy and Birth in Early Modern Europe*. New ed. Cambridge: Polity, 1996.

Giesey, Ralph E. *The Royal Funeral Ceremony in Renaissance France*. Geneva: Droz, 1960.

González Cruz, David. *Guerra de religión entre príncipes católicos: El discurso del cambio dinástico en España y América (1700–1714)*. Madrid: Ministerio de Defensa, 2002.

——— "Actitudes e imagen de las reinas en tiempo de crisis: La transición de los Austrias a los Borbones." In *Vírgenes, reinas y santas: Modelos de mujer en el mundo hispánico*, edited by David González Cruz, 75-104. Huelva: Universidad de Huelva, 2007.

——— "Celebraciones de victorias militares de la monarquía hispánica en sus dominios de Europa y América (siglos XVII y XVIII)." In *Ocio y vida cotidiana en el mundo hispánico en la Edad Moderna*, edited by Francisco Núñez Roldán, 231–244. Sevilla: Editorial Universidad de Sevilla-Secretariado de Publicaciones, 2007.

———, ed. *Vírgenes, reinas y santas: Modelos de mujer en el mundo hispano*. Huelva: Universidad de Huelva, 2007.

——— *Propaganda e información en tiempos de guerra: España y América (1700–1714)*. Madrid: Silex, 2009.

Graeber, David, and Marshall Sahlins. *On Kings*. Chicago: Hau Books, 2017.

Habermas, Jürgen. *The Structural Transformation of the Public Sphere: An Inquiry into a Category of Bourgeois Society*. Translated by Thomas Burger. Cambridge: MIT Press, 1989. First published in 1962.

Hall, James. *Dictionary of Subjects and Symbols in Art*. New York: Routledge, 2018.

Heath, Sean. *Sacral Kingship in Bourbon France: The Cult of Saint Louis, 1589–1830*. London: Bloomsbury, 2021.

Herbermann, Charles George. *The Catholic Encyclopedia: An International Work of Reference on the Constitution, Doctrine, Discipline, and History of the Catholic Church.* New York: Encyclopedia Press, 1913.
Herrero Sánchez, Manuel. "Spanish Theories of Empire: A Catholic and Polycentric Monarchy." In *A Companion to Early Modern Spanish Imperial Political and Social Thought*, edited by Jörg Alejandro Tellkamp, 17–42. Leiden: Brill, 2020.
Hopwood, Nick, Rebecca Flemming, and Lauren Kassell, eds. *Reproduction: Antiquity to the Present Day.* Cambridge: Cambridge University Press, 2018.
Impelluso, Lucia. *Nature and Its Symbols.* Los Angeles, Getty Publications, 2004.
Iñurritegui, J. M. "Las virtudes y el jurista: El emperador político de Francisco Solanes y el amor a la patria." *Pedralbes: revista d'història moderna* (January 2004), 285–310.
Kagan, Richard L. *Lucrecia's Dreams: Politics and Prophecy in Sixteenth-Century Spain.* Berkeley: University of California Press, 1990.
—— *Clio & the Crown: The Politics of History in Medieval and Early Modern Spain.* Baltimore: Johns Hopkins University Press, 2009.
Kagan, Richard L., and Fernando Marías Franco. *Urban Images of the Hispanic World, 1493–1793.* Yale University Press, 2000.
Kamen, Henry. *Philip V of Spain: The King Who Reigned Twice.* New Haven: Yale University Press, 2001.
—— *Spain in the Later Seventeenth Century, 1665–1700.* London: Longman, 1980.
—— *The War of Succession in Spain, 1700–1715.* Bloomington: Indiana University Press, 1969.
—— "The Destruction of the Spanish Silver Fleet at Vigo." *Bulletin of the Institute of Historical Research* 39, no. 100 (1966), 165–175.
Katzew, Ilona, ed. *Painted in Mexico, 1700–1790: Pinxit Mexici.* Los Angeles: LosAngeles County Museum of Art and Fomento Cultural Banamex, 2017.
Kertzer, David I. *Ritual, Politics, and Power.* New Haven: Yale University Press, 1988.
Klaits, Joseph. *Printed Propaganda under Louis XIV: Absolute Monarchy and Public Opinion.* Princeton: Princeton University Press, 1976.
Kuethe, Allan J., and Kenneth J. Andrien. *The Spanish Atlantic World in the Eighteenth Century: War and the Bourbon Reforms, 1713–1796.* New York: Cambridge University Press, 2014.
Kuffner, Emily. "Mandrake and Monarchy in Early Modern Spain." *Journal of the History of Sexuality* 29, no. 3 (September 2020), 335–363.
Leahy, Chad and Ken Tully, ed. *Jerusalem Afflicted: Quaresmius, Spain, and the Idea of a 17th-Century Crusade.* London: Routledge, 2020.
Leddy Phelan, John. *The Millennial Kingdom of the Franciscans in the New World.* 2nd ed. Berkeley: University of California Press, 1970.
Lira Saucedo, Salvador Alejandro. "El discurso visual en la transición dinástica de Austrias a Borbones." In *Semiótica e historia*, edited by Carmen Fernández Galán Montemayor, Alfredo Tenoch Cid Jurado, and Víctor Manuel Chávez Ríos, 65–98. Zacatecas: Universidad Autónoma de Zacatecas, 2018.

López Alonso, Antonio. *Carlos II el hechizado*. Madrid: Ediciones Irreverentes, 2003.
López Anguita, José Antonio. "El matrimonio de Felipe V y la alianza borbónico-saboyana de 1701." *Hispania* 77, no. 257 (2017), 735–762.
López Cantos, Ángel. *Juegos, fiestas y diversiones en la América Española*. Madrid: Editorial MAPFRE, 1992.
Lotman, Yu M. and B. A. Uspensky. "On the Semiotic Mechanism of Culture." *New Literary History* 9, no. 2 (1978), 211–232.
MacKay, Ruth. *The Baker Who Pretended to Be King of Portugal*. Chicago: University of Chicago Press, 2012.
Magnier, Grace. *Pedro de Valencia and the Catholic Apologists for the Expulsion of the Moriscos*. Leiden: Brill, 2010.
Maravall, José Antonio. *Culture of the Baroque: Analysis of a Historical Structure*. Translated by Terry Cochran. Minneapolis: University of Minnesota Press, 1986. Originally published 1975.
Marcos, David Martín. *El papado y la Guerra de Sucesión española*. Madrid: Marcial Pons Historia, 2011.
Marin, Louis. *Portrait of the King*. Translated by Martha M. Houle. Minneapolis: University of Minnesota Press, 1988. Originally published in 1981.
Marías, Fernando, ed. *Otras Meninas*. Madrid: Siruela, 1995.
Marley, David. *Wars of the Americas: A Chronology of Armed Conflict in the New World, 1492 to the Present*. Santa Barbara, CA: ABC-CLIO, 1998.
Mayer, Alicia. *Lutero en el paraíso: la Nueva España en el espejo del reformador alemán*. Fondo de Cultura Económica, 2008.
Mayer, Alicia, and Ernesto de la Torre Villar, eds. *Religión, poder y autoridad en la Nueva España*. Universidad Nacional Autónoma de México, 2004.
McCusker, John J. *How Much Is That in Real Money? A Historical Price Index for Use as a Deflator of Money Values in the Economy of the United States*, 3rd ed. Worcester, MA: American Antiquarian Society, 2001.
Melvin, Karen. "Charity without Borders: Alms-Giving in New Spain for Captives in North Africa." *Colonial Latin American Review* 18, no. 1 (2009), 75–97.
Milhou, Alain. "La chauve-souris, le nouveau David et le roi caché (Trois images de l'empereur des derniers temps dans le monde ibérique : XIIIe–XVIIe s.)." *Mélanges de la Casa de Velázquez* 18, no. 1 (1982): 61–78.
Colón y su mentalidad mesiánica en el ambiente franciscanista español. Las Palmas, Spain: Casa-Museo de Colón, 1983.
"Esquisse d'un panorama de la prophétie messianique en Espagne (1482–1614) : thématique, conjoncture et fonction." In *La prophétie comme arme de guerre : Pouvoirs (XVe–XVIIe siècles)*, edited by Auguste Redondo, 11–29. Paris: Presses de la Sorbonne Nouvelle, 2000.
Mínguez, Víctor. "La monarquía humillada: Un estudio sobre las imágenes del poder y el poder de las imágenes." *Relaciones* 77, no. 20 (1999), 123-148.
La invención de Carlos II: apoteosis simbólica de la casa de Austria. Madrid: Centro de Estudios Europa Hispánica, 2013.
Mínguez Cornelles, Víctor. *Los reyes solares: iconografía astral de la monarquía hispánica*. Publicacions de la Universitat Jaume I, 2001.

"Los emperadores taumaturgos: curaciones prodigiosas desde Trajano a Napoleón." *Potestas*, no. 5 (2015), 43–81.

"Reyes enfermos e imperio renovado. Las muertes de Felipe IV, Carlos II, Luis XIV, Luis I y Felipe V en la Nueva España (1665–1746)." *Romance Notes* 56, no. 3 (2016), 413–422.

Mitchell, Silvia Z. "Introduction: The Spanish Habsburg Court during the Reign of Carlos II (1665–1700)." *The Court Historian* 23, no. 2 (2018), 107–112.

"Women and Children First: Court Ceremonial during Carlos II's Minority, 1665–1675." *The Court Historian* 23, no. 2 (2018), 135–151.

Montes González, Francisco. *Mecenazgo virreinal y patrocinio artístico: El ducado de Alburquerque en la Nueva España*. Seville: Real Maestranza de Caballería de Sevilla, 2016.

Morán, Miguel. *La imagen del rey. Felipe V y el arte*. Madrid: Editorial Nerea, 1990.

Moreno Cebrián, Alfredo and Núria Sala i Vila. *El "premio" de ser virrey: Los intereses públicos y privados del gobierno virreinal en el Perú de Felipe V*. Madrid: Consejo Superior de Investigaciones Científicas, 2004.

Muñoz, José Ángel del Barrio. *Filipinas y la Guerra de Sucesión Española: avatares y sucesos en un frente secundario (1701–1715)*. Valladolid: Castilla Ediciones, 2015.

Nieves, Elienahí. "Donativo de los hacendados de Nueva España para financiar la Guerra de Sucesión Española, 1709–1716." *América Latina en la historia económica* 28, no. 3 (2021), 1–19.

Nunn, Carlos F. *Foreign Immigrants in Early Bourbon Mexico*. Cambridge: Cambridge University Press, 1979.

Nalle, Sarah T. "Revisiting El Encubierto: Navigating between Visions of Heaven and Hell on Earth." In *Werewolves, Witches, and Wandering Spirits: Traditional Belief and Folklore in Early Modern Europe*, edited by Kathryn Edwards, 77–92. Kirksville, MO: Truman State University Press, 2002.

Navarro García, Luis. "La administración virreinal en México en 1703." *Revista de Indias*, no. 115–118 (December 1969), 359–370.

"Los oficios vendibles en Nueva España durante la Guerra de Sucesión." *Anuario de Estudios Americanos* 32 (1975), 133–154.

"Cambio de dinastía en Nueva España." *Anuario de Estudios Americanos* 36 (1979), 111–168.

Conspiración en México durante el gobierno del Virrey Alburquerque. Valladolid: Casa-Museo de Colón; Seminario Americanista de la Universidad de Valladolid, 1982.

Olivari, Michele. *Avisos, pasquines y rumores: Los comienzos de la opinión pública en la España del siglo XVII*. Madrid: Ediciones Cátedra, 2014.

Olivas, Aaron Alejandro. "Loyalty and Disloyalty to the Bourbon Dynasty in Spanish America and the Philippines during the War of the Spanish Succession (1700–1715)." PhD University of California, Los Angeles, 2013.

"Performance and Propaganda in Spanish America during the War of the Spanish Succession." In *Performances of Peace: Utrecht 1713*, edited by

Roger E. de Bruin, Cornelis van der Haven, Lotte Jensen, and David Onnekink, 197–206. Leiden: Brill, 2015.

Oliver Sánchez, Lilia V., ed. *Convergencias y divergencias: México y Perú, siglos XVI–XIX*. Guadalajara: University of Guadalajara, 2006.

Olsen, E. *The Calabrian Charlatan, 1598–1603: Messianic Nationalism in Early Modern Europe*. New York: Palgrave Macmillan, 2002.

Osorio, Alejandra B. "The Copy as Original: The Presence of the Absent Spanish Habsburg King and Colonial Hybridity." *Renaissance Studies* 34, no. 4 (2020), 704–721.

"The King in Lima: Simulacra, Ritual and Rule in Seventeenth-Century Lima." *Hispanic American Historical Review* 84, no. 3 (2004), 447–474.

Pagels, Elaine. *Revelations: Visions, Prophecy, and Politics in the Book of Revelation*. New York: Penguin Books, 2012.

Pearce, Adrian J. *The Origins of Bourbon Reform in Spanish South America, 1700–1763*. New York: Palgrave Macmillan, 2014.

Pérez-Mallaina Bueno, Pedro E. *Política naval española en el Átlantico (1700–1715)*. Seville: Escuela de Estudios Hispano-Americanos de Sevilla, 1982.

"La Guerra de Sucesión y la reforma del sistema de comunicaciones con América." In *La Guerra de Sucesión en España y América Actas X Jornadas Nacionales de Historia Militar, Sevilla, 13–17 de Noviembre de 2000*, 347–360. Madrid: Deímos, 2001.

Pérez Picazo, María Teresa. *La publicitista española en la Guerra de Sucesión*, vols. 1–2. Madrid: Consejo Superior de Investigaciones Científicas, 1966.

Phelan, John Leddy. *The Millennial Kingdom of the Franciscans in the New World*. 2nd ed. Berkeley: University of California Press, 1970.

Ramos, Frances L. "War, Legitimacy, and Ceremony in 18th–Century Mexico City: The Annual Funerary Honors for Fallen Soldiers." In *A Companion to Viceregal Mexico City, 1521–1821*, edited by John F. López, 114–133. Leiden: Brill, 2021.

"Custom, Corruption, and Reform in Early Eighteenth–Century Mexico: Puebla's Merchant Priests versus the Reformist Bureaucrat." In *Corruption in the Iberian Empires: Greed, Custom, and Colonial Networks*, edited by Christoph Rosenmüller, 151–169. Alburquerque: University of New Mexico Press, 2017.

"'Un puñal, un tóxico, que quita la vida de toda una monarquía':ceremonias públicas, sermones panegíricos, y el discurso anti-inglés en la víspera de Utrecht." In *Resonancias imperiales: América y el Tratado de Utrecht*, edited by Iván Escamilla González, Matilde Suoto Mantecón, and Guadalupe Pinzón Ríos, 121–148. Mexico City: Instituto de Investigaciones Dr. José María Luis Mora, 2015.

"Memoria colectiva y disensión política en la Puebla del Siglo XIII, México: el motín en honor del obispo Juan de Palafox y Mendoza." *Historia Mexicana* 62, no. 3 (2013), 1019–1074.

Identity, Ritual, and Power in Colonial Puebla. Tucson: University of Arizona Press, 2012.

"Arte efímero, espectáculo, y la reafirmación de la autoridad real en Puebla durante el siglo XVIII: La celebración en honor del Hércules Borbónico." 25, no. 97 (Winter 2004), 179–218.

"Succession and Death: Royal Ceremonies in Colonial Puebla." *The Americas* 60, no. 2 (2003), 185–215.

Ramos, Frances L., and Iván Escamilla González. "Sucesión y renovación del cuerpo de la monarquía: Las representaciones de Felipe V y la familia real en Nueva España durante la Guerra de Sucesión." *Colonial Latin American Review* 31, no. 3 (2022), 381–410.

Rawlings, Helen. *The Debate on the Decline of Spain*. Manchester: Manchester University Press, 2012.

Redondo, Auguste, ed. *La prophétie comme arme de guerre: Pouvoirs (XVe-XVIIe siècles)*. Paris: Presses de la Sorbonne Nouvelle, 2000.

Reeves, Marjorie. "The 'Arbores' of Joachim of Fiore." *Papers of the British School at Rome* 24 (1956), 124–136.

The Influence of Prophecy in the Later Middle Ages: A Study in Joachimism. Notre Dame: University of Notre Dame Press, 1993.

Ribot, Luis. *Carlos II: el rey y su entorno cortesano*. Madrid: CEEH, Centro de Estudios Europa Hispánica, 2009.

"El rey ante el espejo: historia y memoria de Carlos II." In *Carlos II: El rey y su entorno cortesano*, edited by Luis Ribot, 13–52. Madrid: Centro de Estudios Europa Hispánica, 2009.

Ribot García, Luis Antonio and Luis Miguel Enciso Recio, *Orígenes políticos del testamento de Carlos II: La gestación del cambio dinástico en España*. Madrid: Real Academia de la Historia, 2010.

Rosenmüller, Christoph. *Patrons, Partisans, and Palace Intrigues: The Court Society of Colonial Mexico, 1702–1710*. Alberta: University of Calgary Press, 2008.

ed. *Corruption in the Iberian Empires: Greed, Custom, and Colonial Networks*. Albuquerque: University of New Mexico Press, 2017.

Corruption and Justice in Colonial Mexico, 1650–1755. Cambridge: Cambridge University Press, 2019.

Rosenthal, Earl. "Plus Ultra, Non plus Ultra, and the Columnar Device of Emperor Charles V." *Journal of the Warburg and Courtauld Institutes* 34, no. 1 (1971), 204–228.

Rowlands, Guy. *The Financial Decline of a Great Power: War, Influence, and Money in Louis XIV's France*. Oxford: Oxford University Press, 2012.

Rubial García, Antonio. *El paraíso de los elegidos. Una lectura de la historia cultural de Nueva España*. Mexico City: Fondo de Cultura Económica, 2011.

"El apocalipsis en Nueva España. Los cambios de una tradición milenaria." In *Conocimiento y cultura: Estudios modernos en la Facultad de Filosofía y Letras*, edited by Adriana Álvarez Sánchez, 19–58. Ediciones y Gráficos Eón, 2018.

Rubio Mañé, José Ignacio. *El virreinato: Expansión y defensa*. Part 2, vol. 3. Mexico City: Fondo de Cultura Económica, 1961.

Ruíz, Teofilo F. *Spain's Centuries of Crisis: 1300–1474*. Oxford: Wiley, 2008.

Bibliography

Sandoval Villegas, Martha. "'Traje español' vs. traje de francés'. La transición de la casa gobernante, un problema de identidad personificado en la imagen del funcionario. El caso de Nueva España (finales del siglo XVII, principio del siglo XVIII)." In *El imperio de lo visual. Imágenes, palabra y representación*, edited by Roberto Domínguez Cáceres and Víctor Gayol, 313–360. Zamora, Michoacán: Colegio de Michoacán, 2018.

Schrader, Jeffrey Albert. *The Virgin of Atocha and Spanish Habsburg Devotion to Miraculous Images*. PhD diss., New York University, 2003.

Serra Desfilis, Amadeo. "A Search for the Hidden King: Messianism, Prophecies and Royal Epiphanies of the Kings of Aragon (circa 1250–1520)." *Arts* 8, no. 4 (2019), 1–27.

Sierra Silva, Pablo Miguel. "Afro-Mexican Women in Saint-Domingue: Piracy, Captivity, and Community in the 1680s and 1690s." *Hispanic American Historical Review* 100, no. 1 (2020), 3–34.

Stein, Stanley J. and Barbara H. Stein, *Silver, Trade, and War Spain and America in the Making of Early Modern Europe*. Baltimore: Johns Hopkins University Press, 2000.

Stoichita, Víctor I. "Imago regis: teoría del arte y retrato real in *Las Meninas* de Velázquez." In *Otras Meninas*, edited by Fernando Marías, 186–194. Madrid: Siruela, 1995.

Storrs, Christopher. *The Resilience of the Spanish Monarchy, 1665–1700*. Oxford/New York: Oxford University Press, 2006.

"Disaster at Darien (1698–1700)? The Persistence of Spanish Imperial Power on the Eve of the Demise of the Spanish Habsburgs." *European History Quarterly* 29, no. 1 (1999), 5–38.

Tellkamp, Jörg Alejandro. *A Companion to Early Modern Spanish Imperial Political and Social Thought*. Leiden: Brill, 2020.

Töle, Tom. *Heirs of Flesh and Paper: A European History of Dynastic Knowledge around 1700*. Berlin: De Gruyter Oldenbourg, 2022.

Torres Puga, Gabriel. *Opinión pública y censura en Nueva España: Indicios de un silencio imposible (1767–1794)*. Mexico City: Colegio de México, 2010.

Urrejola Davanzo, Bernarda. "Felipe Quinto, de Austríaco a Borbón, según sermones de la época (Nueva España, 1701–1747)." *Colonial Latin American Historical Review* 25, no. 4 (2016), 465–491.

Valle Pavón, Guillermina del. "Servicios financieros del consulado de México para la Guerra de Sucesión Dinástica." *Mélanges de la Casa de Velázquez* 46, no. 46-1 (2016), 77–88.

Vallejo García Hevia, José María. "Los navíos de aviso y los correos marítimos a Indias (1492–1898)." *Ius fugit: Revista interdisciplinaria de estudios* 7 (1998), 197–268.

Van Young, Eric. *The Other Rebellion: Popular Violence, Ideology, and the Mexican Struggle for Independence, 1810–1821*. Stanford: Stanford University Press, 2001.

Varela, Javier. *La muerte del rey: el ceremonial funerario de la monarquía española, 1500–1885*. Madrid: Turner, 1990.

Vinson, Ben. *Bearing Arms for His Majesty: The Free-Colored Militia in Colonial Mexico*. Stanford: Stanford University Press, 2001.

Weckman, Luis. *The Medieval Heritage of Mexico*. New York: Fordham University Press, 1992.
Wunder, Amanda. *Baroque Seville: Sacred Art in a Century of Crisis*. College Station: Penn State University Press, 2017.

Bibliography

1 This bibliography includes sermons and published descriptions of ceremonies in New Spain, as well as printed, book-length sources. All broadside-like printed texts (decrees, pastoral letters, or *relaciones*), newspaper articles, and short pamphlets with imprint material, are simply cited in the notes, along with the abbreviations of the libraries where they are located.

Index

Page numbers for figures are in *italics*.

Abarsuza, José de, 126
absolutism, 11, 145, 151
Acuña y Bejarano, Juan de, 145
Ágreda, María de, 115, 124
Aguilera Izaguirre, Francisco de, 88, 110–111
Alamany, Johan (Juan Unay), 98
Alburquerque, Francisco Fernández de la
    Cueva, 10th Duke of, 21, 30, 57
  ceremonies organized by, 81, 117, 121–122
  corruption investigation, 39
  divine aid, requests for, 114
  Felipe V, donations to, 36–39
  illicit business dealings, 38
  and military conscription, 31
  of pro-Austrian/Habsburg propaganda, 50
  pro-Austrian/Habsburg propaganda, control and censorship of, 49–50
Alcácer Quibir, Battle of (1578), 93
Alcalá, Joseph de, 105
alcaldes mayores (heads of municipalities), 32, 36, 71
  criticism of, 31
  as king's representatives, 82
  pro-Austrian/Habsburg, 52–53
  sale of appointments, 41
alcaldes ordinarios (annually elected magistrates), 83
Alencastre, Fernando de *see* Linares, Fernando de Alencastre, 1st Duke of,

alférez real (royal standard bearer), 82–83, 87, 119–120
Allende, Ignacio, 149
Almansa, Battle of (1707), 15, 25, 59, 66
Alonso XIII of Castile, 63
Altamira, Luis Sánchez de Tagle, 1st Marquess of, 83
Ambrose, Saint, 129
Anderson, Benedict, 17
Andrien, Kenneth J., 12
Andújar Castillo, Francisco, 12
Ángeles Jiménez, Pedro, *138*
Anne of England and Scotland, 3
Antequera, 113
antisemitism, 62
Anton Florian of Liechtenstein, 49
Aragon, 24–25
Aragon monarchy, 4, 98–99
arbitristas (reformist thinkers), 6
Ardemans, Teodoro, *106*
Argüello, Manuel de, 63, 117
Arriola, Andrés de, 21, 41
astrology, 101
Atrisco, 1st Duke of *see* Moctezuma, José Sarmiento de Valladares, Count of,
Austrian monarchy *see* Habsburg monarchy,

Bacallar y Sanna, Vicente, Marquis of San Felipe, 107
Baltasar Carlos, Prince of Asturias, 124

209

Baños y Sotomayor, Diego, 28
Barbosa, Francisco de la Concepción, 144
Barcelona, 24, 26
  Charles VI (Archduke Charles), loyalty to, 15
  English occupation, 1705, 56
  pro-Austrian/Habsburg material printed in, 49
  Siege of (1697), 24
  Siege of (1706), 25
Bay, Battle of Vigo (1702), 39
Belluga y Moncada, Luis, 56, 61–62
beneficios (bureaucratic appointments), 40
Bernard of Clairvaux, Saint (San Bernardo), 74, 127, 131
Bible
  botanical metaphors in, 128–129
  Felipe V, associated with, 107
  Revelation, 2, 5, 95, 100, 108, 115
    prophecies from, 101, 112–113, 136
    and sacrality of Bourbon monarchy, 134–135
black people
  abductions of, 27
  in New Spain militias, 28, 33
body of Christ, 70
  body politic/of the king, connection to, 86–91
  political appropriation of, 72
  see also Eucharist,
body of the king (*cuerpo del rey*), 9, 17–18, 70
  allegiance to, 150
  beauty of, 74–75
  body of Christ/Eucharist, connection to, 86–91
  body politic as integral to, 86
  health, influence on Empire, 73–74
  present in portraits, 57, 69–70, 78
  subjects' union with, 47, 79, 127
body politic, 18, 70–72
  body of Christ/Eucharist, connection to, 86–91
  body of the king, integral to, 86
  internal relationships of, 71–72
  interrelated bodies within, 18, 79–80
  king as head of, 70, 82
  officials as "limbs" of, 82–83
  resurrection/rebirth of, 89–90
  subjects, relationship with, 71, 79–80
Borges, Analola, 11

Borja, Juan de, 129
Bourbon, Louis Joseph de, Duke of Vendôme, 24, 26
Bourbon monarchy
  continuity offered by, 63, 75–76, 78
  disloyalty to, 17
    accusations of, 51
    as demonic possession, 61, 63
    among grandees, 59
    punishments for, 45
    as sin, 48, 56
  Eucharist, devotion to, 90
  fertility, 123, 128
  legitimacy, 123
  loyalty to, 82–83
  New Spain's mythology of, 9
  opposition to, 45–46
  propaganda campaign, 5–6, 13, 15
  reforms, 11–13
  renewal through, 7–8, 78–79, 121
  sacrality, 4, 132–139, 145–151
  succession, 120–121, 128
  supporters, 13, 59
  visual representations of, 57
  see also Felipe V of Spain; Luis I of Spain,
Bouza, Fernando, 46
Brabo, José (Joseph), 63, 90, 112
Brading, David, 20
Brihuega, Battle of (1710), 15, 26, 59, 78–79, 110–112
buccaneer attacks, 27, 29
Buen Retiro palace, 64
Bula de la Santa Cruzada, 35, 54
bureaucratic appointments, sale of, 22, 53, 83
Burgundian Order, 76
Butrón y Moxíca, Manuel, 136

Calderón, Miguel, 73
Camaño, Juan López, 51, 92
Campeche, 27, 29–30
Capocelato, Don Bartolomé, Count of Antería, 28
Caracas, 28, 50
Carlos II of Spain, 2, 6–7, 40
  ambassadors to court of, 6
  and commemoration of fallen soldiers, 148
  death, 1, 45
    catafalque, Mexico City, 1
    funerary honors, 5, 80, 84, 86, 130
    funerary sermons, 89, 130

Index

Despacho Universal, use of, 55
Eucharist, devotion to, 87
fertility of, 124
illnesses of, 6–7, 73–75
named successors, 2
solar eclipse as image of, 2–3
will and testament, 1, 45, 58, 130
'Carlos III' of Spain *see* Charles VI, Holy Roman Emperor,
Carlos III of Spain (1716–88), 11–12, 141, 147–148
Carlos V, Holy Roman Emperor (Carlos I of Spain), 64, 103
Carrasco y Aguilar, Pedro, 42
Carrera, Baltazar de, 111
Cartagena, 27
Cartagena, Benito, 53, 65
Castilian monarchy, 4
Castorena y Ursúa, Juan Ignacio de
  calificador, 19
  on Felipe V prophecies, 101, 108–109, 115
  on Luis I, 131–132
  on Virgen de Guadalupe, 116
  on war victories, 60, 89
Castro y Romero, Don Manuel de, 86
catafalques
  Carlos II of Spain, 1
  Felipe IV of Spain, 4
  in funerary honors for fallen soldiers, 82, 102
  María Luisa Gabriela de Saboya, 132, *141*, 141
Catholicism
  confessional, prohibition of political influence in, 48, 54
  defense of, 60–61, 104
  of Felipe V of Spain, 48, 57
  Protestantism, conflict with, 47–48, 60–63
  see also Eucharist; masses,
cavalcades, 38, 79
censorship, 19, 46–47, 147
  through control on travel, 49
  of pro-Austrian/Habsburg propaganda, 48–50
  of War of the Spanish Succession narrative, 47–48, 55–56
ceremonies
  and absolutism, 11
  of body politic, 70–72
  cavalcades, 38, 79

commemorations
  for fallen soldiers, 81–82, 102, 108, 148
  pro-Bourbon, 8
  for victories, 102, 107–108, 122
coronations, 4
  costs and funding of, 83
funerary honors, 80, 84, 86
  for Carlos III, 148–149
  genealogies in, 104
  for Louis XIV of France, 105
  for María Luisa Gabriela de Saboya of Spain, 141, *141*
funerary masses, 84
geographical distribution of, 10
jura del rey (royal oath ceremony), 23, 69–70, 80, 83
  botanical metaphors in, 128–130
  clothing in, 78
  indigenous people's participation in, 85–86
  for Luis I, 80, 86, 119–120, 134
  royal portraits in, 76–78, 83, 119
  warrior-king metaphors in, 105, 108
loyalty, demonstrated through, 73
municipalities' participation in, 80
pennants in, 4, 82–83
print descriptions of, 16
as pro-Bourbon propaganda, 47
processions, 84, 147
public rogations, 120
royal portraits in, 76–79, 83, 119, 137–139
and sacred kingship, 4
social stability through, 147–148
subject-audiences, impact on, 13
succession, 4, 80, 87
thanksgiving, 79
  for birth of Luis I, 84, 121–123, 133–134
  hymns, 64
  for military victories, 26, 84–85
  for royal fertility, 125–128
victory celebrations, 26, 78–79, 84–85
Virgen de Atocha, veneration of, 65
visual representations in, 73–74
Charlemagne, 137
Charles VI, Holy Roman Emperor (Archduke Charles of Austria), 23
  Atocha, hears mass at, 66
  as 'Carlos III', King of Spain
    acclaimed by Habsburgs, 23
    books dedicated to, 49

Charles VI, Holy Roman Emperor
(Archduke Charles of Austria) (cont.)
    oaths of loyalty to, 15, 50, 59
    papal recognition of, 25
    support for, 37, 54
    manifesto, 50
    prophecies of victory of, 101
    sacrilege, accused of failure to prevent, 88
    succeeds as Holy Roman Emperor, 26
    in War of Spanish Succession, 23–24, 26
Childers, William, 46
Christian universalism, 103
Christianity *see* Bible; Catholicism; clergy;
    Eucharist; Jesus Christ; Mary,
    Virgin; masses; piety;
    Protestantism; sin,
Cienfuegos, Juan Álvaro, 51
Clement XI, Pope, 25, 48, 79, 114, 121
clergy
    Charles VI (Archduke Charles), support
        for, 37
    Creoles, 115
    disloyalty, criticism of, 66
    loyalty, control of, 48
    New Spain, control on travel to, 49
    pro-Austrian/Habsburg, punishment of,
        54, 56
clothing
    French styles of, 78, 137, *138*
    Spanish styles of, 69, 76, 85, 107
    traditional indigenous, 85
Coatepec, 86
Cohn, Martin, 102
Cohn, Norman, 96
Colbert, Jean Baptiste, Marquis of Torcy,
    25, 75
Collazo de Soto, Pedro, 54, 59, 62
Columbus, Christopher, 98
commemorations
    for fallen soldiers, 81–82, 102, 108, 148
    supporting Bourbon rule, 8
    for victories, 102, 107–108, 122
communication
    between metropole and New Spain, 57–59
    oral, 46, 62–63
    post, 45, 57
    visual, 46, 62–63, 75–79
Company of Scotland for Trading with
    Africa and the Indies, 27
confessional, prohibition of political
    influence in, 48, 54

Constans, Roman Emperor, 96
contraband, 35, 38, 42, 92
Coreth, Anna, 64
Cornaro, Giovanni, 6
coronations, 4
Correa, Juan, 137, *138*
corruption, 42
    anti-corruption measures, 22
    bribery, 39
    illicit business dealings, 38
    tolerance of, 40
Council of the Indies, 81
    fake communications, fear of, 59
    Marian veneration by, 65
    sale of appointments, objections to,
        41–42
Council of Trent, 87
Creoles
    clergy, 115
    sale of appointments to, 22, 41
    stereotypes about, 33
    and Virgen de Guadalupe, 116
Croix, Carlos Francisco de, 1st Marquis,
    147
Cruzat, Fausto, 38
Cruzat, Ignacia, 38
Cuba, 28
cuerpo del rey see body of the king,
Cundoacán, 31
Curcio-Nagy, Linda, 11

Dampier, William, 29
Daniel (biblical figure), 129
Darién, 27, 35–36
David (biblical figure), 20, 74, 94–95,
    109–113
    Savoy family as descendents of, 132–135
David, New (in prophecies), 94, 98–99
Despacho Universal (Universal Dispatch
    Office), 55
Díaz, Porfirio, 151
Díez de Bracamonte, Juan, 41, 117
Diez, Alonso, 24
disease, 6–7, 73–75
du Casse, Jean-Baptiste, 30
Durango, 80, 84, 86, 126–127

Edelinck, Gérard, *106*
Eissa-Barrosa, Francisco, 12
Elizabeth (biblical figure), 126
emblem books, 1–2

Index

Encubierto (Hidden/Sleeping king), 93–94, 98–100, 108, 150
England, 60–61
engravings, 76, 77
Enriquez de Cabrera, Juan Tomas, Admiral of Castile, 50–51, 54
enslaved people
  abductions of, 27
  indigenous, 30
Escamilla González, Iván, 12, 14, 107
Escoto, Antonio de, 139
etymology, 102
Eucharist, 2, 72, 78
  and body of Christ/body of the king, 86–91
  Bourbon devotion to, 90
  feast day, 15
  Fiesta de Desagravios al Santísimo Sacramento, 15, 90–91, 139, 145
  Habsburg devotion to, 86–87
  and Jesus Christ, 72, 87
  monarchy, association with, 90
  monstrances, 88, 90
  representations of, 146
  sacrilege against, 87
exorcism, 4, 7, 61

Factor, Nicolás, 100
feast days
  Fiesta de Desagravios al Santísimo Sacramento, 15, 90–91, 139, 145
  Immaculate Conception, 114
  John the Baptist, 126
  Marian, 65, 114, 139
  San Felipe, 113
  San Fernando, 147
Felipe II of Spain, 64, 93, 99
Felipe III of Spain, 64, 99
Felipe IV of Spain, 1–2, 4–5, 64–65, 124
Felipe V of Spain (Philip of Anjou), 2
  abdication and return to throne, 141, 145
  accession, 23
  anti-corruption measures, 22
  Armada de Barlovento, restoration of, 35
  breaks off diplomatic relations with Pope Clement XI, 25
  Catholic faith of, 48, 57
  clothing, Spanish style of, 69, 76
  commemoration of, 148
  David, associated with, 109–113
  Eucharist, compared to, 89

faith and piety
  as Spanish characteristic, 63
  Virgin Mary, devotion to, 63–64, 66
  Habsburgs, continuity with, 14, 91
  health of, 7
  insignia
    cordon bleu du Saint-Esprit, 76
    Toisón de Oro (Order of the Golden Fleece), 69, 76
  jura del rey (royal oath ceremony), 56, 69–70, 83
    botanical metaphors in, 128–130
    indigenous people's participation in, 85–86
    royal portraits in, 76–78, 83
    warrior-king metaphors in, 105, 108
  legitimacy
    genealogical, 103–104, 137
    through military leadership, 55
    propaganda on, 46, 62, 103
    prophecies of, 101, 109
    questions of, 56, 62
  marriage, 23
  messiah, characterized as, 94
  metaphors and symbols of, 5
    as Christ, 76, 102
    as David, 74, 95
    light, 102–103
    lions, 99, 102
    as Solomon, 76
  Nueva Planta decrees, 11, 25
  reforms, 12
  religious orders' activities dedicated to, 24
  renewal through, 7, 75
  representations of
    as French, 78
    Habsburg heritage in, 75–76
    portraits, 69–70, 75–79, 77, 145–146, 146
    as Spanish, 75–78
    as warrior-king, 105, 107
    written descriptions, 74–75
  succession, security of, 139
  support for, 5–6, 73
  in War of Spanish Succession, 25
  as warrior-king, 105–109, *106*, 110–112
Felipe Próspero, Prince of Asturias, 124
Fernández de la Cueva, Francisco *see* Alburquerque, Francisco Fernández de la Cueva, 10th Duke of,

Fernando II (Ferdinand) of Aragon (the Catholic), 98–99
Fernando III of Castile (San Fernando), 4, 79, 93, 108, 137
Fernando VI of Spain, 141
Fernando VII of Spain, 149
Feros, Antonio, 9
fertility, 7, 20, 124–132
  botanical metaphors for, 128–132
  of Bourbon monarchy, 123
  infertility, 7, 124–125, 127
    symbolic, 127–128
  treatments, 124
Fiesta de Desagravios al Santísimo Sacramento, 15, 90–91, 139, 145
Fiore, Joachim de, 20, 94, 97–98, 100
flowers, 128–129, 145
  lilies, 129–130, 132, 141
  roses, 129–130, 132
Foscarini, Sebastiano, 7
France
  anti-French sentiment and violence, 24
  Bourbon reliance on, 39
  contraband trade with, 38
  mail ships, 57
  New Spain, wartime trade with, 39
  and Spain
    cooperation, 23, 47
    defenders of Catholicism, 60–61
    hostility between, 60–61
    Spanish delegation to, 58
    withdrawal of troops, 59
Franciscan Order, 24, 98–100, 137
Franco Rubio, Gloria Angeles, 120
Frazier, James, 3
Freire, Antonio, 62
funerary honors, 80, 84, 86
  for Carlos III, 148–149
  genealogies in, 104
  for Louis XIV of France, 105
  for María Luisa Gabriela de Saboya of Spain, 141, *141*

Gabriela de San José, Sister, 101
Garcia Valdés, Antonio, 134
Garikoetxea, Juan de, 82, 92, 116
Gasco, Gregorio, 51, 53–54, 92
Gazeta de Madrid (newspaper), 7, 64, 73–74
genealogies, 103–104, 137

George Louis of Hessen-Darmstadt, 24
Gibraltar, 24, 56, 103
Graaf, Laurent le (Lorencillo), 27, 42
Gómez de Aguilera y Saavedra, Rodrigo, 99
Gómez de la Parra, Joseph, 87, 104, 130, 137
González Cruz, David, 13
González de Sancha, Lorenzo Antonio, 111
González Figueroa, Lorenzo, 54
González Valdeosera, Miguel, 126–127
Gorospe e Irala, Diego de, Bishop of Nueva Segovia, 36
governors, 71, 83
Grand Alliance, 13, 23
  declaration of war, 23
  Duchy of Savoy in, 58
  iconoclasm/sacrilege, accused of, 60–61, 88
  Madrid, occupation of, 25–26, 58–59, 66
  military victories, Bourbon censorship of, 47
  Portugal in, 23, 93
  victories of, 26
grandees, 59
Grimaldo, José de, 42, 55, 60
Guadalajara, 75, 78, 82–83, 85
Guevara, Antonio de, 18
Guevara, Juan de, 88, 107, 111

Habermas, Jürgen, 46
Habsburg monarchy, 1
  faith and piety, 64, 86–88
  infertility, 124, 130
  Monarquía Hispánica, 11
  propaganda campaign, 13
  reforms, 12
  and sacrality, 4
  support for, 47
    among grandees, 59
    as identity, 53–54
    as sin, 56
haciendas
  overseers, 54–55
  visitor position, sale of, 41
Hannah (biblical figure), 126
harvest failures, 74
Heras y Alcocer, José (Joseph) de las, 103, 125, 135
Herederos de la Viuda de Miguel de Ribera, 141
Hidalgo, Miguel, 149–150
Hidalgo Revolt (1810–11), 150
Hidden/Sleeping king (Encubierto), 93–94, 98–100, 108, 150

hierarchies, social, 70, 72, 85
Hieronymite Order, 145
Holy Sacrament *see* Eucharist,
Holy Shroud (relic), 133

Ibáñez de la Riva Herrera, Antonio,
    Archbishop of Zaragoza, Inquistor
    General, 9, 56, 101
iconoclasm, 60–61, 65–66, 88
    sermons, reported in, 88, 90
identities
    anti-Bourbon, 46
    composite, 18, 115–117, 143
    Habsburg support as, 53–54
    Spanish, 116
        genealogy, based on, 103–104
        and Immaculate Conception, 114–117
        military prowess in, 108
        pietas austriaca in, 88
    Spanish imperial, 9, 17, 47, 103, 143
imagery *see* metaphors; sun metaphors and
    symbolism,
imagined community, 143
Immaculate Conception, 146
indigenous people
    cabildo members, 85
    ceremonies, participation in,
        85–86
    encomiendas, taxation of, 35
    enslavement, 30
    fears of uprising of, 32
    magistrates, 86
    representations, in royal ceremonies, 69
    in War of the Spanish Succession, 29, 31
inequality, social, 70, 72
infertility, 7, 124–125, 127
    symbolic, 127–128
information
    circulation of, 45–46
    limited access to, 46
    oral communication of, 46
    transfer of, 17
    uncensored, 46
Innocent III, Pope, 132
Inquisition, 48–49, 54, 61
Isabel of Portugal, Saint (Elizabeth of
    Portugal), 137
Isaiah, prophet, 132–133, 135
Isidoro de Sevilla, 104, 109
    *Historia Gothorum Wandalorum
    Sueborum*, 96–97

Isla de Sacrificios, 27–28

Jacinto de Mesa, Agustín, 101
Jalpan, 29
Jamaica, 28, 49
James, Saint (Santiago), 103, 108
Jáuregui y Barcena, Juan de, 37
Jerome, Saint, 129
Jerusalem, 95, 99
    hopes for conquest of, 108–109,
        112
    New, 95, 108, 117
        Mexico City as, 95
        New Spain as, 94, 100
        Seville as, 98
        Spain as, 103
    in prophecies, 93, 98
Jesuit Order, expulsion from New Spain,
    147–148
Jesus Christ
    body of, 70, 72, 86–91
    in Book of Revelation, 95
    Crown of Thorns, 131
    and Eucharist, 72, 87
    Felipe V compared with, 76, 102
    Holy Shroud (relic), 133
    Luis I compared with, 104–105
    monarchs, associated with,
        18, 76, 78
    resurrection of, 88–89
Jiménez, Diego, 21
John of Patmos, 95, 108
John the Baptist, 126
Joseph Ferdinand of Bavaria, 2
Joseph I, Holy Roman Emperor,
    26, 50
Juan Unay (Johan Alamany), 98
Juárez, Nicolás Rodríguez, 107
Julius II, Pope, 99
jura del rey (royal oath ceremony), 23,
    69–70, 80, 83
    botanical metaphors in, 128–130
    clothing in, 78
    indigenous people's participation
        in, 85–86
    for Luis I, 80, 86, 119–120, 134
    royal portraits in, 76–78, 83, 119
    warrior-king metaphors in, 105, 108

Kagan, Richard L., 103
Kertzer, David, 18

kings
    body of the king (*cuerpo del rey*), 9,
        17–18, 70
        allegiance to, 150
        beauty of, 74–75
        body of Christ/Eucharist, connection
            to, 86–91
        body politic as integral to, 86
        health, influence on Empire, 73–74
        present in portraits, 78
        subjects' union with, 47, 79, 127
    as head of body politic, 70, 82
    kingdom, unity with, 71–72
    prophecies of
        Hidden/Sleeping, 93–94, 98–100, 108,
            150
        warrior-king, 95–96
    sun as symbol of, 88
    warrior-kings, 105–109
kingship, sacred, 3–4, 7, 9, 15–20, 133–139,
    145–151
    challenges to, 151
    continuity of, under Bourbons, 13
    Luis I as symbol of, 120
Kuethe, Allan J., 12
Kuffner, Emily, 124

Laguna de Términos, 27, 29–30
Landaeta, Manuel de, 32
Lazarus (biblical figure), 18, 89–90
legitimacy, 123
    genealogical, 103–104, 137
    through military leadership, 55
    propaganda on, 46, 62, 103
    prophecies of, 101, 109
    questions of, 56, 62
León, Lucrecia de, 99
Leopold I, Holy Roman Emperor, 26, 124
Lérida, 25
Levanto, Dionisio, 131
Linares, Fernando de Alencastre, 1st Duke
    of, 21, 35, 50, 102, 108
Lion of Judah, 76, 99, 102, 109, 112, 137
lions, as symbol, 69, 112, 133
    Felipe V as, 99, 102, 135
    and Luis I, 102, 137
    and New David, 98
    and Solomon, 76
    and war, 101
loas (laudatory poems), 119–120
López de Pro, Maximiliano, 5

López, Gregorio, 100
López Lovato, Bernardo, 51
Lorencillo (Laurent le Graaf), 27, 42
Louis IX of France, Saint, 4, 79, 102, 108, 137
Louis XIV of France, 1–2, 4
    fertility, 128
    funerary honors, 105
    marriage, 124
    peace negotiations, 25, 107
    petitions to, 59
    portraits of, 79, 105
    portraits of Felipe V commissioned and
        circulated by, 75–76
    sale of appointments, 40
Luis I of Spain, 79
    accession, 141, 144–145
    birth of, 15, 20, 25
    communication of news of, 57, 121
    prophecies based on, 101, 103
    sermons, 89, 104–105, 130–137
    thanksgiving ceremonies, 80, 103,
        121–122, 131, 133–134
    death, 141, 145
    funerary honors, 145
    genealogy, 137
    miraculous powers attributed to, 137
    oaths of loyalty to, 37, 80
    portraits of, 79, 137–139, *138*
        in prophecies, 123
        Christ, associated with, 104–105
        as descendent of Virgin Mary,
            133–134
        Hercules, associated with, 137
        as millenarian "Prince of Peace",
            135–136
Luther, Martin, 60
Luzzara, Battle of (1702), 66

Maccabees, Spanish army compared with,
    107
Madrid
    Grand Alliance occupation of, 25–26,
        58–59
    relaciones de sucesos on, 66
    jura del rey (royal oath ceremony), 69,
        108
    Real Alcázar, 70, 76
    Virgen de Atocha, 64–67
magistrates
    alcaldes ordinarios, 83
    indigenous, 86

mail, 45, 57
Maldonado, Ángel de, 90, 113, 115
Mañer, Salvador, 54–55, 59
Manrique, Joseph, 119
manuscripts, 46
Margarita Teresa of Spain, 124
Maria Anna of Neuburg, 6
María Luisa de Orleans, 6, 124–125
María Luisa Gabriela de Saboya of Spain, 15, 20, 23, 120–121
   death, 123, 132, 141
   as descendent of Virgin Mary, 132–134
   funerary honors, 140, 141
   piety of, 63–64
   popularity, 120–121
   portraits of, 79
   pregnancies, 25, 103, 125–128
      sermons on, 131
   receives Golden Rose from Clement XI, 121, 133
   as regent, 121
   Woman of the Apocalypse, compared to, 134
María Teresa of Spain, Queen consort of France, 2, 62, 124
Maríana de Neuburgo (Mariana of Austria), 2, 6, 40, 125
Mariana, Juan de, 18–19
Mariano del Río, Alfonso, 137
Mary, Virgin, 61, 63–65, 113–117
   Bourbon devotion to, 63–64, 66
   feast days, 65, 139
   and fertility/pregnancy, 126, 131
   Habsburg devotion to, 64
   Immaculate Conception, 2, 5, 88, 90, 114–117
      as dogma, 115
      as obligatory belief, 114
   New Spain, veneration in, 65
   Our Lady of the Rosary, 64
   representations of, 115
   Savoy family as descendents of, 132–134
   Spanish Crown, association with, 63
   Virgen de Atocha, 64–65
   Virgen de Guadalupe, 60, 63–65, 116–117
   Virgen de la Soledad, 113
   Virgen de los Remedios, 104–105, 114–115, 122, 126
   Virgen del Pilar, 64
   Virgin of Montserrat, 64

masses, 66
   funerary, 84
   thanksgiving, 84–85
Maximilian I of Mexico, 151
Mayan Indians, 29
messianism, 95–100, 112–113, 123, 132, 150
metaphors
   Austrian/Habsburg
      alemanisca (huckaback cloth), 53
   of the body, 70–91, 144
      and body of Christ/Eucharist, 86–91
      resurrection/rebirth, 89–90
      Spanish Empire as, 89
   for (dis)loyalty, 53
   familial, 124
   flowers, 145
   light, 102–103
   phoenix, 3, 5
   reality, blurred with, 79
   transubstantiation as, 145
   trees, 129
   see also sun metaphors and symbolism, Mexico, 114
   court of, 80
   First Mexican Empire, 151
Mexico City, 7
   cabildo (municipal council), 73, 121–122
   Calle de los Mercaderes (Street of the Merchants), 52–53
   Carlos II of Spain catafalque, 1
   casta uprising, 32
   cathedral, 36, 73, 101, 140, 141, 148
   ceremonies, 109–110
      funerary honors, Carlos II, 80, 84
      jura del rey (royal oath ceremony), 69–70, 73, 76–78
      thanksgiving, 121–122, 125
      victory commemorations, 79, 122
   consulado (merchant guild), 37–38
   cuerpo de ciudad (municipal council), 80
   forced conscription in, 31
   Marian shrines in, 115
   in millenarian prophecies, 95
   pro-Austrian/Habsburg propaganda in, 51–52
   riot (1692), 114
   Virgen de los Remedios, 104–105
Mexico, University of, 79
military appointments, sale of, 41
millenarianism, 92, 94, 102–103, 123, 150

Mínguez, Victor, 4, 76
Mitchell, Silvia Z., 6
Moctezuma, José Sarmiento de Valladares, Count of, 1st Duke of Atrisco, 21, 27–28, 80–81
Molina, Tirso de, 129
monarch *see also* kings,
monarchs
　appearance as evidence of character, 73
　authority of, 147
　divinity of, 3–5
　health of, 18
　representations of, 17–18, 69–70
　sainted, 4
　as saints, 133–139
monarchy
　absolutist, 11, 145, 151
　allegiance to, 150
　Christian religious foundation of, 18, 88
　composite, 18
　continuity of, 14
　corporeal metaphors of, 70
　debts of, 37
　at Independence, 150
　Monarquía Hispánica, 11, 18, 71, 99, 126
　permanency of, 2
　sacred, 133–139, 145–151
　solar metaphors and symbols, 1–3, 5
　Universal Catholic Monarchy, 98–99, 103, 136
　see also kingship,
Monségur, Jean de, 121
Montaño, Tomás, 108, 112
Morena Cebrián, Alfredo, 12
Moses (biblical character), 104
Muir, Edward, 71
mulatto people, 28
Murillo y Velarde, Tomás de, 124

Napoleon Bonaparte, 149
nationalism
　Portuguese, 92–93
　Spanish, 103
Navarro García, Luis, 11–12
navios de aviso (dispatch/mail ships), 45, 57
Netherlands, 61–62
New Galicia, 83
New Spain
　altepetls (ethnically based political units), 85

audiencias (high courts), 1, 3, 9, 27, 41, 82–83
　body politic of, 71–73, 79–86
　and Bourbon monarchy
　absolutist representations of, 11
　accession response, 5
　loyalty to, 55, 65
　"presence" through visual representations, 57, 69–70, 78
　propaganda, 7–8, 10, 13–14, 57–58
　buccaneer attacks, 27
　cabezas (head towns), 56, 71–72, 82
　cabildos (municipal councils), 71, 80, 82, 84
　Christianization, 100
　clergy
　　Habsburgs, support for, 36
　　loyalty of, 36–37
　　war donations from, 36
　convents, 84
　Council of War, 28, 30, 32–33
　defence of, 28
　elites, 59, 82–83
　empire, importance to, 145
　English and Dutch, expulsion of, 29–30
　fortification, 110
　and Habsburg monarchy, 11
　　support for, 48, 51–54
　Hercules as symbol in, 103
　historiography, 20
　independence movements, 147, 149–151
　Jesuit Order expulsion from, 147–148
　loyalty of, 36–39
　Madrid, relationship with, 8
　merchants
　　Bourbon loyalty of, 37–40
　　pro-Austrian/Habsburg, 51–54
　municipalities, 8–9, 10, 80–81
　as New Jerusalem, 98
　officials
　　alcaldes ordinarios (annually elected magistrates), 83
　　alférez real (royal standard bearer), 82–83, 87, 119–120
　　beneficios (bureaucratic appointments), 40
　　as body politic, 82
　　calificador (approver of sermons), 19
　　governors, 71, 83
　　oidores (judges), 41, 45
　　padrino (godfather), 83

pro-Bourbon, 101–105, 109
  of rebirth, 94
  Sebastianism, 92–93
  of war, 101–102
Protestantism
  Catholicism, conflict with, 47–48, 60–63
  colonies of, 27
  criticism of, 66
  pro-Habsburg propaganda, suspected of circulation of, 49
  sacrilege, accusations of, 87
  spread of, supposed war objective, 56
Pseudo-Methodius prophecy, 96
public rogations, 120
public sphere, 46–47
  baroque, 46–47, 51
  definitions, 46
  diversity of opinion in, 147
  reading/writing cultures in, 46
  visual/oral cultures in, 46
Puebla, 34, 36
  Bourbons, loyalty to, 50
  cathedral chapter, 36–37
  ceremonies, 83
    funerary honors, Carlos II, 80
    jura del rey (royal oath ceremony), 105
    succession, 87
    thanksgiving, 84
  propaganda circulation in, 47
  pro-Austrian/Habsburg, 48
Pulgar, Blas de, 5, 73, 104–105, 127, 135
Puyol, Joaquin, 53, 60

Rachel (biblical figure), 125
Rada, Antonio de, 52–53
Rawlings, Helen, 6
rebirth
  metaphors of, 89–90, 128–129
  prophecies of, 94
religion *see* Bible; Catholicism; clergy; Eucharist; Jesus Christ; Mary, Virgin; masses; piety; Protestantism; sin,
renewal
  through Bourbon monarchy, 78–79, 121
  Felipe V, 7–8, 75
  Luis I, 123
  metaphors of, 131
  solar, 5, 89
resurrection
  of Jesus Christ, 88–89

  metaphors of, 89–90
  of Spanish Empire, 18, 70, 90
  sun as symbol of, 88
Revolt of the Catalans (1640–52), 65
Ribadeneyra, Pedro de, 18
Ribera, Bernardez de, 133
Ribot, Luis, 6
Rigaud, Hyacinthe, 76
Rincón, Lucas del, 132
ritual *see* ceremonies; Eucharist,
Robles, Antonio de, 31, 125
Robles Porres, Don Joseph de, 83
Rodrigo (Roderic, Visigoth King), 104
Rodríguez Juárez, Juan, 69, 76–78
Rogers, Woodes, 116
Ronquillo, Francisco, 56
Rooke, George, 24, 52
Rosenmüller, Christoph, 12, 40, 51
Rubial García, Antonio, 20, 100
Rudolf I of Habsburg (of Germany), 87, 91
Ruiz de Tagle, Juan Domingo, 38
rumor, 46, 48
  of Charles VI's death, 58
  of disloyalty to Bourbons, 59
  of Felipe V's abandonment of Spain, 50, 58
  gossip, 51
Ruzzini, Carlo, 7

Saavedra Fajardo, Diego de, 18
sacrilege, 60–61, 66
  against Eucharist, 87
  sermons, reported in, 88, 90
Sala i Vila, Nuria, 12
Salazar, Antonio de, 125, 131, 133–134
Salazar, Juan de, *Política Española*, 99
Samson (biblical figure), 89, 136
San Agustín, 30, 34
San Juan Santa Cruz, Francisco, 42
San Luis Potosí, 107
San Marcos presidio, siege of, 30
San Miguel, Juan de, 19, 74, 108, 126–127, 136
Sánchez de Figueroa, Don Lorenzo, 92
Sánchez de Tagle, Luis, 1st Marquess of Altamira, 83
Sánchez, Lorenzo, 62
Sánchez, Miguel, 116
Sánchez Tagle, Andrés, 43
Sánchez Tagle family, 37–39, 42
Sánchez Tagle, Luis, 37

Sánchez Tagle, Luis Antonio, 43
Sánchez Tagle, Pedro, 37, 42
Sandoval Villegas, Martha, 76
Santa Anna, Antonio López de, 151
Santiago (Saint James), 103, 108
Santibañéz, Juan Antonio, 126
Sarmiento de Valladares, José *see*
    Moctezuma, José Sarmiento de
    Valladares, Count of,
Sebastián of Portugal, 93
Sebastianism, 92–93
sermons, 14, 17
  on Battles of Brihuega and Villaviciosa
    (1710), 60
  on birth of Luis I, 80, 89, 104–105,
    130–137
  body metaphors in, 89
  Felipe V
    as New David, 112–113
    as warrior-king, 107–108
  on fertility, 125–128, 131
  for *Fiesta de Desagravios al Santísimo
    Sacramento*, 90
  flower metaphors in, 129–132
  funerary, 74, 89, 130
  on Grand Alliance iconoclasm, 88
  Marian devotion in, 115
  for military victories, 26, 84–85
  printed material cited in, 62–63, 74
  pro-Bourbon, 47
  resurrection symbolism in, 89–90
  thanksgiving, 103
  on Virgen of Atocha, 66–67
Serruto y Nava, José, 148–149
Seven Years' War (1756-1763), 147
Seville
  consulado (merchant guild), 39, 57
  as New Jerusalem, 94, 100
shipping, 35
  Armada de Barlovento, 21, 34–35, 39
  flota (merchant fleet), 23
  losses of, 35, 57
  navios de aviso (dispatch/mail ships), 45,
    57
Sibylline oracles, 95–96, 99
Silva, Felipe de, 145, *146*
sin
  disloyalty as, 48, 56
  infertility as punishment for, 124, 127
slave trade, 27, 29
smuggling, 35, 38, 42, 92

Solanes, Francisco, *El emperador politico, y
    politica de emperadores*, 48
Solis Cachero, Don Diego de, 139
Solomon (biblical figure), 4, 76, 89, 95
Sousa y Prado, Don Manuel de, 53
Spain
  foundation and origin myths, 103–104
  and France
    cooperation, 23, 47
    defenders of Catholicism, 60–61
    hostility between, 60–61
  Muslim conquest, 96–97
  Reconquest, 61
  symbolic infertility of, 127–128
Spanish Empire
  autonomy in, 11
  body metaphors for, 6, 89, 143
  body politic of, 73
  emblems and mottos, 103
  as imagined community, 17, 47
  perceived decline of, 6
  perceived threats to, 61
  resurrection of, 18, 70, 90
  sun as symbol of, 88
  Virgen de Atocha, significance to, 65
Stanhope, James, 26, 56, 60, 66
Starhemberg, Guido, 26, 66
Stein, Stanley and Barbara, 34
Storrs, Christopher, 6, 12
Suárez, Francisco, 18
succession
  Bourbon, 120–121, 128, 141
  from Carlos II of Spain, 2
  ceremonies, 4, 80, 87
sun metaphors and symbolism, 2–3, 88–89, 136
  divinity, association with, 2
  eclipses, 90, 112
  as force of renewal, 5, 89
  as metaphor for monarchy, 1–3, 5
  setting of, and death, 145
symbolism
  biblical, 4
  condensation of, 18
  nature, 20
  religious, 18
symbols
  Austrian/Habsburg
    eagles, 52
  botanical, 128–132
    lilies, 129–130, 132, 141
    roses, 129–130, 132

Felipe V as, 99, 102, 135
  and Luis I, 102, 137
  and New David, 98
  and Solomon, 76
  and war, 101
  Hercules, as founder of Spain, 103
  lions, 69, 112, 133
  Pillars of Hercules, 103
  trees, 129
  see also sun metaphors and symbolism,

Tabasco, 29–30
taxation
  alcabala (sales tax), 37–38
  for war finance, 34–35
Tenorio, Gregorio, 115
thanksgiving ceremonies, 79
  for birth of Luis I of Spain, 80, 84, 103, 121–123, 133–134
  hymns, 64
  masses, 84
  for military victories, 130
  for royal fertility, 125–128
  sermons, 110–111
Thomas Aquinas, Saint, 145
Tiburtina prophecy, 96
Tlaxcala, 80, 85–86
Toisón de Oro (Order of the Golden Fleece), 38, 69, 76
Torcy, Jean-Baptiste Colbert, Marquis of, 25, 75
Toro Altamirano, Fernando de, 137
Torres Puga, Gabriel, 147
transubstantiation, 87, 145
Tubal (biblical character), 103
Turuley, Acham, 96, 100–101

Ubilla y Medina, Antonio, 55, 65, 105, *106*, 137
Unibárbia, Bernardo, 63, 66, 111–112
United Kingdom
  buccaneers, 29
  England, 60–61
  New Spain, military raids in, 30
  traders, expulsion of, 29–30
University of Mexico, 108–109
uprisings, 58, 74
  casta uprising, Mexico City, 32
  fears of, 32
  Hidalgo Revolt (1810–11), 150
  Revolt of the Catalans (1640–52), 65

Urrejola Davanzo, Bernarda, 14
Ursúa y Arizmendi, Martín de, 37

Valencia, 25
Valle Pavón, Guillermina del, 38
Valtierra, Antonio de, 19, 102, 130
Van Young, Eric, 150
Vendôme, Louis Joseph de Bourbon, Duke of, 24, 26, 111
Venezuela, 28
Veracruz, 27
  defense of, 28, 32
  evacuation, 28
  governor position, sale of, 42
Vermeulen, Cornelius, 76, 77
Veytia y Linaje, Juan José de, 34, 37
viceroy role
  in body politic, 71
  ceremonial responsibilities, 81, 84
  news, amplification of, 58–59
  proxy for king, 71
viceroys
  Alburquerque, Francisco Fernández de la Cueva, 10th Duke of, 21, 30, 57
    ceremonies organized by, 81, 117, 121–122
    corruption investigation, 39
    divine aid, requests for, 114
    Felipe V, donations to, 36–39
    illicit business dealings, 38
    and military conscription, 31
    pro-Austrian/Habsburg propaganda, control and censorship of, 49–50
  Linares, Fernando de Alencastre, 1st Duke of, 21, 35, 50, 102, 108
  Moctezuma, José Sarmiento de Valladares, Count of, 1st Duke of Atrisco, 21, 27–28, 80–81
  Ortega y Montañés, Juan, Archbishop of Mexico, 21, 36, 58, 114
Victor Amadeus II, Duke of Savoy, 58
Vigo, 39
Villagutierre, Alonso de Cevallos, 83
Villalobos, Joaquín Antonio, 107
Villanova, Arnau de, 98
Villars, Claude Louis Hector de, 1st Duke, 26
Villars, Pierre de, Marquis of, 6
Villaviciosa, Battle of (1710), 15, 26, 59, 78–79, 145–146, *146*

Villerías y Roelas, José Antonio de, 145
Visigothic Empire, 96–97
Vivien, Joseph, 76, 77

War of the Spanish Succession (1701–14), 8
  Battle of Almansa (1707), 15, 25, 59, 66
  Battle of Brihuega (1710), 15, 26, 59, 78–79, 110–112
  Battle of Luzzara (1702), 66
  Battle of Vigo Bay (1702), 39
  Battle of Villaviciosa (1710), 15, 26, 59, 78–79, 145–146, *146*
  Bourbon morale, 25
  declaration, 23
  financing of, 33–36
    donations, 36, 42
    fines for contraband trade, 35
    Peruvian silver, 33–34
    religious funds, appropriation of, 35–36
    salaries, collection from, 35
    through sale of appointments, 40–43
    taxation, 34–35
  historiography, 11–14
  as holy war, 13, 36, 47–48, 56, 60
    defense of Holy Sacrament in, 87
  miracles, reporting of, 61, 63
    Virgen de Atocha shrine, control of, 65
  Madrid, recapture of, 130
  narrative
    control and censorship of, 47–48, 55–56
    doubt of, as indicator of disloyalty, 52
  New Spain, impact on, 14, 21–22, 26, 28–33
    financial, 33–36
    and trade, 39–40
  prophecies of, 101–102
  Siege of Barcelona (1706), 25
  Siege of Cádiz and Santa María (1702), 52, 56
  in Spain, 24–26
Weckman, Luis, 20

Xardon, Antonio, 101, 131

Yamasee soldiers, 30
Yañez de Aviles, Pablo, 60

Zacharias (biblical figure), 126
Zacharias of Rome, 104
Zaragoza, 26, 88

CAMBRIDGE LATIN AMERICAN STUDIES
(continued from page ii)

129. *A Colonial Book Market: Peruvian Print Culture in the Age of Enlightenment*, Agnes Gehbald
128. *Veracruz and the Caribbean in the Seventeenth Century*, Joseph M. H. Clark
127. *We, the King: Creating Royal Legislation in the Sixteenth-Century Spanish New World*, Adrian Masters
126. *A History of Chile 1808–2018, Second Edition*, William F. Sater and Simon Collier
125. *The Dread Plague and the Cow Killers: The Politics of Animal Disease in Mexico and the World*, Thomas Rath
124. *Islands in the Lake: Environment and Ethnohistory in Xochimilco, New Spain*, Richard M. Conway
123. *Journey to Indo-América: APRA and the Transnational Politics of Exile, Persecution, and Solidarity, 1918–1945*, Geneviève Dorais
122. *Nationalizing Nature: Iguazu Falls and National Parks at the Brazil–Argentina Border*, Frederico Freitas
121. *Islanders and Empire: Smuggling and Political Defiance in Hispaniola, 1580–1690*, Juan José Ponce-Vázquez
120. *Our Time is Now: Race and Modernity in Postcolonial Guatemala*, Julie Gibbings
119. *The Sexual Question: A History of Prostitution in Peru, 1850s–1950s*, Paulo Drinot
118. *A Silver River in a Silver World: Dutch Trade in the Rio de la Plata, 1648–1678*, David Freeman
117. *Laboring for the State: Women, Family, and Work in Revolutionary Cuba, 1959–1971*, Rachel Hynson
116. *Violence and the Caste War of Yucatán*, Wolfgang Gabbert
115. *For Christ and Country: Militant Catholic Youth in Post-Revolutionary Mexico*, Robert Weis
114. *The Mexican Mission: Indigenous Reconstruction and Mendicant Enterprise in New Spain, 1521–1600*, Ryan Dominic Crewe
113. *Corruption and Justice in Colonial Mexico, 1650–1755*, Christoph Rosenmüller
112. *Blacks of the Land: Indian Slavery, Settler Society, and the Portuguese Colonial Enterprise in South America*, John M. Monteiro, James Woodward, and Barbara Weinstein
111. *The Street Is Ours: Community, the Car, and the Nature of Public Space in Rio de Janeiro*, Shawn William Miller
110. *Laywomen and the Making of Colonial Catholicism in New Spain, 1630–1790*, Jessica L. Delgado
109. *Urban Slavery in Colonial Mexico: Puebla de los Ángeles, 1531–1706*, Pablo Miguel Sierra Silva
108. *The Mexican Revolution's Wake: The Making of a Political System, 1920–1929*, Sarah Osten

107. *Latin America's Radical Left: Rebellion and Cold War in the Global 1960s*, Aldo Marchesi
106. *Liberalism as Utopia: The Rise and Fall of Legal Rule in Post-Colonial Mexico, 1820–1900*, Timo H. Schaefer
105. *Before Mestizaje: The Frontiers of Race and Caste in Colonial Mexico*, Ben VinsonIII
104. *The Lords of Tetzcoco: The Transformation of Indigenous Rule in Postconquest Central Mexico*, Bradley Benton
103. *Theater of a Thousand Wonders: A History of Miraculous Images and Shrines in New Spain*, William B. Taylor
102. *Indian and Slave Royalists in the Age of Revolution*, Marcela Echeverri
101. *Indigenous Elites and Creole Identity in Colonial Mexico, 1500–1800*, Peter Villella
100. *Asian Slaves in Colonial Mexico: From Chinos to Indians*, Tatiana Seijas
99. *Black Saint of the Americas: The Life and Afterlife of Martín de Porres*, Celia Cussen
98. *The Economic History of Latin America since Independence, Third Edition*, Victor Bulmer-Thomas
97. *The British Textile Trade in South America in the Nineteenth Century*, Manuel Llorca-Jaña
96. *Warfare and Shamanism in Amazonia*, Carlos Fausto
95. *Rebellion on the Amazon: The Cabanagem, Race, and Popular Culture in the North of Brazil, 1798–1840*, Mark Harris
94. *A History of the Khipu*, Galen Brokaw
93. *Politics, Markets, and Mexico's "London Debt," 1823–1887*, Richard J. Salvucci
92. *The Political Economy of Argentina in the Twentieth Century*, Roberto Cortés Conde
91. *Bankruptcy of Empire: Mexican Silver and the Wars between Spain, Britain, and France, 1760–1810*, Carlos Marichal
90. *Shadows of Empire: The Indian Nobility of Cusco, 1750–1825*, David T. Garrett
89. *Chile: The Making of a Republic, 1830–1865: Politics and Ideas*, Simon Collier
88. *Deference and Defiance in Monterrey: Workers, Paternalism, and Revolution in Mexico, 1890–1950*, Michael Snodgrass
87. *Andrés Bello: Scholarship and Nation-Building in Nineteenth-Century Latin America*, Ivan Jaksic
86. *Between Revolution and the Ballot Box: The Origins of the Argentine Radical Party in the 1890s*, Paula Alonso
85. *Slavery and the Demographic and Economic History of Minas Gerais, Brazil, 1720–1888*, Laird W. Bergad
84. *The Independence of Spanish America*, Jaime E. Rodríguez
83. *The Rise of Capitalism on the Pampas: The Estancias of Buenos Aires, 1785–1870*, Samuel Amaral
82. *A History of Chile, 1808–2002, Second Edition*, Simon Collier and William F. Sater

81. *The Revolutionary Mission: American Enterprise in Latin America, 1900–1945*, Thomas F. O'Brien
80. *The Kingdom of Quito, 1690–1830: The State and Regional Development*, Kenneth J. Andrien
79. *The Cuban Slave Market, 1790–1880*, Laird W. Bergad, Fe Iglesias García, and María del Carmen Barcia
78. *Business Interest Groups in Nineteenth-Century Brazil*, Eugene Ridings
77. *The Economic History of Latin America since Independence, Second Edition*, Victor Bulmer-Thomas
76. *Power and Violence in the Colonial City: Oruro from the Mining Renaissance to the Rebellion of Tupac Amaru (1740–1782)*, Oscar Cornblit
75. *Colombia before Independence: Economy, Society and Politics under Bourbon Rule*, Anthony McFarlane
74. *Politics and Urban Growth in Buenos Aires, 1910–1942*, Richard J. Walter
73. *The Central Republic in Mexico, 1835–1846, 'Hombres de Bien' in the Age of Santa Anna*, Michael P. Costeloe
72. *Negotiating Democracy: Politicians and Generals in Uruguay*, Charles Guy Gillespie
71. *Native Society and Disease in Colonial Ecuador*, Suzanne Austin Alchon
70. *The Politics of Memory: Native Historical Interpretation in the Colombian Andes*, Joanne Rappaport
69. *Power and the Ruling Classes in Northeast Brazil, Juazeiro and Petrolina in Transition*, Ronald H. Chilcote
68. *House and Street: The Domestic World of Servants and Masters in Nineteenth-Century Rio de Janeiro*, Sandra Lauderdale Graham
67. *The Demography of Inequality in Brazil*, Charles H. Wood and José Alberto Magno de Carvalho
66. *The Politics of Coalition Rule in Colombia*, Jonathan Hartlyn
65. *South America and the First World War: The Impact of the War on Brazil, Argentina, Peru and Chile*, Bill Albert
64. *Resistance and Integration: Peronism and the Argentine Working Class, 1946–1976*, Daniel James
63. *The Political Economy of Central America since 1920*, Victor Bulmer-Thomas
62. *A Tropical Belle Epoque: Elite Culture and Society in Turn-of-the-Century Rio de Janeiro*, Jeffrey D. Needell
61. *Ambivalent Conquests: Maya and Spaniard in Yucatan, 1517–1570, Second Edition*, Inga Clendinnen
60. *Latin America and the Comintern, 1919–1943*, Manuel Caballero
59. *Roots of Insurgency: Mexican Regions, 1750–1824*, Brian R. Hamnett
58. *The Agrarian Question and the Peasant Movement in Colombia: Struggles of the National Peasant Association, 1967–1981*, Leon Zamosc
57. *Catholic Colonialism: A Parish History of Guatemala, 1524–1821*, Adriaan C. van Oss
56. *Pre-Revolutionary Caracas: Politics, Economy, and Society 1777–1811*, P. Michael McKinley

55. *The Mexican Revolution, Volume 2: Counter-Revolution and Reconstruction*, Alan Knight
54. *The Mexican Revolution, Volume 1: Porfirians, Liberals, and Peasants*, Alan Knight
53. *The Province of Buenos Aires and Argentine Politics, 1912–1943*, Richard J. Walter
52. *Sugar Plantations in the Formation of Brazilian Society: Bahia, 1550–1835*, Stuart B. Schwartz
51. *Tobacco on the Periphery: A Case Study in Cuban Labour History, 1860–1958*, Jean Stubbs
50. *Housing, the State, and the Poor: Policy and Practice in Three Latin American Cities*, Alan Gilbert and Peter M. Ward
49. *Unions and Politics in Mexico: The Case of the Automobile Industry*, Ian Roxborough
48. *Miners, Peasants and Entrepreneurs: Regional Development in the Central Highlands of Peru*, Norman Long and Bryan Roberts
47. *Capitalist Development and the Peasant Economy in Peru*, Adolfo Figueroa
46. *Early Latin America: A History of Colonial Spanish America and Brazil*, James Lockhart and Stuart B. Schwartz
45. *Brazil's State-Owned Enterprises: A Case Study of the State as Entrepreneur*, Thomas J. Trebat
44. *Law and Politics in Aztec Texcoco*, Jerome A. Offner
43. *Juan Vicente Gómez and the Oil Companies in Venezuela, 1908–1935*, B. S. McBeth
42. *Revolution from Without: Yucatán, Mexico, and the United States, 1880–1924*, Gilbert M. Joseph
41. *Demographic Collapse: Indian Peru, 1520–1620*, Noble David Cook
40. *Oil and Politics in Latin America: Nationalist Movements and State Companies*, George Philip
39. *The Struggle for Land: A Political Economy of the Pioneer Frontier in Brazil from 1930 to the Present Day*, J. Foweraker
38. *Caudillo and Peasant in the Mexican Revolution*, D. A. Brading, ed.
37. *Odious Commerce: Britain, Spain and the Abolition of the Cuban Slave Trade*, David Murray
36. *Coffee in Colombia, 1850–1970: An Economic, Social and Political History*, Marco Palacios
35. *A Socioeconomic History of Argentina, 1776–1860*, Jonathan C. Brown
34. *From Dessalines to Duvalier: Race, Colour and National Independence in Haiti*, David Nicholls
33. *Modernization in a Mexican ejido: A Study in Economic Adaptation*, Billie R. DeWalt
32. *Haciendas and Ranchos in the Mexican Bajío, Léon, 1700–1860*, D. A. Brading
31. *Foreign Immigrants in Early Bourbon Mexico, 1700–1760*, Charles F. Nunn

30. *The Merchants of Buenos Aires, 1778–1810: Family and Commerce*, Susan Migden Socolow
29. *Drought and Irrigation in North-east Brazil*, Anthony L. Hall
28. *Coronelismo: The Municipality and Representative Government in Brazil*, Victor Nunes Leal
27. *A History of the Bolivian Labour Movement, 1848–1971*, Guillermo Lora
26. *Land and Labour in Latin America: Essays on the Development of Agrarian Capitalism in the Nineteenth and Twentieth Centuries*, Kenneth Duncan and Ian Rutledge, eds.
25. *Allende's Chile: The Political Economy of the Rise and Fall of the Unidad Popular*, Stefan de Vylder
24. *The Cristero Rebellion: The Mexican People between Church and State, 1926–1929*, Jean A. Meyer
23. *The African Experience in Spanish America, 1502 to the Present Day*, Leslie B. RoutJr.
22. *Letters and People of the Spanish Indies: Sixteenth Century*, James Lockhart and Enrique Otte, eds.
21. *Chilean Rural Society from the Spanish Conquest to 1930*, Arnold J. Bauer
20. *Studies in the Colonial History of Spanish America*, Mario Góngora
19. *Politics in Argentina, 1890–1930: The Rise and Fall of Radicalism*, David Rock
18. *Politics, Economics and Society in Argentina in the Revolutionary Period*, Tulio Halperín Donghi
17. *Marriage, Class and Colour in Nineteenth-Century Cuba: A Study of Racial Attitudes and Sexual Values in a Slave Society*, Verena Stolcke
16. *Conflicts and Conspiracies: Brazil and Portugal, 1750–1808*, Kenneth Maxwell
15. *Silver Mining and Society in Colonial Mexico: Zacatecas, 1546–1700*, P. J. Bakewell
14. *A Guide to the Historical Geography of New Spain*, Peter Gerhard
13. *Bolivia: Land, Location and Politics Since 1825*, J. Valerie Fifer, Malcolm Deas, Clifford Smith, and John Street
12. *Politics and Trade in Southern Mexico, 1750–1821*, Brian R. Hamnett
11. *Alienation of Church Wealth in Mexico: Social and Economic Aspects of the Liberal Revolution, 1856–1875*, Jan Bazant
10. *Miners and Merchants in Bourbon Mexico, 1763–1810*, D. A. Brading
9. *An Economic History of Colombia, 1845–1930*, W. P. McGreevey
8. *Economic Development of Latin America: Historical Background and Contemporary Problems*, Celso Furtado and Suzette Macedo
7. *Regional Economic Development: The River Basin Approach in Mexico*, David Barkin and Timothy King
6. *The Abolition of the Brazilian Slave Trade: Britain, Brazil and the Slave Trade Question, 1807–1869*, Leslie Bethell
5. *Parties and Political Change in Bolivia, 1880–1952*, Herbert S. Klein

4. *Britain and the Onset of Modernization in Brazil, 1850–1914*, Richard Graham
3. *The Mexican Revolution, 1910–1914: The Diplomacy of Anglo-American Conflict*, P. A. R. Calvert
2. *Church Wealth in Mexico: A Study of the 'Juzgado de Capellanias' in the Archbishopric of Mexico 1800–1856*, Michael P. Costeloe
1. *Ideas and Politics of Chilean Independence, 1808–1833*, Simon Collier

For EU product safety concerns, contact us at Calle de José Abascal, 56-1º, 28003 Madrid, Spain or eugpsr@cambridge.org.

www.ingramcontent.com/pod-product-compliance
Lightning Source LLC
Chambersburg PA
CBHW031105050526
RI82441I0000IB/R182441PG44191CBX00001B/1